TRIANGLE OF
DE△TH

TRIANGLE OF
DE△TH

The Shocking Truth About the Role of

South Vietnam and the **French Mafia**

in the Assassination of JFK

Brad O'Leary and L. E. Seymour

THOMAS NELSON
Since 1798

Published in Nashville, Tennessee, by WND Books.

Library of Congress Cataloging-in-Publication Data

O'Leary, Bradley S.
    Triangle of death : the shocking truth about the role of South Vietnam and the French mafia in the assassination of JFK / Brad O'Leary and L. E. Seymour.
      p. cm.
    Includes bibliographical references.
    1. Kennedy, John F. (John Fitzgerald), 1917–1963—Assassination. 2. Mafia—United States—History—20th century. 3. Organized crime—France—History—20th century. 4. Vietnam (Republic)—Politics and government—20th century. 5. Vietnam—Politics and government—1945–1975. 6. Vietnamese Conflict, 1961–1975—Influence. I. Seymour, L. E. II. Title.
E842.9.O344 2003
364.152'4'092—dc22   ISBN 978-1-59555-282-2   2003016093

Printed in the United States of America

03 04 05 06 07 BVG 5 4 3 2

To my former political mentors, Governor John Connally and U.S. Senator John Tower, who taught me never to be afraid of speaking what I believe to be the truth.

–B.S.O.

Contents

Foreword

AS PRESIDENT of the United States, John F. Kennedy authorized the overthrow of the Catholic government of South Vietnam and the assassination of Ngo Dinh Diem, South Vietnam's democratically elected, constitutional president.

Most readers will find this difficult to accept because for years Kennedy had ostensibly supported Diem. As president, Kennedy had generously pledged American troops, military equipment, and tax dollars to protect South Vietnam from the threat of communism. But although the notion of the U.S. government intentionally eliminating an ally does strain credulity, the fact remains that Diem was overthrown—and immediately assassinated.

Three weeks after Diem's assassination, Kennedy himself was assassinated. Few may be familiar with or even aware of the story of Diem's death, but everybody knows about the JFK assassination, the most intriguing murder mystery of our time. Yet, in spite of the dozens of theories that have surfaced regarding Kennedy's assassination and the almost constant attention given to them over the past forty years, only two official investigations have ever been conducted.

The investigative bodies of the U.S. government have made numerous claims—among them that a lone gunman named Lee Harvey Oswald was the assassin; that only two shots hit their target on November 22, 1963, with one shot missing; that the bullets fired that day all came from the sixth floor of the Texas Schoolbook Depository; and that Kennedy was killed because he was preparing to pull all U.S. troops out of Vietnam.

All of these claims are false and are designed to placate the American public and distract them from the facts of the case. But recently declassified federal documents relating to the Vietnam War, the KGB, the U.S. Mafia, the French Secret Services, and the international heroin syndicate provide vital new clues to help solve the forty-year-old mystery that surrounds the assassination of one of America's most beloved presidents. In this book, we provide an analysis of the whole body of evidence in order to give a more complete picture of what actually happened.

Here are some of the disturbing facts revealed in this book:

- Robert Kennedy didn't want his brother's death investigated because the investigation might uncover the fact that he, along with the president and the rest of the Kennedy White House, had drawn up operational plans to assassinate Fidel Castro after the Bay of Pigs Invasion.

- Kennedy's brain—a crucial piece of forensic evidence—was stolen by a U.S. Navy admiral on Robert Kennedy's orders.

- Just days before his death, the president had secretly planned and carried out the overthrow and eventual assassination of the Catholic leaders of Vietnam, turning the Vietnamese government over to a Buddhist military junta.

- Kennedy personally asked a high-ranking U.S. military officer to assassinate South Vietnam's President Diem.

- Mafia chieftain Carlos Marcello personally met with Jack Ruby and Lee Harvey Oswald, and Marcello verifiably confessed to federal officers that he had been directly involved in Kennedy's murder.

- The United States and the Soviet Union both went on high military alert immediately after Kennedy's death, bringing the human race one hair's-width away from nuclear annihilation.

But more important than any of that, this book reveals an official CIA document that may well be the most shocking piece of evidence ever to arise from the enigma surrounding Kennedy's murder.

The document affirms that an international assassin had been captured by U.S. authorities in Dallas, Texas, less than two days after

Kennedy was shot, and that instead of arresting him, those same U.S. authorities secretly flew the assassin out of the country to freedom.

Using that document, along with other relevant information, we will present our theory that the contract to murder President John F. Kennedy was not originated by the CIA or the military-industrial complex but by a partnership between the U.S. Mafia, the French heroin syndicate, and the government of South Vietnam.

Bradley S. O'Leary
L.E. Seymour

1

A Young Man in a Hurry

"Ask not what your country can do for you . . ."

— JOHN F. KENNEDY

IN 1960, when John F. Kennedy became the thirty-fifth president of the United States, America was in tumult. Cuba, just ninety miles off the coast of Florida, lay in the hands of an eccentric communist dictator. A strange new "cold" war was being waged between the U.S. and the Soviet Union, and World War III seemed inevitable with both countries frantic to aim as many missiles at the other as possible. The economy was constricting. Racial tensions were intensifying. Americans were living in fear.

At age forty-three, Kennedy's youth and vision of a New Frontier gave America what it needed most at that time—hope.

His murder in Dallas, Texas, on November 22, 1963, would become what many regard as the crime of the century. But the focus on his assassination deflects attention from his prodigious accomplishments, both leading up to and during his brief presidency.

Kennedy first proved his resolve and leadership abilities in World War II, receiving Navy and Marine Corps medals for heroism after he gallantly led his surviving crewmen to safety from their sinking patrol torpedo boat.

Politically, Kennedy distinguished himself by openly criticizing Senator Joseph McCarthy's anti-communist crusades in the early '50s, in spite of the facts that Kennedy himself was a staunch anti-communist and that his father sternly disapproved.

Kennedy was a popular author, making the bestseller list with his first book, *Why England Slept*, in 1940 and winning the esteemed Pulitzer Prize in 1957 with his next book, *Profiles in Courage*.

1

Kennedy was elected to three consecutive terms in the House of Representatives (1947-53) and then went on to win a Massachusetts Senate seat, soundly defeating hardline anti-Catholic Republican Henry Cabot Lodge. He won his second term as Massachusetts senator by the biggest margin of any senate race that year. Indeed, John F. Kennedy never lost an election.

Kennedy seemed to be a new kind of conqueror, destroying all opponents in their tracks with a concise, conversational oratory and a focused command of the issues that most concerned the voters. One journalist appropriately described him as a "young man in a hurry."[1]

As president, he stuck to issues that resonated with the American people: advocating drastic civil rights reform, supporting America's share in the space race, and pressuring France to grant independence to Algeria. He declared war against the common enemies of men: "tyranny, poverty, disease, and war itself."[2] All Americans are familiar with his famous "Ask not" speech, and most informed readers know that Kennedy founded the Peace Corps, but few remember that he also founded the popular Alliance for Progress, an aid incentive for Latin America. Kennedy also signed the first nuclear test ban treaty, and, though he was a liberal Democrat, he considered one of his most important ventures to be a sweeping tax cut. It can even be said that Kennedy's massive tax-cut strategy, which resulted in monumental economic stimulus, would eventually prove to be a model for the conservative tax-cut ideologies of the early eighties, which slashed inflation and unemployment and, in fact, produced more government revenue by increasing jobs.

Kennedy was indeed a "young man in a hurry." But little did he know, he was also hurrying toward his death, for as president, Kennedy would inherit one predicament that would eclipse all others: Vietnam.

2

Taproot to Chaos

"All men are created equal. They are endowed by
their Creator with certain inalienable rights."

— Ho Chi Minh, 1945

IN TRUTH, there were many Vietnam wars, and if ever there were a
people weaned on violent conflict, it's the Vietnamese. Historically, war
has been as much a part of Vietnamese life as birth and death. It was
China, in fact, that waged the very first wars against the Vietnamese
people; China was very interested in the Red River Delta's excellent
farmland and its value as a port. The Chinese not only tried to enslave
Vietnam's peasant population for their own means but also attempted to
overwrite Vietnamese culture and religious beliefs with their own. This
didn't work, and in 40 A.D. two Vietnamese women, the Trung Sisters,
successfully staged a rebellion against the Chinese military outposts and
secured Vietnam as an independent nation for three full years.

Thus began the predilections of the true Vietnamese spirit. The
Vietnamese people would, in effect, be ruled by China for some time to
come, but they would never stop fighting for their own identity. Nor would
they ever fully succumb to Chinese domination. No matter how hard they
were oppressed, the Vietnamese never stopped fighting against their
oppressors.

In the late 1850s, a new oppressor arrived. France, with its advanced
weaponry and superior field tactics, began colonizing what are now
Vietnam, Cambodia, and Laos in order to procure desperately needed overseas commerce. It took sixteen years for the French to solidify their hold on
this new colony, which they named Indochina. They came down hardest in
Vietnam, and they intentionally segmented the area into separate colonial

districts to shatter the people's cultural identity, committing unspeakable acts of cruelty to crush their spirit. The French force-fed them Catholicism and starved them when they failed to meet production quotas. From the 1860s to the 1940s, thousands died building roads, railways, docks, and canals. Thousands more died in the mines, the rice fields, and the irrigation ditches. When peasants begged for tax relief during droughts, the French said no. When workers got sick in the cement and textile factories, it was deemed more cost effective to just let them die without medical attention and replace them with fresh workers.

But things would only get worse. In September of 1940, after France surrendered to the Nazis, the French governor-general in Vietnam cut a deal allowing the Japanese to admit thirty thousand troops to take over all Vietnamese airports for their war efforts against Allied powers.[1] The Japanese offered no relief from French oppression because the collaborative deal they had made did not involve any actual governance. "Take your complaints to the French," they advised the peasants. Meanwhile, close to two million Vietnamese starved to death during a famine, even as the French and Japanese ate well and exported surplus rice to Japan. The French did not object because their tenuous administrative rule was dependent on keeping the Japanese happy.

When the Japanese began to realize that defeat was imminent, they threw all French military personnel into prison for fear of insurrection. But by this time, there were more insurrectionists about—native insurrectionists—who rebelled against French and Japanese oppression alike. Under harsh Chinese rule, the Vietnamese had honed their skills of rebellion, which they perfected under the French. The rebellion took form in a group called the Viet Minh, a well-organized guerilla militia around whom the country immediately rallied. Its leader was a man who would later become the only chief of state to ever win a war against the United States: Ho Chi Minh.

It's a little known fact, though, that at the end of World War II, Ho was an ally of the United States, or at least that's what he was led to believe. Initially, President Roosevelt spoke out strongly against foreign imperialism and oppression in Asia, and Ho Chi Minh believed him. Ho was not yet a true Communist at that time; his endeavor was purely nationalistic, an effort to depose all imperialistic rule over the country and give Vietnam back to the Vietnamese. Near the end of the war, U.S. and British intelligence operatives worked closely with the Viet Minh under Ho Chi Minh to undermine Japanese control in Vietnam. The Viet Minh were already actively stealing rice stockpiles from the Japanese as well as rescuing prisoners and downed pilots for the Allies. And it was Ho Chi Minh who helped immeasurably by disclosing the Japanese troop locations so the British could disarm them.

Believing he had our support, Ho then officially declared the independence of his country—the Democratic Republic of Vietnam—fashioning his declaration of independence after America's. But when Ho Chi Minh asked Harry Truman, the new U.S. president, for official U.S. support, Truman ignored his pleas, having already decided that the U.S. State Department should do everything in its power to help restore postwar France as quickly and effectively as possible. This included allowing France to reclaim Laos, Cambodia, and Vietnam as part of the French colonial empire.

To add insult to injury, the British then cunningly rearmed the Japanese army and used them to overthrow Ho's newly-declared democratic government in the southern half of the country. To Ho Chi Minh—as well as the majority of the population who supported him—this was the ultimate lesson in Western treachery.

Cambodia and Laos accepted "partial" independence within the "French Union." But Ho Chi Minh would not concede. When he began to challenge the newly re-installed French, they boasted that Ho's Viet Minh army would be swept aside in eight days.

But in 1954, after eight years, the French hadn't swept aside anything but their own arrogance. Even with two and a half billion dollars in United States aid for re-establishing their "colony" in Vietnam, the French pulled out after the catastrophic loss of their military garrison at Dienbienphu. The Viet Minh out-thought, out-maneuvered, and out-fought the French at every turn. Ho Chi Minh's total destruction of French imperialism in Vietnam was so severe that a multinational conference was convened. The resulting Geneva Accord determined that the country of Vietnam would be temporarily divided in half, at the 17th Parallel, until 1956 when a popular election would be held to determine the leadership of the entire nation; an international control committee would oversee these elections and make sure that the reunification of North and South Vietnam was fair, legitimate, and uncorrupted. Ho Chi Minh, now the recognized leader of the North, abided by the stipulations of the accord.

The government of the South, backed by the United States, did not.[2]

This period of Vietnam history was the taproot from which utter chaos would soon bloom, and the flower would be a smug and solidly-U.S.-supported Catholic eccentric named Ngo Dinh Diem.

3

The Puppet Who Pulled His Own Strings

"Diem doesn't want to hold elections, and I believe
we should support him in this."

— JOHN FOSTER DULLES
U.S. SECRETARY OF STATE[1]

THE DIVISION of Vietnam was clearly intended to be temporary until a nationwide election could be held. The election was slated for 1956, allowing two years for political parties to solidify and present themselves to the electorate. Ho Chi Minh's Communist party in the north waited contentedly, while in the south, the American CIA propped up the Catholic intellectual Ngo Dinh Diem (pronounced "Zee-em"), whom they believed to be a perfect puppet to rubberstamp U.S. interests. Back in the days of the "Domino Theory" (a theory that purported if one country fell to communism, then all of the other countries in the region would also fall to communism), this was serious business. Ho Chi Minh was now solidly backed by the Soviet Union and the Red Chinese, and the United States needed a suitable Vietnamese leader in the south to keep the U.S. in a legitimate position to counterbalance the Communists.

At this point, Diem was prime minister, serving under yet another political puppet, Bao Dai, who had long served as "emperor" for the French. But Bao Dai was a brash womanizer and gourmand who spent most of his time partying in France while his country languished in turmoil and starvation. The United States needed Bao Dai out of the picture, but before this could be achieved, Diem's own political opponents had to be dealt with.

7

Thus, the Saigon Military Mission was formed, supposedly as an advisory corp. In actuality, it was a CIA front, and one of its key figures, Colonel Edward Lansdale, was charged exclusively with seeing to it that Diem was viewed by his populace in a positive light.

Formerly with the OSS (the Office of Strategic Services, precursor to the CIA), Lansdale was a master of psychological warfare, and his resumé included assisting the leader of the Philippines, Ramon Magsaysay, in crushing a Communist rebellion in that country. Lansdale was a contradiction: on the outside he seemed soft-spoken, eloquent, and low-key, but on the inside he was an aggressive man of action and a mastermind of deception and dirty tricks. Upon his arrival in Vietnam in June of 1954, Lansdale caused great anti-communist dissension by concocting rumors of Red Chinese soldiers burning Vietnamese villages. He also hired native fortunetellers to tell their patrons that Ho Chi Minh would bring only death and destruction to the country. (The Vietnamese were and always had been very superstitious; a trip to the neighborhood fortuneteller was as common as a trip to the market.) Lansdale even manufactured phony Viet Minh documents to terrorize the populace.[2]

But this was only the beginning. In 1955, Diem's major opponents were three political factions: the Cao Dai, the Hao Hao, and the Binh Xuyen. Lansdale quickly swept one coup attempt aside by luring the conspirators away on a pleasure trip to Manila. When other opponent leaders began to rally, Lansdale simply paid them off with CIA funds, giving as much as $3 million to each man to guarantee his public support for Diem.[3] As Lansdale anticipated, many of these chieftains immediately retired to the French Riviera.

The Cao Dai and the Hao Hao factions were rendered harmless, but there remained the Binh Xuyen, the quasi-military faction that ran the secret police. The Binh Xuyen were originally common bandits and river pirates formed of bands of laborers who had sneaked away from the mines, plantations, and factories where they had been enslaved by the French. But by the early '50s, these bandits, under the leadership of Bay Vien, a former street thug who could not read or write, had grown into a small organized crime network throughout Saigon. Vien was the Al Capone of the city, and he and his force of forty thousand controlled all the brothels, gambling casinos, and opium dens in the region.[4] Even Lansdale's enormous bribes couldn't buy off Vien, whose profits from drug smuggling made Lansdale's bribe money look like pocket change.

But it was Diem, not Lansdale, who made the next move, and this surprised the entire Saigon Military Mission. Until then, Diem had appeared as little more than an ineffectual, smiling yes-man in a white suit. His true zeal showed now, and with the help of his brother Nhu—who governed a strong political faction of his own—he decided to fight the powerful Binh Xuyen. Lansdale strongly advised against this (he didn't think Diem could win), but when Diem's mind was made up, Lansdale helped in the strategizing. The result proved even more surprising than the gesture. In April and May of 1955, Diem's forces did battle with Bay Vien's in the streets of Saigon. Five hundred were killed in the operation, whole city districts were turned to rubble, and twenty thousand citizens were left homeless; but at the end of the fight, Diem stood victorious.[5] All of his major political opponents were now sufficiently neutralized.

Diem's show of bravado, planning, and organization duly impressed the Eisenhower administration, reaffirming that Diem was their perfect puppet. And with Diem's adversaries vanquished, there was only one more thing for Lansdale to do. He needed to secure Diem as the bona fide leader of South Vietnam, which meant removing Bao Dai, the official chief of state.

Assassination would have been too risky, and bribery was not an option since Bao Dai was already fabulously wealthy. Instead, Lansdale urged Diem to call for an election. Initially, this seemed daunting to Diem (as a Catholic, he wasn't terribly popular with the Buddhist majority), but Lansdale assured him he could win. Utilizing his specialized skills, Lansdale helped rig the election. Ballot boxes were stuffed. Voters were coerced and threatened. Knowing the penchant for superstition among the population, Lansdale made sure that the ballots for Diem were red (symbolizing good fortune), and those for Bao Dai were green (the color of ill-omen). In the end, Diem won the election by more than 98 percent of the vote, and in many districts, he received more votes than there were voters.[6]

Thus began Diem's reign and the strange power he would soon wield over all of South Vietnam. As the "legitimate" president, he immediately appointed his brother Nhu as his chief advisor and director of the secret police. (Eventually it would be learned that Nhu was the real power behind Diem, and it was a tainted power indeed.) But there was still one more obstacle before Diem could establish his full control over the country—the Geneva Accord.

Nineteen fifty-six was fast approaching, and with it, the Accord's call for a free election to be held for all of Vietnam, allowing the people to choose one leader for their reunified country. Lansdale and the CIA had no control in the north, so tampering with the election would have been fruitless. Diem and Lansdale both knew full well that in a legitimate nationwide election, Ho Chi Minh would almost certainly win because of his broad support among the peasants who comprised most of the population.[7] The situation seemed grim. But there was a quick fix, and it was a fix that the United States wholly endorsed.

With Lansdale's assurance that he'd get away with it, Diem simply refused to allow elections. After all, he'd already won an election, and an additional election would only serve to allow local dissidents to gain power while leadership remained in question.

Diem was the leader of this country now, and as the default bastion of anti-communism, the United States stood solidly behind him. With the Soviets backing the north, it only seemed fair for the United States to back the south.

Now Diem was free to rule South Vietnam. This early in the game, America was only seeing things in black and white. Diem was anti-communist; therefore Diem must be supported. What the administration didn't realize at the time was that Diem viewed things very differently than they did. Diem was primarily motivated by his lust for power and his fanatical Catholicism, not by politics.

As a result, the religious conflict in Vietnam was much more significant than the political conflict. South Vietnam was a quagmire of contradiction. Buddhists comprised the majority of the population, while Catholics accounted for only 10 percent. Soon after Diem's rise to power, however, he filled all the major government posts with family members and other fellow Catholics. During what he called "land reform," the best farmland was given to Catholics, while Buddhist peasants were displaced to lower quality tracts. U.S.-supplied high-quality fertilizers and rodent poisons quickly found their way to Catholic peasants, while the Buddhists got products that were diluted with inert materials. In South Vietnam, the banks were all run by Catholics, so only Catholics got bank loans. Health care in the cities was easily accessible to Catholics, but not Buddhists. This was how Diem began his leadership, and these were the injustices that gave rise to the anti-Diem factions that would eventually become his greatest bane—the Vietcong.

Initially a disorganized amalgam of farmers who would work the land by day and fight at night, the Vietcong would eventually become a formidable guerilla force that Diem's army was hard-pressed to counter. The Vietcong weren't necessarily Communists; they were simply rebels opposed to Diem's favoritism toward the Catholic minority. This rebellion soon developed into an outright war against Diem's government.[8]

To counter this new threat, the U.S. helped train and equip Diem's Civil Guard, but instead of dispatching these troops to protect citizens from the Vietcong, Diem used them to protect his Presidential Palace and government buildings where family members and/or appointed Catholics worked. Diem was fully aware that the United States needed him to maintain a strong stance against communism, and this gave him great power. Though many Eisenhower State Department players didn't approve of Diem at all (envoy John Collins, in fact, was recalled for being a bit too vocal about his dislike of Diem), the overall consensus was that Diem, though not a convincing national leader, was about the best that could be procured at the time. Besides, the U.S. had supported his rise to power; it risked an intractable loss of credibility if it withdrew its support.

Diem used this leverage to his fullest advantage. He and his brother loved the weapons and material that the U.S. heaped upon them, but they used them as they pleased, refusing to take advice from the Americans. The same went for Diem's army (the Army of the Republic of Vietnam, or ARVNs), whom Diem forbade to take orders—or even to consider operational suggestions—from U.S. personnel.[9] This was an unfortunate choice, considering that the United States had considerably more expertise in warfare than the ARVNs. Diem chose instead to use his military forces and police to capture and kill the Viet Minh "stay-behinds," even though these actually posed little or no threat to the country, since a good share of them were simply not Communists and those that had been had either recanted in favor of the Diem government or returned to the north. In his award-winning (and shocking) national bestseller *A Bright Shining Lie,* Neil Sheehan reveals a terrifying practice of Diem's. Diem regarded any stay-behind or ex-member of the Viet Minh as "evil," and he gave the order that anyone even suspected of being a stay-behind should be arrested without trial or investigation. To Diem, suspicion equated to guilt. Those not shot on sight were methodically tortured for names of more "offenders," a process which re-fed itself exponentially. Women bore the brunt: they were raped and tortured, for rape was considered part of the interrogation protocol. In the end, thousands of South Vietnamese were killed, and as many as one hundred thousand more were placed in concentration camps.[10]

Diem persecuted the inactive Viet Minh stay-behinds in much the same way that Hitler persecuted the Jews. Diem created an enemy out of non-aggressors and then viciously and systematically purged them. But if Diem was the Hitler of South Vietnam, his brother Nhu was the Himmler. Nhu ran the secret police, which was a kind of private army for Diem and his family, similar to Hitler's SS. In fact, it was under Nhu's command that the secret police enthusiastically undertook the previously mentioned chores of interrogation, torture, and rape.

But with the stay-behinds vanquished, Diem needed a new scapegoat in order to demonstrate to the populace that he was protecting them from an enemy, however imagined. Now, Diem turned to a religious rather than a political enemy. Diem was a zealous, eccentric Roman Catholic; in 1950, before becoming South Vietnam's prime minister, he lived at the Maryknoll Seminary in New Jersey (where, incidentally, he met and duly impressed a dashing young Massachusetts congressman named John F. Kennedy), praying, meditating, and considering the priesthood.[11] He obviously declined that prospect in favor of politics, but he chose to remain celibate nonetheless. Later, as president, even as he was ordering mass-executions and throwing tens of thousands into concentration camps, he attended Mass nearly every day. Until the day he died, Diem and his entire family considered themselves absolutely devout Catholics. (It is thought that Diem's religious zeal was largely influenced by his eldest brother, Ngo Dinh Thuc, who would become a Catholic archbishop and the Vatican's prelate of South Vietnam. Thuc was principal in many of Diem's controversial actions and policy decisions in the early '60s.)

The natural choice for the new scapegoat, then, was the Buddhists. As mentioned earlier, Diem's unfairness and repression of the Buddhist majority in South Vietnam actually started when he became president; it was just more subtle back then. When nine hundred thousand Vietnamese Catholics were allowed to leave the north and come to the south (a stipulation of the Geneva Accords), Diem immediately granted them better land, jobs, etc., than the Buddhists who had been there in the first place.[12] But in the early '60s life got dramatically worse for the Buddhists. Any problems they brought to the Diem government were ignored. Diem's shock troops forced the Buddhists to either burn their Altars to the Ancestors and convert to Catholicism or suffer the consequences.[13]

Aware of the intricate filaments of Buddhist culture, Diem and Nhu stooped even lower in activating their hatred of Buddhism. In the Buddhist faith, nothing is held more sacred than a cemetery, nothing is deemed more spiritually critical than proper burial of the dead, and nothing is considered more obscene than the desecration of a graveyard. Under Diem's orders, national troops and police began to dig up and desecrate Viet Minh war memorials and Buddhist graveyards,[14] often urinating on and even dismembering the corpses.

As Diem's term drew on, his audacity and madness grew. No longer satisfied with oppression and desecration, in the 1960s, Diem's regime began treating the Buddhists as it had the placid remnants of the Viet Minh, treating them to execution, torture, and concentration camps—and all this from a man that Lyndon Johnson had referred to as "the Winston Churchill of Asia."[15]

4

Triumvirate of Hatred

"If the Buddhists wish to have another barbeque,
I will be glad to supply the gasoline and the match."
— NGO DINH NHU, 1963[1]

IT WAS a sweltering day on May 8, 1963, when crowds of Buddhists congregated at the Tu Dam pagoda in the ancient city of Hue, which was situated near the coast of the Gulf of Tonkin in the northernmost sector of South Vietnam. It was Buddha's 2,527th birthday, and his worshipers had come to joyfully and peacefully celebrate this religious occasion.

Nhu's Civil Guard security forces, led by a Catholic commander, arrived quickly in armored cars, shut down the local radio station, and then engaged in dispersion operations. As part of the celebration, the Buddhists had raised their official flag. Hence, the excuse for the dispatch of government troops was that the assembly violated one of Diem's laws, which forbade religious banners to be flown (despite the fact that a week previously, Diem's brother, Bishop Thuc, had freely flown the papal flag on his limousine). The crowd rebelled, and the order to open fire was given. A woman and eight children were killed. The crowd stampeded into a riot, and when it was all over hundreds had been beaten, arrested, and taken to concentration camps. Protests then began to pop up on a regular basis; students joined the Buddhists in picketing, public denunciation of the Diem regime, and outbursts of rock-throwing. And all were met with the same swift response by Nhu's troops.

By this time, John F. Kennedy was well into his first term as president, and he had essentially maintained his predecessor's posture of supporting South Vietnam in the fight against communism. Kennedy's State Department had ordered Diem to cease Buddhist harassment, but even when the order was ignored, Kennedy wasn't terribly worried about what Washington viewed as a single countercultural skirmish. (Diem claimed that the Vietcong had caused the May 8th riot and had fired into the crowd; when autopsy reports on the dead proved otherwise, Diem confiscated the reports.[2])

Then, on June 11, 1963, a Buddhist leader named Quang Duc calmly sat down in a Saigon street, soaked himself with gasoline, and lit a match. The monk burst into flames but never moved, never screamed or shouted, never even flinched. Instead he remained seated in the standard lotus position, praying, as the fire consumed him. Eventually he slumped over dead.

This self-immolation was actually a traditional form of Buddhist protest; throughout the history of the Buddhist faith, high-ranking monks would set themselves ablaze as a symbolic gesture—they would become willing torches to shine a light through the darkness of oppression. The news of Quang Duc's self-sacrifice swept through South Vietnam, but something else happened that hadn't been foreseen.

The news also swept through the world.

South Vietnam, by this date, was a hotbed of reporters, photo-journalists, and wire-service correspondents. And this was big news.

The day after Quang Duc's suicide, news photos of the incident appeared on the front pages of every major newspaper in the world, along with articles explaining the roots of the tragedy. The world was shocked, and so was President Kennedy. Prior to Quang Duc's self-immolation, the world had been kept relatively ignorant of Diem's abuses of the Buddhists, and even though Kennedy and his State Department had—through diplomatic back channels—complained to Diem about it, the abuses were not considered a big deal.

But it was definitely a big deal to Kennedy on June 12, 1963. In one night, America and the rest of the world learned the truth about the "Winston Churchill of Asia," and the Kennedy administration couldn't have been more embarrassed. With the news out on the full extent of Diem's brutality toward the Buddhists, America immediately began to ask itself the obvious questions: Why is the U.S. supporting a foreign government that engages in religious persecution? Why is President Kennedy sending U.S. military personnel to help the government of a man who puts his own people into concentration camps?

Until then, America had understood that the increasing number of

U.S. men and women being sent to South Vietnam (close to 15,000 by June 1963) and the 1.2-million-dollar-per-day aid package were to help the South Vietnamese fight the deadly Vietcong. But suddenly it seemed that Diem was more concerned with fighting unarmed, pacifist monks in saffron robes. Literally overnight, the United States was internationally perceived as a bunch of buffoons who were propping up a tyrant. Kennedy was infuriated; moreover, he and his political consultants were scared. The next election was just over a year away, and Kennedy had won his first term by an unimaginably narrow margin (he beat Richard Nixon by 118,000 votes out of 68.3 million cast).³ Sending U.S. tax dollars and U.S. blood to the Hitleresque Diem would make Kennedy appear completely inept to American voters and make him an easy target for Republicans, who were still seething from their defeat in 1960. They already believed that Kennedy had stolen the election, based on suspicious vote-counting in Illinois; a Catholic U.S. president supporting a Catholic fanatic who was intent on persecuting another religious group would provide them with all the ammunition they needed in November of '64.

Of course, Kennedy immediately ordered his State Department to rebuke Diem and order him to desist. This single self-immolation had presented Kennedy with his worst problem since the Cuban Missile Crisis, and he was determined to fix it.

As ordered, Diem was severely reprimanded by U.S. officials, who made it plain that if Buddhist repression continued, Diem would lose his cherished U.S. aid.

Diem's response only proved his breathtaking arrogance. Instead of kowtowing to his only major supporter, he and his brother spin-doctored the incident in a smear campaign, ridiculously painting the Buddhists as Communists and undercover agents for the Vietcong. Nhu would make appallingly brazen public statements, offering to supply the gasoline and the match for further immolations, insisting that the Buddhists were operatives for the enemy. Additionally, Nhu's wife, the controversial Madame Nhu (also called "The Dragon Lady" and "The First Lady of Vietnam") stepped closer to the forefront not only to support the groundless accusation that the Buddhists were Communists but also to propagate even more rancor. In a film interview, she absurdly claimed that the first sacrifice would have been more efficient if the Buddhists had used local instead of imported gasoline,⁴ and later would refer to continued self-immolations as "*bonze* barbeques," adding, "Let them burn, and we shall clap our hands."[5]

Diem, Nhu, and Madame Nhu were now presenting themselves as an oligarchy or a triumvirate, not as officials of what was supposed to be a democratic government. When Diem ignored further U.S. insistence that he cease his repression of the Buddhists, Kennedy yanked the current U.S. ambassador (Frederick Nolting) and appointed Henry Cabot Lodge as his replacement, a man with strong anti-Catholic roots and, of all things, a hardline Republican. Kennedy chose Lodge for three reasons. One, as a Republican, Lodge's appointment would defuse rising Republican objection in the Congress to Kennedy's handling of Vietnam. Two, with Lodge in place, Kennedy had a Republican to cast blame on if the Vietnam situation turned into a debacle during his administration. And, three—and perhaps foremost—this was the strongest message sent to Diem thus far that he'd better shape up. Nolting had not only been a staunch supporter of Diem, he was a personal friend.

But Kennedy's plan backfired. Diem would not be shaken, threatened, or intimidated. Recalling Nolting was like a blow to the face, but instead of bowing down, Diem punched back, continuing his Hitlerian onslaught against the Buddhists.

Throughout July and August, Diem and his entourage persisted with public statements vilifying the Buddhists as Communists, continued with their poor-taste comments and "barbeque" remarks, and, worse, continued raiding and ransacking Buddhist temples, continued killing and beating, and began throwing even more Buddhists—thousands now—into the camps.[6]

As a result, more Buddhist monks burned themselves alive in protest, and the Kennedy administration continued to take a critical pounding, because now the atrocities against Buddhists were getting more coverage in the press than the Vietnam War itself, despite the fact that the Vietcong were in full swing, bombing public buildings, assassinating Diem's officials, and killing peasants, ARVN troops, and U.S. military advisors.

Even before Henry Cabot Lodge assumed his new post as U.S. ambassador, South Vietnam was going to hell in a handbasket. And so was John F. Kennedy's reputation.

Diem, Nhu, Madame Nhu—this tyrannical triumvirate of hatred was making a fool of the entire United States.[7]

5

The Network

After Nhu guaranteed his opium shipments safe
conduct, Francisci's fleet of twin-engine
Beechcrafts began making regular clandestine
airdrops inside South Vietnam.[1]

AS PREVIOUSLY recounted, Diem's forces, with CIA-plant Edward Lansdale's help, defeated and expelled the notorious Binh Xuyen sect and its thug overlord General Bay Vien. After they were removed, their previous enterprises (gambling, prostitution, and drugs) were left to founder. After a short time, however, the casinos and brothels were quietly permitted to renew their operations, but one vice that Diem could not abide was opium use. Diem sponsored public burnings of opium paraphernalia as a means of publicly denouncing the evils of Vien and his crimelords. And when his defeat of the Binh Xuyen closed down all the opium dens, he was determined to keep those dens closed until it became expedient for them to be reopened.

His brother Nhu had inherited the country's secret police (formerly controlled by Vien), and he also maintained a vast intelligence network. United States aid to Diem was hefty indeed (it would grow to close to half a billion dollars per year by 1963), but Diem needed these funds to maintain his regular army and his government, not to mention his own indulgence. Popular history seems to ignore or overlook Diem's gross abuse of U.S. economic aid, but for students who look more closely, it's no secret at all. The very best firsthand synopsis of this abuse that we've seen comes from a letter that wasn't declassified until 2003. The letter is to Maryland 1st District Congressman Thomas F. Johnson from Nguyen-Thai-Binh, a Vietnamese scholar and political science student. The date is November

20, 1961. Johnson had recently toured South Vietnam on a fact-finding mission with other U.S. congressmen, and in this monumental letter, Binh acknowledges Johnson's visit and adds some interesting supplemental information. Binh's perspectives are important because they offer us a true insider's look at the situation in South Vietnam at the time. His insights and revelations so alarmed Congressman Johnson that he forwarded the letter to the Secretary of State. Here's what Binh had to say to Johnson about the way Diem was ruling South Vietnam in general:

> During the past seven years our country has received enough financial aid from the United States to rebuild the entire country on a scale of any large American city. But instead of any social or economic improvement the money has been used to support a familial dictatorship whose tyrannical methods have incurred the hatred and compounded the misery of the Vietnamese people. Ngo Dinh Diem, with the aid of his brothers, in-laws, and cousins, who hold all the key administrative posts in the government, has unscrupulously suppressed freedom and civil liberties and indulged in extensive graft and corruption. Instead of new homes, factories, civil enterprises, etc., they have used the money to build concentration camps and prisons, to maintain a secret police force which is used to police the Vietnamese people, to control the press, rig elections, and for propaganda in favor of their regime.

Binh goes on,

> Under the guise of war security measures, Diem has constructed concentration camps that now hold 30,000 prisoners whose greatest crime is their belief in freedom. The camps are described as a revival of the cruelest period of Nazi methods of suppression. Communism can only be fought with strong nationalistic support, and Diem puts the nationalist leaders in prison!

Keep in mind, U.S. troops in military advisory roles were also in the country at the time, some taking fire, some being injured and killed. None of them knew that they were putting their lives at risk for this tyrannical farce. Ideally, the U.S. presence in South Vietnam existed to preserve democracy, while actually our men were being made cannon fodder to support a liar, thief, and despot. Binh points out how far removed Diem's regime was from promoting democracy: "Elections are a notorious farce. Recently a popular candidate outdistanced the ballot-stuffers and won. His seat in the National Assembly was promptly denied him on the grounds that he had made 'false promises' in his election campaign."

In a democracy, citizens are entitled to a free press, but Binh writes that,

> Press control is extensive and effected through both direct pressure and "guidance memos" to newspaper and radio directors. The extent of expenditure of propaganda to support the Diem regime is incalculable. Foreign embassies are assigned the task of disseminating [circulating] information favorable to Diem on a large scale . . . . These elusive propaganda campaigns over the years have distorted the problems of South Vietnam beyond recognition.

But these first few paragraphs of Binh's shocking testimony are tame compared to what we learn next, and this information is much more pertinent to the more specific abuses of powers we're about to highlight. Referring to a recent exposé in the French newspaper *Combat*, Binh writes:

> The corruption, embezzlement, and nepotism of the Ngo Dinh Diem regime are notorious. Everyone in Vietnam talks about it, and here are some names and facts:
>
> Ngo Dinh Nhu, Diem's brother, head of the Can-Loa [a supposedly nationalistic political group], controls the entire economic life of the country. The article goes on to give facts and dates about some of the notorious scandals in the government, including: Ngo Dinh Can's [another Diem brother, the governor of Central Vietnam] traffic of rice to the Vietminh; the embezzlement of 22 million dollars of American foreign aid . . . [and] traffic in opium organized by the Can Loa [Nhu's political party] through diplomatic valises.

This last bit of news takes us right back to the major point of this chapter. As the regime's internal power began to escalate, so did its need for security and self-preservation. Security costs money, however, and although Diem was able to cleverly—and illicitly—harness a lot of money via the misuse and misappropriation of U.S. financial aid (which Binh grimly verifies), only so much U.S. cash could be reaped. It was not enough, and Nhu's private intelligence operations suffered from under-funding as a result.

The solution to this fiscal problem was simple. In 1958, they simply reopened the opium dens in order to cultivate the commerce of Saigon's multitude of hungry addicts.[2]

A few pro-Diemists will assert that Nhu did this on his own, without his brother's approval, but this is unlikely in the extreme. Nhu's intelligence network was so vast that it employed as many as 100,000 part-time operatives.[3] It would have been impossible for him to finance the entire operation without his brother, the president, ever figuring it out.

It only makes sense that Diem knew about this and approved it, for Nhu's spy network was essential in keeping tabs on all of the government's many enemies, information about whom Diem needed in his Stalin-like paranoia. As far as Diem was concerned, it was not a sin to profit off of sinners.

In this pursuit, Nhu employed a corporate expertise like that of a Fortune 500 executive. In order to provide a profitable quantity of opium to Saigon's innumerable addicts, he needed to construct a reliable supply route. This would be from Laos, in the northwest, from the abundant poppy fields that were part of the famed Golden Triangle. And it was a leftover operative from the old days of French rule who would become Nhu's exclusive partner.

Bonaventure Francisci, nicknamed "Rock," was a debonair, handsome Frenchman fond of imported white silk jackets, jewelry, and fineries. With his slicked-back dark hair, pencil-line moustache, intriguing, eloquent charm, and primped manner, he could have been a well-funded pimp; or he could have been a diamond dealer. But Francisci dealt in something far more valuable than diamonds. He had lucrative, long-since-established procurement connections with the Laotian opium market. Francisci worked for a man named Antoine Guerini who headed the heroin syndicate back in Marseille in southern France. The Marseille Mob drew extensively from the *Union Corse* for its personnel resources.*

It was the Marseille Mob's heroin laboratories that provided product to underworld bosses in the United States using a long-standing deal

---

*The *Union Corse* refers to the Corsican Mob, which was comprised of ex-patriots, thugs, deserters from the French military who elected to pursue a life of crime as hitmen, drug-peddlers, extortionists, etc. Often the Marseille Mob and the Corsican Mob are referred to as synonymous entities, and this is because the mainstay of personnel in the Marseille underworld originally came from the island of Corsica to forge more lucrative careers in organized crime. From here on, for simplicity's sake, we'll refer to this underworld entity as the "Marseille Mob."

made by New York crime-hierarch Meyer Lanksy in the early '50s. Since that time, most of the heroin being sold to U.S. addicts was made in Marseille,[4] and Rock Francisci was the middleman between raw product and delivery.

Rock Francisci worked expressly for the Marseille enterprise, which was then run by Antoine Guerini and his brother Barthélemay. It's accurate to say that the heroin franchise in the U.S. and in Western Europe was controlled almost entirely by the Guerinis. In 1958, when Diem and Nhu reopened opium traffic into Saigon, Francisci couldn't have been happier. This revitalized his old business of transporting opium from his sources in Laos over to South Vietnam by way of a fleet of private planes he owned. But there was even more money to be made by simply marketing opium to Saigon's hundreds of dens and thousands of addicts. Opium production in other parts of the world—particularly Turkey and Mexico—was becoming erratic and unreliable due to increased intervention by law-enforcement authorities. This situation worked to the advantage of the Guerinis in that it increased their cut of the heroin pie when Nhu and Rock Francisci cut a landmark distribution deal. Francisci would transport the opium to Saigon for Nhu's opium dens, but in addition he would also transport even more opium to Saigon drop-points where it would then be shipped by supply freighters to Marseille's labs. In Marseille, the opium would be processed into high-grade heroin and then resold to druglords in the United States such as Santos Trafficante, Carlos Marcello, and Sam Giancana. Everyone made money on this deal, and it was as safe a deal as anyone could imagine because Nhu had no law-enforcement entity to worry about or answer to. He was the law, and he utilized this power to guarantee Francisci—and his Marseille buyer—a constant supply of opium for heroin production.

Nhu, given his position of power in the South Vietnamese government, could guarantee that Francisci's opium-heavy charter planes (under the auspices of "diplomatic" transport) could slip into Saigon from Laos and make their deliveries with no worry of intervention. Nhu even increased the steady stream of product in 1961 and 1962 by utilizing his own 1st Transport Group (an aerial intelligence operation which sometimes flew jointly with the CIA) to do the same.[5] Between 1958 and 1963, Saigon became a veritable warehouse of raw opium, much of which was spirited to Marseille to eventually satisfy the needs of America's heroin addicts.

But Nhu provided further incentives for the lucrative agreement. While

Francisci's own charter planes—called Air Laos Commerciale—flew opium daily into Saigon with no law-enforcement worries, other smaller suppliers were not afforded the same protection. Nhu's police force would quickly take care of any opium supplier that dared to cut into Francisci's "turf."[6]

The Guerini syndicate couldn't have been more elated with Francisci's deal, nor could they have been happier with Nhu for making it all possible. This deal made the Guerinis the heroin lords of the globe in the late '50s and early '60s, and it forged a rock-solid criminal alliance between Nhu and the Marseille Mob. Nhu, Diem, and the entirety of the Ngo Dinh family gained phenomenal personal wealth due to this alliance (while also procuring the necessary under-the-table funding for their secret police and intelligence branch). More important than that, the Guerini crime family amassed even more wealth, and so did their primary heroin buyer: the U.S. Mafia.

In essence, the Marseille Mob, the U.S. Mafia, and the Diem government became mutual business partners in a global heroin network.

This of course meant enormous profit for all involved, and the source of this money and power was Ngo Dinh Nhu.

6

Kennedy's Coup

"The United States Government
will support a coup . . ."

— DEAN RUSK
U.S. SECRETARY OF STATE,
AUGUST 29, 1963[1]

THE ABOVE epigraph is from a cable sent by Dean Rusk to U.S. Ambassador of Vietnam Henry Cabot Lodge. Bear in mind, Rusk was not only Secretary of State but also one of Kennedy's primary yes-men. He transmitted this cablegram on August 29, 1963, immediately after a national security meeting, and in it stipulated the initial guidelines for a U.S.-endorsed coup d'etat against their allies, the government of South Vietnam.

Lodge had been in place at his new post as ambassador for only a week, and this is the kind of cable traffic he was already receiving from Washington. Lodge was a strong supporter of an overthrow of the Diem government, as were Rusk, Attorney General Robert Kennedy, Assistant Secretaries for Far Eastern Affairs Averrel Harriman and Roger Hilsman, National Security Chief McGeorge Bundy, and Bundy's brother William in the defense department.

These were the men closest to the president's ear—exceedingly powerful officials who were capable of and often responsible for carrying out Kennedy's orders.

Readers who question the assertion that Kennedy and his team wanted President Diem's government toppled and destroyed should investigate the Government Printing Office publication entitled *Foreign Relations of the United States, 1961-1963, Volume IV, Vietnam: August-December*

1963, which remained classified for more than two decades. This document is a printing of the official record of U.S. foreign policy regarding Vietnam during that time period. It contains assessment reports, government memorandums, reviews of White House meetings with Kennedy, and of particular interest, all U.S. cable-traffic between the White House and the U.S. Embassy in Saigon. The pages of this book expose the conscience of the Kennedy administration related to the government of President Ngo Dinh Diem and comprehensively prove that the Kennedy administration engaged in one of the most traitorous of acts: sponsoring the overthrow of an allied chief of state.

But before probing into the president's culpability and its perilous consequences, let's take a look at the crisis-point of the Diem regime and the events that happened soon thereafter.

△

On August 21, 1963, despite strong warnings by the Kennedy administration, Diem and Nhu launched yet another series of violent, repressive strikes against the Buddhists, principally the Xa Loi Temple, which was the Buddhists' most sacred shrine in Saigon. During this surge of strikes, Nhu's soldiers plundered pagodas with reckless abandon and incarcerated thousands of monks and nuns. In addition, many of these "public offenders" simply disappeared,[2] never to be seen again.

Alarm bells had been going off at the White House since June of '63 because of Diem's hostile treatment of the Buddhists. Successive protests that involved monks burning themselves to death had begun to make international headlines and were beginning to cast the United States in a darker light for its support of such a repressive government. But even before those horrific displays, on March 8, 1963—seven months before the Diem coup actually took place—the South Vietnamese Ambassador to the United States (Tran Van Chuong, Madame Nhu's father and Nhu's father-in-law) told National Security Council staff member Michael Forrestal, "We could not win with Diem. Therefore there was only one course open to us and that was to bring about a change in government, which could probably only be done with violence."[3]

A U.S. intelligence assessment report delineates the feeling of the White House at the time: "The Buddhist Crisis in South Vietnam has highlighted and intensified a widespread and long-standing dissatisfaction with the Diem regime and its style of government."[4]

Kennedy could see this colossal accident waiting to happen, and he could also see his chances for reelection, in little more than a year, going straight down the drain. After all, Diem was a president America was supporting with considerable tax dollars and material (not to mention thousands of personnel), and yet he continued to embarrass the U.S. in the global spotlight. Naturally, Kennedy ordered a salvo of threats. Diem was told to cease all affronts against the Buddhists, or else.

Clearly, without U.S. support, Diem and Nhu and their seat of power in South Vietnam would not be long-lived. Nevertheless, they ignored the U.S. warnings altogether. As the crisis grew hotter, Lodge was sent to assume his ambassadorial post early, now that Frederick Nolting had been yanked out for his pro-Diem views. (Nolting was a friend of Diem, and even with the pile of repressive evidence at his feet, he continued to insist that Diem was a hallmark of "democratic principles" and "social justice."[5]) Lodge immediately met with Diem at the Presidential Palace and couldn't have been more insulted by Diem's attitude. "I brought up this question of getting Nhu out of the country," Lodge said in a 1983 interview, "and Diem absolutely refused to discuss any of the things I was instructed [by Kennedy] to discuss. And it gave me a little jolt, frankly. I think that when an ambassador goes to call on a chief of state, and he has been instructed by the president to bring up certain things, the chief of state ought to at least talk about them."[6]

Diem's position and arrogance were obvious. He would not betray his brother Nhu or change his stance on the Buddhists to save his presidency. Kennedy couldn't help but see this as a flagrant insult; Diem was biting the hand the fed him.

Diem's major military generals were growing more and more dissatisfied with the direction of the current government (many of these generals were not Catholic; they had Buddhist roots), and it was known, even earlier in the year, that there was talk of overthrowing Diem. The White House got wind of this from a variety of channels: the Military Assistance Advisory Group; Army, Navy, and Air Force intelligence sectors; and the CIA. Smart governments always consider worst-case scenarios, and Kennedy had been doing exactly that, well before the Buddhist repression hit the papers and threatened to smear his grasp of foreign policy. Kennedy had called for numerous assessment reports on not only the progress of the war but also Diem's competence as president of the nation.[7] The cogs were turning. Kennedy knew how to calculate potential political obstacles; he was constantly considering the present for its implications, good or bad, toward the future. Kennedy carefully weighed every White House move, judging how the Republicans might use it against him in the next election.

At 1 P.M. on November 1, 1963, a coup d'etat commenced against the Diem government, led by South Vietnamese General Duong Van Minh (a.k.a "Big Minh"). As a precaution, Big Minh ordered the executions of an influential pro-Diem naval commander as well as the commanders of South Vietnam's special forces shortly before the coup had officially started, nipping potential rallying in the bud. Then the fight began in the form of prompt military strikes on communication centers and radio stations, the national police headquarters, and Diem's luxurious Presidential Palace. Meanwhile, the major military units that could have been used to defend Diem had cleverly been moved out of striking distance. When the rebellion began, Lodge was immediately notified by the CIA desk. Diem called the ambassador himself and asked what the United States' attitude was. Lodge replied, "I do not feel well-informed enough to be able to tell you."[8]

America would not communicate with their former ally anymore; Diem was a marked man.

The coup was executed with speed and precision. But as a fierce battle raged at the Presidential Palace, Diem and Nhu managed to escape through an underground passageway and find safe harbor in Cholon (Saigon's Chinatown), where Nhu had close confidants via his opium network.*

Diem eventually capitulated—having little choice—and the fighting ceased. After a bit of haggling, Diem agreed to reveal his location and publicly surrender to Big Minh and his insurgent generals if they promised Diem and his brother Nhu safe passage out of the country. Minh agreed.

Diem then disclosed that he and Nhu were hiding at a Catholic church in Cholon, and he guaranteed that they would wait to be picked up by

---

*It's interesting to note here, as an addendum to Diem and Nhu's character, that the loyal presidential security forces at the palace continued to fight and die for many hours to come, never knowing that the president they were fighting for had long since abandoned them. Once he'd reached safe distance from the palace, Diem could have easily placed an untraceable phone call to his security forces at the palace and told them to surrender and save their lives. Instead, Diem chose to let them die.

Minh's soldiers and taken back to staff headquarters to officially abdicate. Minh dispatched his bodyguard and a platoon of vehicles and troops to make the pickup. When they arrived at the church, Diem and Nhu cordially turned themselves in, whereupon they were escorted out of the church and placed inside an armored personnel carrier.

When the personnel carrier's door was shut, Diem and Nhu were immediately beaten, hog-tied, and then shot to death.[9]

△

The above account seems cut and dried. Dissatisfied South Vietnamese generals overthrew the government and executed its president and chief of staff. No U.S. soldiers participated. So what does this have to do with complicity on the part of the Kennedy administration?

First, there's the case of Lucien Conein, the rough and tough paratrooper and French Resistance fighter who was—as of 1963—a high-priority clandestine operative for the CIA. Lodge chose Conein to be his secret middleman between the insurgent generals and Lodge's office. Conein was French by birth; he knew the language as well as the customs, which was important because Big Minh and many of his rebel generals were raised in French culture too. Conein could immediately relate to these men in a way that other U.S. operatives couldn't. Conein's function—which he carried out flawlessly—was to assure Big Minh and his general staff that the United States would support them in a coup against Diem. Conein was the messenger (the secret messenger, as most of his meetings with the insurgent generals were deliberately never reported to the U.S. military commanders in South Vietnam) between the generals and Lodge, ferrying information back and forth under Lodge's orders.[10] Conein was also Big Minh's man on the inside, a trusted comrade who insulated their coup plans from the pro-Diem U.S. Military Mission. Conein was even cementing crucial friendships before Lodge arrived as ambassador, with the likes of General Tran Van Don,[11] who was Big Minh's right-hand man during the coup.

Hence, Conein was the CIA's main operator in Saigon as far as the coup was concerned. (It certainly wasn't Station Chief John Richardson who, like ex-Ambassador Nolting and U.S. Military Advisory Mission Commander General Paul Harkins, was stridently opposed to a coup against Diem and was fired by Kennedy in October of 1963.[12])

But what exactly did Conein do with regard to Diem's overthrow besides pass messages back and forth between Lodge and the plotting generals?

- Before the coup officially began, Conein was summoned to Big Minh's general staff headquarters and given a direct line of communication to the Saigon CIA outpost.[13] (To support this point, more recently, it's been revealed that during the coup, Conein was also in steady cable contact with McGeorge Bundy at the White House Situation Room. Bundy was Kennedy's closest NSC advisor.)[14]

- The greatest concern of Big Minh and his generals was receiving the United States' "blessing" for their endeavor to overthrow Diem. They wanted to know if U.S. troops would intervene, and it was Conein who assured them they would not. They also wanted to be assured that U.S. military aid would continue once Diem was gone, and it was Conein who assured them it would. What Big Minh and his generals wanted—what they needed— more than anything else was a green light from the United States to begin the coup. "I know that I gave them a green light prior to the coup," Conein stated in an interview years later, "upon the instructions of my government."[15]

- Lodge, as well as CIA channels, provided Minh and his insurgents with money and weapons for the coup.[16] They also received intelligence information about the locations of combat units likely to remain loyal to Diem, as well as the locations of weapons and ammunition that Nhu had been secreting about Saigon for several months. The day before the overthrow began, Lodge made it clear that last-minute funds could be delivered to the generals if necessary. "I believe we should furnish them," he said.[17] So when Conein was invited by Minh to staff headquarters just before the coup commenced, he brought a bag full of cash (the equivalent in Vietnamese piasters to forty thousand U.S. dollars, which would be equal to several hundred thousand dollars today) as a last minute emergency fund and as escape money for the generals in the event that the coup failed.[18]*

---

*As recently as April 2000, it's become known that Diem himself, on the night of the coup, had in his possession a suitcase containing 1 million U.S. dollars. Big Minh took possession of that money, and to this day, no one knows where it came from or what Minh did with it.[19]

• When Diem phoned the general staff headquarters and agreed
to capitulate in return for a guarantee of safe passage, Minh
agreed. But then Minh gave the order to execute Diem and
Nhu anyway. Allegedly, when Minh asked Conein for a plane
to fly Diem and Nhu out of the country, Conein said a plane
couldn't possibly be requisitioned in less than twenty-four
hours.[20] Big Minh knew that if Diem and Nhu weren't flown
out of the country immediately, a counter-coup could result.
This isn't merely speculation, because records attest that the
United States was thinking the exact same thing. On August
30, 1963, Assistant Secretary of State for Far Eastern Affairs
Roger Hilsman prepared a list of contingencies regarding the
coup that by this point appeared unavoidable. It's a six-page
top secret memo that forecasts multiple coup scenarios and
cites the most effective U.S. response to each case. The last page
reads: "Under no circumstances [after a successful coup] should
the Ngo's be permitted to remain in Southeast Asia in close
proximity to Viet-Nam because of the plots they will try to
mount to regain power." Earlier in the same paragraph,
Hilsman recommends, "We should be prepared, with the
knowledge of the coup group, to furnish a plane to take the
Ngo family to France or other European country which will
receive it." Yet, despite his promises, no plane was ever
furnished. One would assume that for a campaign of this
importance, the United States could have provided a plane
instantly (the general staff headquarters for the coup was
located at the officers' club at Ton Son Nhut airport where the
United States had dozens if not hundreds of aircraft that could
have easily been relegated for this task). Conein was, after all,
the same man who had given Big Minh the green light, upon
the instructions of his government, to begin a coup, and he was
still operating under those same government instructions to
deny access to a plane for safe-passage, which gave Big Minh
no choice but to order Diem and Nhu's execution.

It can be argued that, from a political standpoint, Kennedy didn't just
want Diem and Nhu dead; he needed them dead. Otherwise, once given
asylum somewhere else, they would crucify Kennedy in the international

press, and this information would be used by those Republican political foes working against his reelection. America was already in a state of communist paranoia. Imagine how voters would react to Kennedy if recently deposed ally Diem launched an international trash campaign against him.

Diem couldn't simply be deposed; he had to be killed. And it had to be Diem's own generals that performed the task. Conein effected this with no effort at all.*

This all provides a pretty clear picture of Lucien Conein. Bypassing and essentially ignoring his own field boss (Richardson, the Saigon Station Chief), Conein worked directly for Lodge, and Lodge worked directly for Kennedy. Indeed, author Neil Sheehan describes Conein best of all: "Few secret agents are ever given an opportunity to scale the professional summit by arranging the overthrow of a government. Conein was transmitting the power of the United States to influence these generals to do its bidding."[22]

To sum up, Kennedy, in actuality, was a staunch enemy of communism, but when Diem's true colors began to show—as a despot, a persecutor, and a chief of state who condemned monks, nuns, and children to concentration camps—Kennedy politically recoiled. But rather than admit his mistake to the American people and publicly call for action against Diem, Kennedy elected to utilize the same ploy that had saved him during the Cuban Missile Crisis: using clandestine back-channels to take care of the problem. Kennedy outright ignored the very people who were most in the know of the precarious situation. Nobody in the U.S. military or government really liked Diem, but as far as the cessation of communism in South Vietnam went, Diem was judged by Kennedy's top field advisors to be the best weapon they had. And as it turns out, these advisors—men like Ambassador Nolting, CIA Station Chief Richardson, MAAG General Harkins, CIA Director John McCone, and his deputy William Colby— were right. Writer and historian Professor C.L. Corey says it most effectively in his March 1999 article: "The Kennedy Administration and the media, by destroying the South Vietnamese government, made the war the headless monster it became."[23]

---

*A final note on Conein's character: A little less than ten years later, CIA "black-bag" man E. Howard Hunt strongly considered recruiting Conein as a member of the discreet-entry team that would later become known as the Watergate Burglars. To this, Conein affirmed, "If I'd been involved, we'd have done it right."[21]

After Diem's death, the South Vietnamese government fell into a succession of flawed, corrupt regimes that never effectively countered communist influence in the country—something Kennedy was warned of by his pro-Diem advisors. Before Diem's assassination, the United States had only seen about 150 U.S. military personnel killed in action; after Diem's assassination, the United States would see 58,000 men and women killed. Kennedy chose to ignore his field advisors in favor of the State Department yes-men who advised and acted only in accordance with the mission of getting him reelected. This meant letting the insurgent generals depose and kill Diem and Nhu, a cleaner (though less diplomatic) way to resolve the rising danger that threatened his public image.

Another expert of the Vietnam War, William J. Rust, describes the administration's resolve to destroy Diem in the book that may detail his execution better than any text ever written:

> Although American officials in Washington and Saigon had advance knowledge of the coup and the danger in which Diem might find himself, no arrangements had been made to fly him out of the country. . . . [S]eventeen hours after the start of the coup, there still had been no attempt to fly Diem out of the country.[24]

A close look at actual cablegram traffic between the White House and the U.S. Embassy in Saigon shows further evidence that Kennedy and his administration willingly prompted this coup d'etat.

On November 1, 1963, 12:04 P.M.—just one hour before the coup began—Secretary Rusk cabled Lodge,

> If coup succeeds, acceptance and understanding of its purpose here will be greatly increased if the Generals and their civilian associates continue to develop strongly and publicly the conclusion reported in one of their broadcasts that Nhu was dickering with the Communists to betray anti-Communist cause.[25]

In essence, Rusk is telling Lodge that U.S. voters will be mollified if Lodge asks the coup generals to publicly state that Nhu was a Communist collaborator.

A statement from Roger Hilsman, assistant secretary of state for far eastern affairs, declared that if Diem "remains obdurate and refuses [to remove his brother Nhu from the government] we must face the possibility that Diem himself cannot be preserved." This message was given to Lodge on August 24, 1963, only two days after he had arrived to assume his post as ambassador.[26] This message, which Rusk also ordered to be communicated to the rebel generals, is a clear signature of the Kennedy administration endorsing the coup.

Stanley Karnow states the implication quite well in his famous compendium of the Vietnam War: "For it [the message] meant, in theory at least, that the United States [hence, the Kennedy administration] reserved the right to manipulate a dependent government that failed to conform to its standards."[27]

On August 29, 1963, Lodge posted this message to the White House, verifying the administration's attitude: "We are launched on a course from which there is no respectable turning back: the overthrow of the Diem government."[28]

Once the ball got rolling, Kennedy expressed some erratic last-minute reservations, fearing the consequences if the coup failed (the same sort of reservations that caused him to renege at the last minute on air support during the Bay of Pigs Invasion, which turned the endeavor [which he knew about and initially authorized] into a catastrophe and became his only major public embarrassment). But his stamp of approval came soon enough when he personally cabled Lodge and said, "But once a coup under responsible leadership has begun . . . it is in the interest of the U.S. government that it should succeed."[29]

In the preeminent documentary *Vietnam: A Television History*, Lodge was interviewed a few years before he died in 1985 and stated rigidly, "I'd been living with it for several weeks but I can't say I was surprised . . . but it was an interesting thing to see people shooting."

Not only does Lodge downplay the gravity of the coup and the ensuing war with that peculiar last statement, but also he seems to have forgotten his pivotal role in the whole effort. Documentation proves that Lodge had been prompting this overthrow not for "several weeks" but for months, even before his White House meetings, before he'd been sent to Saigon in August of 1963.

Seymour Hersh, in his phenomenal *The Dark Side of Camelot*, cites unpublished memoirs left by Lodge after his death: "I was instructed to send my telegrams directly to [President Kennedy]"[30]—more evidence that Kennedy ordered Lodge to circumvent proper channels in favor of the back-channel and deliberately keep the plan of coup support from the knowledge of the U.S. military commanders in South Vietnam and other field-politicos who opposed Kennedy's vision for resolving the problem.

As previously stated, Kennedy's plan wouldn't work if Diem and Nhu survived the coup, but the plan would also fail if certain other members of Diem's family either survived or weren't sufficiently neutralized. The infamous Madame Nhu was touring America at the time of the coup, try-ing—and failing—to drum up faltering U.S. support for the South Vietnamese cause. She was safely out of the way of the coup and couldn't very well be suddenly found dead (like, for instance, so many Kennedy assassination witnesses) because she was too much in the limelight at the time. Lodge saw to it that her children did not remain in harm's way; he had them moved to a mountain retreat just before the coup and ordered them flown to Rome. Diem's oldest brother, the Archbishop Thuc, was conveniently recalled back to the Vatican shortly after Kennedy met with the pope in July. Another of Diem's brothers, Ngo Dinh Can, who acted as Diem's overlord in Central Vietnam didn't fare so well. He was very political and very vocal about U.S. attempts to manipulate Diem's sover-eign government. During the coup, however, Can realized his predicament and contacted Lodge, pleading for asylum, knowing that if captured, Big Minh's forces would kill him. Lodge readily complied, or so it would seem. Can was instructed by Lodge to hide in an American plane, in a diplomatic courier bag, after which he would be flown safely out of the country to the Philippines. But as soon as Can had hidden himself on the plane, the flight was diverted and ordered to land at Ton Son Nhut air-base where Big Minh's soldiers were waiting. Can was immediately arrested and later shot by a firing squad.[31] Lodge had set Can up, leaving him at the mercy of a new government that had no choice but to kill him.

Through it all, Lodge kept America looking clean. After the coup, the esteemed ambassador went public to assert to the American people that the United States was completely innocent of the whole bloody Diem ordeal. "The overthrow," he wrote in a *New York Times* article on June 30, 1964, "of the Diem regime was purely a Vietnamese affair. We never participated in the planning. We never gave any advice. We had nothing whatever to do with it."[32] And yet only five days after Diem and Nhu were executed, Lodge sent a cable to the White House which read, ". . . the ground in which the coup seed grew into a robust plant was prepared by us and the coup would not have happened without our preparation."[33]

The evidence that Kennedy and his close circle of yes-men helped support the toppling of Diem is abundant, and close examination of recently declassified information offers further incontrovertible proof. For instance, the top secret Department of State memorandum of conversation from August 26, 1963 (which was declassified by the National Archives on December 4, 2002, authority #NND 939543), records the summary of a White House meeting between Kennedy and all the State Department, CIA, and Defense Department higher-ups regarding pre-coup possibilities now that Lodge was fully in place in Saigon as U.S. ambassador. Early in the account, the report reads, "General Taylor expressed some doubt as to whether we could get along without Diem."*

However the president didn't listen to Taylor at all; his comment was never addressed. Instead, Taylor was rolled over by Defense Secretary Robert McNamara, who desperately wanted to know "what other generals were associated with Khiem, Khanh, and Don [Buddhist Generals whom America believed to be pro-coup] and what their detailed plans were." Assistant Secretary of State Roger Hilsman immediately responded that these "Generals for security reasons were reluctant to give us the names of their colleagues and their detailed plans," thereby supporting McNamara and the importance of his questions and totally disregarding General Taylor. Later, the report says, "Secretary McNamara's fourth point was that the Generals and the field should be queried as to who their alternative would be to Diem," once again completely ignoring the informed concerns of the military commander in the field.

McNamara concluded this monumental meeting with this: "The Secretary said that if a coup was unsuccessful we would be on an inevitable road to disaster. The decision of the United States would be, therefore, to get out and let the country go to the Communists or to move U.S. combat forces into Viet-Nam and put in a government of our own choosing." Since allowing the Communists to win in Vietnam would be a deathblow to Kennedy's next election, the choice was obvious. The report added, "There was no dissent from the Secretary's analysis."

The importance of this newly declassified memorandum is obvious. It clearly defines Kennedy's attitude toward the volatile political climate

---

*General Maxwell Taylor was Kennedy's senior military official in Saigon, a man who knew the political climate in that city better than anyone and certainly a man whom one would expect the president to listen to with keen interest.

and his worries over ramifications more than two months before the coup would take place. And it's solid proof that the U.S. government was instigating the overthrow of an ally for its own political ends, ignoring the objections of senior experts in the field. In fact, as the records show, Kennedy was concerned about the shaky situation in Vietnam from the very start of his presidency, and his foresight into the impending danger deserves respect. On October 12, 1961, two years before the coup, Kennedy sent instructions to MAAG Chief General Maxwell Taylor, which were specified in a classified "confidential" memorandum, declassified January 27, 2003. In it, Kennedy tells General Taylor,

> I would like you to proceed to Saigon for the purpose of appraising the situation in South Viet-Nam, particularly as it concerns the threat to the internal security and defense of that country and adjacent areas . . . . I would like your views on the courses of action which our Government might take at this juncture to avoid further deterioration . . . .

Later, Kennedy instructs,

> You will necessarily have to discuss with President Diem and his officials some of the courses of action which we have under consideration in order to elicit their views and to assure their cooperation if we take certain decisions.

Here, Kennedy was issuing a rose-colored order that General Taylor strong-arm Diem if necessary to evoke a reaction and to let the South Vietnamese government know that America will not offer military and economic aid until they accept the U.S. way of doing things. In addition, Kennedy noted, "Mr. McNamara also has made available the services of his assistant for guerilla and counter-guerilla operations, General Lansdale, to assist you." Edward Lansdale was the man who'd been in the thick of the situation from the start and who'd helped throw elections in Diem's favor. By propping up Lansdale behind General Taylor, Kennedy was able to subtly intimidate Diem. Lansdale was a reminder to Diem that elections and public propaganda could work both ways. The U.S. helped get Diem in office; hypothetically, they could just as easily get him out.

Before finishing off, Kennedy became more blunt as he finalized his instructions to Taylor:

I suspect there are many unconventional forms of assistance which we might bring to this situation if we apply all our initiative and ingenuity. Will you see that we are not overlooking any possibilities which fall outside of strictly orthodox measures?

Even this early in the game, Kennedy was perceptive enough to recognize a worst-case scenario, and it's easy to see the true nature of this last order. By structuring it as a question, he's prompting Taylor to acknowledge the most unorthodox measure of all. The president wanted all of his men behind him, not just the State Department and the Attorney General's office (on which he already had a firm grasp) but the military and the CIA too. But he would never get the latter two, and the ploy behind this rather coy list of orders to Taylor ultimately backfired. Three weeks after Kennedy issued these instructions, Taylor made his recommendations, which were documented in a top secret Department of State memorandum declassified January 1, 2003. According to the report, Taylor never mentions the "unorthodox measures" that Kennedy was hinting at but instead lists eight summary points of his recommendations, which deal with bolstering U.S. training roles of South Vietnamese government forces, improving military-political intelligence at provincial levels, and improving economic aid for flood-relief programs. It seems that, according to General Taylor, things weren't going that badly in South Vietnam and he clearly didn't see much problem with Diem at the time. In fact, between 1961 and 1963, General Taylor would make many situational assessments and many recommendations to Kennedy, and they would all be in favor of keeping Diem in place as the leader of South Vietnam. This was not what Kennedy wanted to hear. The president wanted a green light; he desperately sought a stamp of approval but would never get it from the people he needed it from most. Ultimately, Kennedy would reject or ignore every critical recommendation that General Taylor would make to him.

Instead, Kennedy asked the State Department to document alternate recommendations for dealing with Diem. In a "Top Secret – Limited Distribution" memorandum issued on November 28, 1961 (marked declassified January 21, 2003, by Authority #NND 949535), which was boldly titled "Possible Contingencies in Vietnam," a possibility is offered, listed as Situation II, A., which reads, "No coup attempt, or, if there is one, it is defeated by Diem." The memo then recommends as

Alternative I., "If this occurs, our problems will by no means be solved. It is quite possible that we will get a formal agreement from Diem which he will then fail to carry out," in which case "we will have to consider whether we should have him replaced." Even then, nearly two years before the coup would commence, the top government officials were casually talking about the need to have the leader of an allied nation "replaced." A few other excerpts from the document, which is actually filled with similar evidence, further illuminates the State Department's attitude at the time:

> The evidence suggests that all we will probably have to ensure that a coup takes place is to indicate clearly, but in an indirect fashion, that we will support a coup effort. In giving such indication, we might be well advised to indicate that we would much prefer an arrangement which provided for the constitutional succession of [a puppet leader].

It continues,

> Our most important action will be to make clear that we will go along with a coup . . . . If we can get the kind of coup we want without evidence of overt U.S. involvement, we shall be better off . . . . We might, at some crucial stage, let coup leaders know privately that we were prepared to fly in forces . . . . If there is any serious hitch indicating the possibility of success by the opposition, we may have to move quickly with military forces. But couldn't the necessary forces, which wouldn't have to be very large, be kept in the Philippines or some considerable distance offshore and flown in to Saigon?

In the end, Kennedy got what he unwittingly asked for by ignoring General Taylor's recommendations: a nightmare in Vietnam.

Convinced that the communist aggression could not be stopped with Diem's government in place, Kennedy and his State Department judged it best to cultivate a coup. Whereas Diem had ruled South Vietnam for nine years, his successor, Big Minh, would remain in office for only two months before he was overthrown by his cohorts. After that point, for the next eleven years, the Vietnam conflict would escalate into a full-scale war that would kill 58,000 Americans and millions of Vietnamese on both sides—the only war that the United States had ever lost and one of the darkest blots on U.S. history. The presidency of South Vietnam would itself become a kind of absurd game of musical chairs with one corrupt military leader after the next clawing and fighting each other for the luxury of occupying the Presidential Palace and reaping the riches that the office provided.

In other words, it must be suggested that Diem's string of successors would never hold the line against communism as well as Diem himself did. Diem's death was merely prologue to the demise of South Vietnam. As it turns out, the nay-sayers, men like General Paul Harkins, CIA director McCone, former-Ambassador Nolting, and particularly Maxwell Taylor, were right. Diem may not have been a good leader, but he was certainly better than any other alternative—as the next decade of blood, death, and horror would prove. And though Diem's treatment of the Buddhists was wholly unacceptable, further diplomatic pressures would have likely prompted Diem and Nhu to end their repressive strikes. After all, the priority in South Vietnam was the effort to keep it free from communist rule, and Diem did this. Hence, Kennedy's "solution," in truth, helped destroy the initial cause. Diem was killed because his repression of the Buddhist majority threatened Kennedy's reelection hopes. But what's worth noting is that after Diem's death, Buddhist repression didn't cease. In fact more monks would burn themselves alive in protest of their government after Diem was gone.[34]

After all this documentation, direct U.S. complicity in the Diem coup cannot be denied. Kennedy's feelings about the success of the coup are apparent in the last line of a cable he sent directly to Lodge on November 6, 1963, just four days after the death of Diem and Nhu: "With renewed appreciation for a fine job, John F. Kennedy."[35]

7

Building the Case

"The [U.S.] government murdered Diem."

— Richard M. Nixon[1]

NOW THAT we've covered the greater extent of the South Vietnamese coup, especially as it pertains to U.S. involvement, we'd like to address the questions that most likely will arise, clearing up any doubts or confusion about specific issues left unclear and solidifying the case established thus far:

1) *Initially wasn't Kennedy resistant to the idea of staging a coup?* The truth is, Big Minh and his conspirators did delay the coup a couple of times, when Conein's insulated messages from the White House indicated that the administration was having cold feet. If the coup failed, Kennedy knew that he and his State Department personnel risked serious repercussions. This would explain the initial wavering back and forth not only in Kennedy's mind but also in the cables transmitted between Washington and Saigon. The same wishy-washy attitude that plagued Kennedy during the U.S.-backed Cuban invasion was influencing his decision here. To verify this, one need only look at the State Department cable traffic in Volume IV of *Foreign Relations of the United States: Vietnam* (particularly in cables sent from the White House to Lodge), which demonstrate Kennedy's uneasiness about the upcoming Diem coup, plus his advisements that Lodge urge the mutinous generals to delay the overthrow. Still, Kennedy's fingerprints, indecisive and otherwise, remain all over the coup. In fact, it would be foolish to believe that the act, which was actively advised against by Harkins, Nolting, Richardson, and CIA Director John McCone, among others, could have

been engineered without the president's approval. After all, when Diem and his brother lay dead in a U.S. M113 armored personnel carrier, it was obvious that Kennedy and his State Department were satisfied with the result.

2) *Can we be sure that CIA Saigon Station Chief John Richardson was opposed to a Diem coup?* Richardson repeatedly and wholeheartedly supported President Diem for the same reason that General Harkins and Ambassador Nolting did, that despite Diem's tremendous shortcomings, he was the best available man to stand up against the Vietcong. The administration realized that the Buddhist crisis could be remedied in time with the proper détente and diplomatic coercion. Yet one cannot easily deny the contrary evidence found in one of the most famous cables in the so-called *Pentagon Papers* (a volume of the most critical and interesting U.S. foreign policy documents related to the Vietnam War). It's a transmission on August 28, 1963, from Richardson that says, "Situation here has reached the point of no return . . . . Conein's meeting with General Khiem [one of Big Minh's comrades] reveals that overwhelming majority of generals . . . are united . . . . Nevertheless, we understand that the effort [the coup] must succeed and that whatever needs to be done on our part must be done." So here is the CIA chief in Saigon essentially endorsing a coup against Diem, when in previous months he opposed one (Richardson was on very good terms with Diem and Nhu). This can be attributed to a number of things. First of all, Richardson could have genuinely changed his mind as time went on, or Richardson could have been tailoring his cables because he knew now that the coup was inevitable. There's also the distinct possibility that Richardson simply decided to get with the Kennedy program to save his job. After Ambassador Nolting's dismissal, Richardson could have finally understood that he was next on the chopping block (although despite being pulled for his initial siding with Nolting and Harkins, Richardson was recalled in October). But the shifting attitudes of Richardson are hardly the point of interest in this cable. What's of greater importance is that this is more verification that Conein, an agent of the U.S. government, was surreptitiously meeting with the plotting generals, which is further evidence of U.S. involvement.

3) *Hasn't it been said that CIA operative E. Howard Hunt actually forged some State Department documents to implicate Kennedy in the Diem*

assassination? Yes. As recounted in *Plausible Denial,* author/attorney Mark Lane was granted the opportunity to cross-examine Hunt during a defamation trial. Lane's job was to destroy Hunt's credibility before the jury, which he did with methodical expertise by forcing Hunt to admit to a string of lies and deceit. During the cross-examination, Lane quite skillfully got Hunt to admit that he fabricated some State Department cables that would lead people to believe that Kennedy ordered the assassination of Diem. Hunt did this in collusion with Nixon administration aide Charles Colson. Hunt manufactured these cables with his own typewriter, made them appear authentic, and then sought to get them published as genuine in *Time* and *Life.*[2] Hunt's shady past is no secret (he helped organize the famed Watergate burglary), and neither is his hatred for John F. Kennedy (Hunt expressly blamed Kennedy for the failure of the Bay of Pigs Invasion and further despised Kennedy for reducing CIA authority in Vietnam). What's crucial to note, however, is that the cables, which Hunt fabricated, are not the official cables cited in this book. Hunt didn't fabricate Volume IV of *Foreign Relations of the United States,* the 793-page official U.S. foreign policy record for August-December, 1963; he fabricated several external documents which have since been exposed. Anyone who still doubts Kennedy's complicity in the Diem overthrow need only check the official record that contains hundreds of pages of cable traffic which clearly show that Kennedy and members of his administration encouraged, aided, and abetted Big Minh and his generals in deposing Diem and Nhu, an act which inevitably led to their murders and promptly got Kennedy out of an international hotseat.

4) *Aren't there contradictions in some history books about Diem's and Nhu's deaths, particularly Conein's refusal to requisition a plane to fly the Ngo brothers to asylum?* Although the minute details of Diem's and Nhu's murders are technically clouded, there's no disputing the fact that they were killed under Big Minh's orders. Whether Big Minh gave the order of his own accord or was forced to do so when Conein could not provide a plane within twenty-four hours is debatable. A number of excellent history books cite slightly different details regarding the actual murders. In Neil Sheehan's exhaustively sourced book, *A Bright Shining Lie,* the author asserts that Big Minh ordered a major to kill the two brothers. The major killed them both with a pistol inside the personnel carrier, after which some overzealous troops attacked Nhu's dead body

with repeated bayonet jabs.[3] In Stanley Karnow's equally voluminous tome, *Vietnam: A History*, the author describes how a tank corps major (Nghia) and Minh's hit-man bodyguard (Nhung) were dispatched to pick up Diem and Nhu under the command of a General Xuan, who had a personal gripe against Diem for job discrimination. Nghia, by Karnow's account, opened fire on the brothers with an automatic weapon from the gun turret (an unlikely scenario since the M113 armored personnel carrier doesn't have a gun "turret," and shooting them outside the vehicle would attract the attention of unwanted witnesses), while Nhung opened fire with a weapon of undisclosed type and then repeatedly stabbed both bodies with a knife.[4] Gruesome details aside, the point is that in both cases Diem and Nhu believed they would receive safe transport from the country but instead were executed immediately. Still, there does seem to be a discrepancy regarding Conein and the plane. Karnow's account plainly reports that Conein claimed to be absolutely unable to supply a plane to transport Diem and Nhu out of the country,[5] a seemingly bogus claim since many U.S. aircraft were indeed available in the area—one of which, via Lodge, was provided with no trouble at all to Diem's ill-fated brother Can. Then again, Seymour Hersh's *The Dark Side of Camelot* cites, much in the same vein, that in 1975 testimony Conein claimed that Minh asked him to provide aircraft to get Diem out but he denied the request as a requisitional impossibility. Then Hersh adeptly concluded, "[A]s Conein knew, Diem was in the hands of military men who would murder him. In any case, a suitable aircraft could easily have been provided in advance but was not. Jack Kennedy had written off Diem, and everyone in Saigon knew it."[6] What's even more interesting, though, is that Conein, in a 1996 interview, stated that there was never any doubt that Big Minh planned to kill Diem and Nhu, and he immediately reported this information to Lodge,[7] who was reporting directly to Kennedy. Regardless of the variety of Conein's testimony and interview answers, in all cases he implicated himself as a rook in the Kennedy administration's plot to get rid of Diem and Nhu.

5) Was Kennedy really going to end U.S. military involvement in Vietnam? There's been as much ink spilled on that question as on the potential identity of the third killer in *Macbeth*. According to one of the more famous Kennedy lines regarding this topic, Kennedy-aide Kenneth O'Donnell claims that Kennedy privately conversed with Senator Mike

Mansfield and implied to the senator that U.S. forces in Vietnam would be pulled out. "But," Kennedy was reported as saying, "I can't do that until 1965—after I'm reelected."[8] As apocryphal as this quote might seem (after all, it's just an aide quoting the senator quoting the president who could have simply been making a joke), the overall implication is quite correct. It would have been political suicide for Kennedy to make a major withdrawal of U.S. personnel from Vietnam before the 1964 elections, and no one knew this better than Kennedy. Most likely, he'd have been branded as a softie on communism and would have lost the election in a landslide (keep in mind, though the Vietnam War would become phenomenally unpopular among U.S. citizens by 1966, in 1963 most voters supported American efforts there). Kennedy knew that the way Americans perceived his handling of U.S. involvement would make or break his chances in the next election.

And yet a favorite cluster of assassination theories—many forming the motivational cornerstone for Oliver Stone's film, *JFK*—asserts that Kennedy was killed by the military-industrial complex and the CIA (with the help of Mob contractors affiliated with the CIA). This theory chiefly stems from a document called National Security Action Memorandum 263 (NSAM 263, which can be found on pages 395-396 of *Foreign Relations of the United States, 1961-1963, Volume IV*), which is commonly cited as proof that the United States would definitely withdraw one thousand U.S. troops by December, 1963, and all U.S. troops by 1965.

But closer examination of the well-worn document suggests a slightly different interpretation. This once top secret document (shown on the facing page) is an announcement from the head of the national security council staff McGeorge Bundy to Secretary of State Dean Rusk, Defense Secretary Robert McNamara, and Chairman of the Joint Chiefs General Maxwell Taylor.

Here, Bundy has, essentially, written a cover letter for a foreign policy matter that existed as a body of several other documents. But what is this reference to Document 179 (as directed by the reference number 2), and what exactly was stated in the report referred to at the president's meeting on October 5, 1963?

Document 179 is a two-page-plus memorandum prepared by NSC staff member Michael Forrestal, and reference number 2 does not refer to the report of the meeting but to an assessment report prepared by Secretary McNamara and General Taylor based on their trip to South

At a meeting on October 5, 1963,[2] the President considered the recommendations contained in the report of Secretary McNamara and General Taylor on their mission to South Vietnam.

The President approved the military recommendations contained in Section I B (1-3) of the report, but directed that no formal announcement be made of the implementation of plans to withdraw 1,000 U.S. military personnel by the end of 1963.

After discussion of the remaining recommendations of the report, the President approved an instruction to Ambassador Lodge which is set forth in State Department telegram No. 534 to Saigon.[3]

---

[2] See Document 179.
[3] Document 181.

Vietnam in September of 1963, which is actually compiled in Document 167, dated October 2, 1963. This is obviously the case simply because there is no "Section I B (1-3)" in the report of the October 5th meeting, but there is a Section I B (1-3) in Document 167. Undoubtedly, the CIA/military-industrial complex assassination reporters discovered in the contents of this report (167), in paragraphs 1 and 2 of Section I B, the following:

B. *Recommendations.*
We recommend that:

1. General Harkins review with Diem the military changes necessary to complete the military campaign in the Northern and Central areas (I, II, and II Corps) by the end of 1964, and in the Delta (IV Corps) by the end of 1965. This review should consider the need for such changes as:
   a. A further shift of military emphasis and strength to the Delta (IV Corps).

    b. An increase in military tempo in all corps areas . . . .

    c. Emphasis on "clear and hold" operations . . . .

    d. The expansion of personnel in combat units to full authorized strength.

    e. The training and arming of hamlet militia to an accelerated rate . . . .

    f. A consolidation of the strategic hamlet program . . . .

2. A program be established to train Vietnamese so that essential functions now performed by U.S. military personnel can be carried out by the end of 1965.[9a]

This part of the assessment report is making recommendations for "review" with Diem, meaning consideration for action by the president. What it is saying is this: *To get out of Vietnam clean, we have to vigorously support the South Vietnamese to be able to effectively hold off the Communists. If we want to get out of here by the end of 1965, here's what we need to do.*

When McGeorge Bundy stated in NSAM 263 that Kennedy had "approved the military recommendations contained in Section I B (1-3) of the report," he wasn't saying that Kennedy was going to withdraw all U.S. troops by the end of 1965. What he was saying was that in order to pursue the possibility of strengthening the South Vietnamese to a level sufficient to preserve their nation against communist takeover, the president would agree to "consider the need for such changes" to effect this best-case scenario, which involved increased U.S. support and U.S. personnel. Kennedy was approving recommendations to try to shorten the war; he wasn't approving a total withdrawal. Observe another excerpt from Document 179:

> The President also said that our decision to remove 1,000 U.S. advisors by December of this year should not be raised formally with Diem. Instead the action should be carried out routinely as part of our general posture of withdrawing people when they are no longer needed.[9b]

Kennedy is acknowledging the decision to remove 1,000 U.S. advisors by the end of 1963, and he has stated this should not be raised "formally" with Diem. But what about informally? Regarding this entire matter, Secretary of State Dean Rusk said this to Lodge in an "Eyes Only" telegram on October 5, 1963, at 5:38 P.M. (TELEGRAM #180):

> As he approved next following detailed cable of instructions, the President asked me to send you this personal message from him.
>
> He thinks it of the greatest importance that . . . we should not open this next stage to the press. The decisions and instructions in following telegram [this is telegram 180; the following telegram is 181, sent one minute later at 5:39 P.M.] are being held most tightly here [at the White House] and we are making every possible effort to limit public knowledge. . . .[10]

Here Rusk is telling Lodge that Kennedy didn't want the American people to hear of this approval to withdraw one thousand U.S. troops. Why? Because there was no withdrawal. Kennedy didn't want Diem to hear about this via the U.S. newspapers because if Diem did, so would America. Instead, Kennedy was leaving it to be communicated to Diem informally, i.e. via intelligence leaks. This entire effort of NSAM 263 was merely a bogus gesture—pretending to be official—manufactured to scare Diem into thinking that the United States was about to withdraw all support. If Diem thought this was true, then he would shape up fast and finally start doing what the U.S. was telling him to do if he wanted to win the war.

And on what do we base this assertion? The original reference number 3 all the way back at the source, NSAM 263. This reference number indicates Document No. 181, the very telegram that Rusk brought to the attention of Lodge. (See Endnote 10.) Now let's go to Telegram 181, sent one minute later, and see what it says about all of the above actions.

Paragraph 2 states to Lodge:

> 2. Actions are designed to indicate to Diem Government our displeasure at its political policies and to create significant uncertainty in that government and in key Vietnamese groups as to the future intentions of the United States . . . .[11]

This official U.S. State Department document plainly states that the foundation piece of NSAM 263 was nothing more than propaganda

designed to scare Diem into improving the way he ran his government—
a typical maneuver of a big government over a little government in order
to maintain public approval of a political endeavor.

Another cornerstone of the theory that Kennedy was assassinated
because he planned to withdraw from Vietnam can be found in National
Security Action Memorandum 273 (NSAM 273), with which many theorists are no doubt familiar. (Incidentally, the basis for this theory is that
the "military-industrial complex" wanted the Vietnam War to continue
so it could make money via a war-based economy.) It's long been propa-
gated that NSAM 273, in its approval for accelerated U.S. military presence in South Vietnam, is a direct reversal of NSAM 263, which declared
a withdrawal of U.S. military presence in South Vietnam. But as we've
already revealed, NSAM 263 did no such thing and instead has been
grossly misinterpreted, to an alarming extent, by certain JFK assassination cliques. Therefore, a closer look at the infamous NSAM 273 and its
fine print may also be illuminating:

The President [Lyndon Johnson, now] had reviewed the discussions of
South Vietnam, which occurred in Honolulu [a meeting of Kennedy's
chief advisors held two days before Kennedy's assassination; check
Endnote 12] and had discussed the matter further with Ambassador
Lodge. He directs that the following guidance be issued to all concerned:

1. It remains the central object of the United States in South Vietnam
to assist the people and the Government of that country to win their
contest against the externally directed and supported Communist conspiracy. The test of all U.S. decisions and actions in this area should be
the effectiveness of their contribution to this purpose.

2. The objectives of the United States with respect to the withdrawal
of U.S. military personnel remain as stated in the White House statement of October 2, 1963. [The McNamara/Taylor recommendations
which called for increased support in the North, Central, and Delta
regions until such a time should come that the South Vietnamese military could fend for itself.]

3. It is a major interest of the United States Government that the present provisional government of South Vietnam should be assisted in con-
solidating itself and in holding and developing increased public support.
All U.S. officers should conduct themselves with this objective in view.[13]

There's more, but the overall point is that the U.S. president has now officially pledged hardline United States military support to the new government of South Vietnam (Diem is dead now, Big Minh is the country's bona fide leader). And what the CIA/military-industrial complex theorists emphasize is that this memorandum was signed by the new president, Lyndon Johnson, just four days after Kennedy's death. They go on to speculate that Johnson must have had something to do with the assassination because the rough draft of NSAM 273 was actually written two days before Kennedy's death.

But once again this is merely the misinterpretation and/or forced manipulation of facts. In Craig Roberts's *Kill Zone* (an interesting book on many points), the author states that NSAM 273 was "written by McGeorge Bundy for LBJ's policy to commit forces and aid to South Vietnam."[14]

Roberts is mistaken. The working draft was written two days before Kennedy was killed. Hence, it wasn't written for Johnson; it was written for Kennedy. To suggest otherwise is to accuse every member of the Honolulu Conference of being directly involved with the Kennedy assassination and of having prior knowledge of it, men such as Secretary of State Dean Rusk, Secretary of Defense Robert McNamara, Ambassador Henry Cabot Lodge, General Paul Harkins, and General Maxwell Taylor. The Honolulu Conference was a meeting of the military and State Department minds to decide what changes should be made in U.S. policy regarding South Vietnam now that their former banes—Diem and Nhu—were dead. More to the point, the Honolulu conference—the basis for NSAM 273—was convened to make recommendations for President Kennedy, who was still alive at that time. And yet, despite these certainties, the myths of the significance of Johnson's participation haven't waned. Even Robert Groden, who has devoted his life to the Kennedy assassination and whose books have been some of the best ever produced on the subject, stated assertively in his book, *The Killing of a President*, that NSAM 273 was "[t]he first directly political result of the Kennedy assassination."[15]

This is not old news either. In fact, it's maintained a global interest for four decades. In the critically acclaimed *The Color of Truth* (published by Simon & Schuster in late-1998), renowned author and contributing editor for the *Nation,* Kai Bird, refers to this National Security Action Memorandum as such: "Indeed, with Diem gone, the attitude in

Washington was that now the business of winning the war could proceed."[16] Bird's book is not only backed by his astounding credentials but also its sources; it's a biography of two of Kennedy's utmost advisors, McGeorge and William Bundy, and built on nearly a hundred interviews with the Bundys and their associates. (In fact, this is probably the most comprehensive book ever written about the close inside circles of the Kennedy White House and, later, the Johnson White House.)

Another widely read book that zeroes in on the NSAM 263 and NSAM 273 is *JFK: The CIA, Vietnam, and the Plot to Assassinate John F. Kennedy* by L. Fletcher Prouty (who supports the chief theory behind the Oliver Stone movie). On page 267, Prouty explains that without the proper reference to the McNamara/Taylor Report, NSAM 263 is of no deductive value (just as we suggested earlier). On page 268 of his book, Prouty states, "Without the report itself in the record this cover letter is all but worthless."

Prouty goes on to cite NSAM 263's provisions in Section I B (1-3) of the report, as we have, but that's where he stops, and unfortunately that's where many assassination theorists have stopped. He makes no mention of the rest of the memorandum's critical stipulations. Moreover, he makes no mention of Telegram 181 to Lodge which explains the actual function and nature of this national security action.

It's somewhat surprising for Prouty to have failed to mention this, especially when Prouty claims to have participated in the authorship of the memorandum. "Much of it," he says, "guided by White House policy, was actually written by my boss at the Pentagon, General Krulak, myself, and others of his staff."[17]

In all, Prouty makes a painstaking effort to convince the reader that any other interpretation of the NSAM 263 issue is a "cover" story manipulated by lazy historians and assassination researchers whose theories merely disagree with his own. Prouty even writes, "I have cited these facts with care in order to demonstrate what the original presidential policy was [we must note that the original presidential policy on October 11, 1963, was clearly undetermined at that point] and to compare it with what has been done with it since those days by those who wish to conceal and obfuscate the facts."[18] Based on this quote and the other essential elements of NSAM 263 that Mr. Prouty didn't mention, predacious critics might easily charge Prouty himself with concealing and obfuscating facts.

This is probably just an oversight. Still, Prouty's book makes the same statement to thousands of readers that Oliver Stone's *JFK* made to millions of viewers—that "Kennedy's NSAM 263 policy would have assured that hundreds of thousands of American soldiers would not have been sent to the war in Vietnam,"[19] when in fact Kennedy's NSAM 263 policy would've done nothing of the sort.

And even again, Prouty states with the same exclusivity, "Had John F. Kennedy lived, Americans would not have fought and died in Vietnam."[20] This statement is simply inaccurate. And *Foreign Relations of the United States, 1961-1963, Volume IV* is the proof.

Prouty then goes on to refer to NSAM 273 as "Johnson's NSAM 273,"[21] again perpetuating the myth that Johnson was somehow responsible. In the groundbreaking 1999 Simon & Schuster release, *Vietnam: The Necessary War*, renowned political historian Michael Lind dismisses the idea that Kennedy had a secret plan to pull out of Vietnam:

> Even more absurd was Oliver Stone's thesis, expressed in his movie *JFK*, that unidentified forces in the U.S. government arranged for the assassination of Kennedy in order to replace him with Lyndon Johnson who would carry out their plan to escalate the war in Vietnam. If Kennedy had lived and abandoned South Vietnam, his record in foreign policy would have been one of unmitigated failure in Cuba, Berlin, and Southeast Asia.[22]

Dick Shultz, author of *The Secret War against Hanoi* and director of international studies at Tufts University, describes the notion of Kennedy wanting to withdraw from Vietnam as a "myth," and in a brilliant January 2000 *Boston Globe* article, he solidly explained that in 1963, Kennedy "sought to escalate the war significantly and covertly, not withdraw from it."[23]

The official record is available via the Government Printing Office to any interested reader, but in *The Assassination of John F. Kennedy* James P. Duffy and Vincent L. Ricci summarize this point and the entire controversy over the issues of NSAM 263 and NSAM 273 better than anyone:

> Proponents of the theory that Kennedy was killed because of his alleged plans to pull out of Vietnam ignore very strong evidence that if Kennedy had lived, the war might well have continued just as it did under Lyndon B. Johnson. John Kennedy was not the "peacenik"

many attempt to paint him as. Many of the men who advised Johnson to expand the war were Kennedy's closest advisors . . . .[24]

After all, if Kennedy really wanted to withdraw all U.S. forces from South Vietnam, why would he say in a support-rallying speech, "Without the United States, Vietnam would collapse overnight"?[25]

6) What of Edward Lansdale, the major CIA field operative who was assigned to help Diem defeat his major adversaries in the mid-'50s? Did he participate in U.S. involvement in the Diem coup? Lansdale wasn't involved in any significant way, but he was intimately familiar with the subversive tactics of America's foreign campaigns. He'd spent much of his early career neck-deep in clandestine operations that revolved around killing Communist rebels. (Neil Sheehan refers to Lansdale as "a legendary clandestine operative."[26]) Previous to his assignment in South Vietnam, Lansdale had helped crush rebel forces in the Philippines, and once in Saigon he was instrumental in securing Diem's presidency. First he'd helped in the CIA effort to get Bao Dia to grant prime-ministership to Diem, and then he'd gotten rid of Dia by rigging a pro-Diem election. It was Lansdale's operational advice that had helped Diem in his victory against the 40,000-man Binh Xuyen sect in 1955. The United States had chosen to prop up Diem as South Vietnam's bona fide leader, and it had been Lansdale who'd done most of the work. But whether or not Lansdale was a killer and one of the fabled CIA "wet-workers" is debatable. It should be noted, however, that Lansdale had no problem with the outright slaughter of the Vietminh "stay-behinds" in the mid-'50s. Lansdale must've known that most of these people weren't really Communists, but since some of them probably were, he readily endorsed their extermination, incarceration, and intimidation, which he casually referred to as a "cleaning-up" process.[27] Still, Lansdale was a hero and a patriot, discharging the assigned tasks of his government, as any good soldier does, without question. But that was in the mid-'50s, and things had changed dramatically by 1963. It's very interesting to cite, then, a revelation in Seymour Hersh's bestseller. In the autumn of 1963, Lansdale was called to meet privately with President Kennedy, whereupon Kennedy, knowing Lansdale's previous close connections to Diem, asked Lansdale if he'd like to return to Saigon to convince Diem to remove his brother Nhu from the South Vietnamese government. Lansdale enthusiastically accepted the offer, as he had always been a close friend to Diem but had never approved of Nhu (who was really the main problem for the Kennedy administration in the first place). Lansdale, who was considering retirement at the time due mainly to boredom, was elated by Kennedy's offer. That was until he heard the rest.

As an aside, Kennedy asked Lansdale if the prospect of removing Nhu from his political association with Diem failed, or if the president changed his opinion and decided that Diem had to be eliminated, would he still be interested in the job? As badly as he wanted it, Lansdale had to turn down the president's offer. Lansdale had "no doubt" that what Kennedy was actually posing to him was the very serious question: *Would you kill Diem if I decided it was necessary?* Lansdale, a CIA deep-cover op from the old school and one-time supporter and defender of Diem, could not.[28]

(A final note: It's not our intention at all to disparage other books written on the subject of the Kennedy assassination. In fact, many of the books specifically sourced in this chapter—Groden's *The Killing of a President,* Hersh's *The Dark Side of Camelot,* Karnow's *Vietnam: A History,* Lane's *Plausible Denial,* Prouty's *JFK: The CIA, Vietnam, and the Plot to Assassinate John F. Kennedy,* Roberts's *Kill Zone,* Sheehan's *A Bright Shining Lie*—are all books that we highly recommend. All are written by consummate experts in their fields with strong credentials. In fact, most are *New York Times* bestselling authors, and Oliver Stone is an Oscar-winning filmmaker. Ultimately, while we disagree with some of his contentions, Stone's film *JFK* is probably the best vehicle produced yet—film or book—to communicate to a large audience the serious problems with the Warren Commission Report and the lies it has injected into the American conscience.)

8

The Usual Suspects

> ". . . President John F. Kennedy was probably assassinated as a result of a conspiracy."[1]
>
> — HOUSE SELECT COMMITTEE ON ASSASSINATIONS, 1979

THE WORLD forgot about Diem's murder very quickly because twenty days later John Kennedy himself was murdered, a crime which would become one of the modern world's most perplexing enigmas.

But since that infamous day in November 1963, a veritable society of Kennedy assassination researchers has surfaced—often prompted by their own simple curiosity or outrage—to attempt to solve what is the equivalent of the holy grail of murder mysteries. In the decades following the assassination, this society examined every conceivable aspect of the Kennedy assassination, down to the last irreducible speck of evidence and false evidence, every witness and every rumor, every photograph and fake photograph, and every Oswald document and Oswald imposture. To say that no stone has been left unturned would be a feeble understatement. The result, for the most part, has been beneficial, allowing seekers of truth to freely seek and then present their own opinions based on their findings to a populace that ardently wants to know.

The never-ending pursuit to find out who killed John F. Kennedy, and why, has forged careers and ended them; it has consumed lives, generated much controversy, and urged Americans to think twice about trusting their government. Lastly, this strident pursuit of the truth has produced over six hundred books, thousands of articles, and millions of words in the effort to render an explanation for the tragic events of Dealey Plaza on an uncharacteristically warm day in November of 1963.

Myriad theories have been formulated, some most intriguing, some not so. The accusatory finger has been pointed at potential killers from Lee Harvey Oswald to E. Howard Hunt, and dozens of characters in between. Depending on whom you ask, Kennedy's murder was ordered by Lyndon Johnson, Richard Nixon, Jimmy Hoffa, or Carlos Marcello and/or Santos Trafficante, and let's not forget Fidel Castro, Nikita Khrushchev, the John Birch Society, and a bunch of Texas oil men. Other theories range from the frightening (the CIA killed Kennedy) to the absurd (Kennedy was killed by the Air Force because he was about to reveal government knowledge of extraterrestrial life forms). On the whole, though, most of the theories presented have been carefully considered interpretations of evidence, facts, and personal accounts and have contributed greatly and honestly to this sojourn toward the truth.

However, one week after Kennedy's death, the very first U.S. investigation was launched into the question of who killed him. It was issued by the new president, Lyndon Baines Johnson, as Executive Order 11130, but it would more infamously come to be known as the Warren Commission.[2] As most readers already know, the Warren Commission turned out to be a sham, an official U.S. government stamp on a lie of monumental proportions. In the end, the Commission's official 26-volume report was supposed to provide the American people with a prompt answer to who killed Kennedy (Oswald, they said—a lone gunman and not a conspiracy) and why (because he was a pro-Cuba nut) and additionally to prove to the people that the United States government was sensitive to their needs and was responding accordingly.

In truth, the Warren Commission and its subsequent report answered none of the questions the American people yearned for. Instead, it deliberately ignored conflicting evidence, refused to call essential witnesses, and was doggedly intolerant of any corroboration, testimony, or documentation that suggested anything but what the Commission wanted to present to America. The Warren Commission was not a fact-finding mission at all; it was a fact-deleting mission designed solely to mislead the American people into believing the most convenient—as well as the most implausible—scenario. Why the Warren Commission did this just provides more good grist for the Kennedy research mill, and it probably always will. What it all boils down to, though, is that some filament of our government decided that it was vital that they never let America know the real story of why one of the most beloved presidents in the country's history was shot and killed during a routine campaign trip.

Though a handful of other investigative ventures would arise and just as quickly peter out, in 1976 the House Select Committee on Assassinations was convened to put the matter to rest. On its surface, the HSCA was formed to finally get to the truth behind Kennedy's death, a polar opposite of what the Warren Commission was by then known to be. The Warren Commission was formed to withhold the truth, while the House Select Committee on Assassinations was supposedly conceived to correct all of that and finally deliver a sound and honest investigation. The end result, regrettably, is debatable. It started off with a controversial bang—to immediate turmoil, bickering, objection, and shady one-upmanship. Arguments persisted over such matters as budget and member time, and the effort was accused of secret CIA intervention. The press did not respond well, and in its internal disarray, the committee went through three chairmen, three directors, and undue months of wasted time. Three years after its formation, it released its report, and there was a definite good side. The HSCA dared to proclaim what the Warren Commission refused to. It openly and publicly asserted the opinion that Kennedy's murder was more than likely the result of a "conspiracy," something researchers had been screaming all along. It stipulated that four shots were fired at Kennedy, not three (as the Warren Commission had insisted); it suggested that organized crime may have been part of the conspiracy (which the Warren Commission deftly skirted); and at least one committee constituent announced his opinion that at least three snipers opened fire on Kennedy.[3]

But there was also a definite down side. It refused to acknowledge the discovery by assassination supremate Robert Groden of forged photographic evidence regarding the Kennedy autopsy (of paramount importance in determining the direction of the fatal shot), and it also refused to entertain the suggestion of an exhumation order for Kennedy's body,[4] an act that would have certainly proven whether Kennedy's fatal head wound was fired from behind (the direction of the Texas Schoolbook Depository) or from the front (the direction of such spots as the grassy knoll). There's also insurmountable evidence, based on witness reports, that at least one rifleman (and probably two) discharged their weapons from behind the grassy knoll's stockade fence or its proximity.

But this book isn't about where the shots were fired from, nor is it a reintroduction of already exhaustively published speculations about Lee Harvey Oswald, motives of the CIA and the U.S. military, irate Cuban exiles, Robert Wilfred Easterling, Roscoe White, Frank Sturgis, etc. Many of the books already scribed about these theories and implications are very convincing; we refer you instead to those (see Bibliography) rather than sourcing and reinterpreting this material. Our assertion is that they can neither be all right nor all wrong.

We agree with the House Select Committee on Assassinations, "that President John F. Kennedy was probably assassinated as a result of a conspiracy."

But here's what we don't believe. We don't believe that the so-called military-industrial complex killed Kennedy because he was planning to withdraw U.S. material, personnel, and support from Vietnam (based on the previous documentation that proves it's not true). Furthermore, we don't believe that it was Richard Nixon, Lyndon Johnson, Fidel Castro, or the Soviet Union that ordered Kennedy's assassination. We don't believe that Corsican mobsters Lucien Sarti, Sauveur Pironti, or Jorge Boccogini, as posited in a late-'80s theory, were anywhere near Dealey Plaza on November 22, 1963. We don't believe that the CIA had Kennedy killed as revenge for the failed Bay of Pigs Invasion.*

However, we do believe that a favorite element—the U.S. Mafia—was involved. We believe that more than three shots were fired from more than one direction, and having said that, we obviously believe that several shooters were involved. We're not even discounting another favorite element—that perhaps rogue members of the U.S. government assisted.

It seems most logical to us that the best way to discern why Kennedy was killed is to positively identify one of the shooters.

---

*Why would the CIA want to kill Kennedy because of the botched invasion? The CIA is run by the National Security Council, and the National Security Council knew full well that Kennedy was planning not only further attempts to invade Cuba but also at least six more clandestine assassination plots against Castro. These facts are plainly cited in the NSC document # NSC F93-1588 (see Appendix N). This weighty document proves that the CIA was completely informed of Kennedy's future intentions of killing Castro and taking Cuba back from communist rule. Hence, the popular conspiracy theories that insist the CIA killed Kennedy because of the Bay of Pigs Invasion make no sense whatever.

9

The French Assassin

IMAGINE THAT a suspected killer and known foreign-national terrorist is on the loose and on the move, seeking escape from United States soil. The U.S. government knows that this terrorist has received rigorous training in a foreign military in the past and is part of a covert paramilitary organization that has already murdered dozens if not hundreds of people and has without conscience initiated public bombings, anti-American propaganda campaigns, and assassinations of military officers, high-ranking police officials, and democratically elected politicians.

One might suspect that such a person might be a member of any number of growing right-wing militia organizations, possessed of the same sort of sentiments that led to, say, the bombing of the Federal Building in Oklahoma City. Or it could be someone connected with a Gadhafi-like sect or a pro–Saddam Hussein faction, or perhaps an operative associated with the notorious Osama bin Laden.

But, no, the terrorist in question is not affiliated with any of these groups.

He's French.

Now, imagine further that the terrorist, this known killer, has been tracked down by the FBI and the U.S. Immigration and Naturalization Service—components of the United States Department of Justice—and these components have caught our suspect after an extensive and well-integrated manhunt. This dangerous terrorist is now safely in the custody of the FBI and INS. Problem solved, right?

Wrong.

He is never charged with any crime. He is never brought before a judge, even though he is wanted by an allied nation. He is not detained, incarcerated, or even officially questioned.

Instead, he is immediately whisked away and deported safely out of the United States without so much as a raised eyebrow.

Since when does the U.S. Justice Department render safe passage to international terrorists? Why wouldn't this man at least have been detained for questioning, and why wouldn't said questioning be officially filed?

These are good questions, but there's one more thing to imagine.

The capture and deportation took place in Dallas, Texas, on November 24, 1963, two days after the assassination of President John F. Kennedy.

Can you imagine such a scenario?

No one need imagine it, because it's all true. And numerous documents prove it.

This deportation, in fact, and the sinister man in question have been the subject of repeated U.S. Justice Department investigations for more than three decades, investigations that have been deliberately withheld from the American public and the world. Furthermore, no aspect of this suspicious expulsion was ever reported to the Warren Commission.

Before we explain further, what follows is a verbatim reproduction of a CIA document which, until very recently, had been filed in U.S. government archives vaults with a classification of "secret." We've reconstructed the document here (on the following page) for easier readability, though a copy of the actual document can be found in Appendix A.

Now, let's look very closely at this (for brevity's sake, from here on, we'll refer to the above document as 632-796) and distill its meaning and overall pertinence.

In its statement, "Mr. Papich advised that the French had hit the Legal Attache in Paris," it's clear that "the French" is a reference to some component of the French government, and the "Legal Attache" refers to the U.S. legal attaché office connected to the U.S. Embassy in France. To simplify, when Government A has a question for Government B, the first and generally the most prompt resource is for Government A to submit that question either orally or in writing to Government B's legal attaché at their embassy. That's what happened here. The French government asked the U.S., via its legal attaché, about knowledge of this man named Jean Rene Souetre. It's unclear exactly who "Mr. Papich" is, but it's ultimately

AAZ-22592
1 Apr 64

SECRET

Jean SOUETRE's expulsion from the U.S.

CIA HISTORICAL REVIEW PROGRAM
RELEASE IN FULL 1995

8. Jean SOUETRE aka Michel ROUX aka Michel MERTZ - On 5 March 1964, Mr. Papich advised that the French had hit the Legal Attache in Paris and also the SDECE man had queried the Bureau in New York City concerning subject stating that he had been expelled from the U.S. at Fort Worth or Dallas 48 hours after the assassination. * He was in Fort Worth the morning of 22 November and in Dallas in the afternoon. The French believe that he was expelled to either Mexico or Canada. In January he received mail from a dentist named Alderson living at 5803 Birmingham, Houston, Texas. Subject is believed to be identical with a Captain who is a deserter from the French Army and an activist in the OAS. The French are concerned because of de Gaulle's planned visit to Mexico. They would like to know the reason for his expulsion from the U.S. and his destination. Bureau files are negative and they are checking in Texas and with INS. They would like to check our files with indications of what may be passed to the French. Mr. Papich was given a copy of CSCI-3/776,742 previously fur-nished the Bureau and CSDB-3/655,207 together with a photograph of Captain SOUETRE. WE/3Public; CI/SIG; CI/OPS/Evans
  * of President Kennedy
  Document Number 632-796

SECRET

(For reference, see Appendix A)

unimportant. (It's reasonable to assume, however, that Papich may have been a CIA asset working discretely in the legal attaché's office, a surveillance operator, or simply an employee who served as a liaison for the U.S. Embassy.) But 632-796 also states that "the SDECE man had queried the Bureau [the FBI] in New York City." This brings in another component of the French government, namely "SDECE," or the *Service de Documentation Extérieure et Contre-Espionage.* To generalize, this is the French equivalent of the CIA—it was their major intelligence agency at the time (and an agency with quite a reputation, which we'll talk about later). At any rate, what we read in 632-796 not only tells us that our embassy in Paris had been questioned about a man named Souetre but also tells us that a SDECE officer sent an inquiry about Souetre to the FBI field office in New York City.

So who is this Souetre?

Based on the limited information contained in 632-796, we only know a few things. We know that he received mail from a Texas dentist named Alderson in January 1964 (which also tells us that SDECE or some other French authority was looking for Souetre; if not, why would they be tracking his mail?), and we also know that he "is believed to be identical with a Captain who is a deserter from the French Army and an activist in the OAS." (Since this is a CIA document, why would the CIA suspect such a thing? More on that later.) Now we know that Jean Rene Souetre is a former French Army officer who deserted and joined an activist organization called the OAS. Hence, in what seems a minimal amount of data, this secret document tells us an awful lot about the mysterious man named Jean Rene Souetre. The OAS (*Organisation de l'Armée Secrète,* or the Secret Army) was a right-wing extremist group composed of men who had deserted from the French Army in opposition to French President Charles de Gaulle's rather sudden policy to grant the African nation of Algeria its independence from French rule. The OAS was indeed a "secret army" because during their heyday, they participated in countless acts of terrorism and assassination.

So here is the real meat of 632-796's significance. The OAS partook in political assassination, and one of its members, Jean Rene Souetre, was captured by U.S. authorities less than forty-eight hours after John F. Kennedy's assassination.

Let's reiterate the lines from the document: "He [Souetre] was in Fort Worth on the morning of 22 November and in Dallas in the afternoon."

On that morning in Fort Worth, Kennedy was giving a speech in front of the Hotel Texas. In the afternoon, in Dallas, he was assassinated.

Certainly, this is shocking enough. But it gets even more shocking when we read 632-796 in its entirety. The French had information that this same terrorist was "expelled from Fort Worth or Dallas 48 hours after the assassination."

Here is verification that Souetre was caught and then "expelled" from the United States. The reason for French concern is so stated: "The French are concerned because of de Gaulle's planned visit to Mexico. They would like to know the reason for his expulsion from the U.S. and his destination." We'll explain the history and significance of the OAS in detail later, but what must be understood immediately is that the OAS considered Charles de Gaulle their primary enemy; in fact, they made repeated attempts on de Gaulle's life. Typically, the destination for U.S. deportations was either Mexico or Canada, and de Gaulle planned to visit Mexico in the summer of 1964. And so we see why the French are alarmed. Somehow, they knew that Souetre was deported, and if he was in fact deported to Mexico, the French needed to know.

But what about our concerns?

Not only does 632-796 tell us that Souetre was deported from Texas shortly after Kennedy's assassination—an inexplicable occurrence in the first place—but it also tells us, given the target of the French queries, that it was some U.S. authority that deported Souetre. All U.S. deportations are executed by an arm of the United States Justice Department (the Immigration and Naturalization Service).

Why would an authority of the United States Justice Department deport a known terrorist? One would believe that Souetre, instead, would've been apprehended and imprisoned, or at least sent back to France where the legal authorities there had already clearly deemed him an enemy of the state. But there's no evidence to suggest that Souetre was ever even questioned about his presence in Dallas so soon after Kennedy's murder.

Instead, Souetre was picked up and quickly and quietly flown out of the United States. He was deported under a cloak of secrecy. The deportation was never reported to the Warren Commission, which officially formed only five days after the event. And in April 1964—the actual date of 632-796—the Warren Commission's investigation into Kennedy's assassination was in full swing. Yet no one in the CIA, the FBI, the INS, or the legal attaché's office ever reported the existence of this crucial document to the Commission or the American people.

The document's history, however, goes back twenty years, and this history is briefly outlined in Henry Hurt's *Reasonable Doubt*.[1] Existence of 632-796 was unveiled essentially by accident, by Texas-based independent assassination researcher Mary Ferrell. Ferrell is world-famous in her research expertise (she was the one who provided the Dallas Police Department's famed "dictabelt" tapes to the House Select Committee on Assassinations. These dictabelt recordings provided critical sonic evidence: the actual sounds of the gunshots fired at Kennedy).[2]

By 1977, Ferrell had secured thousands of declassified CIA documents by filings through the Freedom of Information Act, a treasure trove of data—or so she may have thought. Like the majority of "declassified" CIA documents, most in this parcel were barely legible—multiple photocopies of old carbon copies, or "redacted" documents, which means they were edited by a declassification officer. (In other words, a photocopy was made of the document, and then specific sentences of the photocopy were crossed out with a magic marker.) But Ferrell was not discouraged—after all, she was and remains an expert document examiner, and she knew a few tricks of her trade. With quality magnifying lenses and backlights, she was able to decipher enough of 632-796 to disclose its true meaning.[3] Hence, the name Souetre was made available to the eager Kennedy-research community. Reference to this deciphered document appeared as early as 1980 in Anthony Summer's *Conspiracy*[4] which many critics cite as the forerunner to the most popular assassination theories of today.

Though Ferrell's painstaking decryption of 632-796 may have missed a few lines or words (see Appendix A for an unblemished, unedited look at the actual document), it revealed enough to let us know that a French assassin was deported out of Texas by U.S. authorities within forty-eight hours of Kennedy's murder. This revelation can only be described as colossal in the realm of assassination research, and one would accordingly expect the league of Kennedy researchers to jump all over it, examine it to every degree, and then include its startling importance in the overall field of their work.

But that never happened.

As far as we can tell, in the hundreds of books written about the Kennedy Assassination, none of them pay very much attention to existence of 632-796 and its mysterious Jean Rene Souetre. In fact, the major writers in the field seem to have brushed it aside altogether, or if they have mentioned it, the reference seems only to have been made as an inconsequential afterthought. For instance, Summers' book, a 640-page tome, refers to Souetre's deportation and 632-796 only in a short, one-paragraph footnote.[5] Henry Hurt's *Reasonable Doubt* devotes less than six pages to this data, and in no way does he attempt to utilize it in the rest of his 555-page analysis. As for later books, we find nothing of note about 632-769 in Mark Lane's *Plausible Denial,* Robert Groden's *The Killing of a President,* or Colonel Prouty's *JFK,* and no incorporation of 632-796's revelations in the movie inspired by Prouty's book, Oliver Stone's *JFK.* In Groden's excellent *The Search for Lee Harvey Oswald,* the author inserts two photographs and one sentence about Souetre on the last page of the book but relates nothing whatever to the importance of this information.

This is curious. It's no secret that a good many authors have made millions of dollars writing about the Kennedy assassination, nor is it a secret that various critics have charged that many authors in the so-called Kennedy research community have spent the last twenty years propping up their own theories, and ignoring all others, solely in order to maintain their lucrative careers. We're not suggesting anything of the sort ourselves (we value all these books, and we find their theories essential components of this tremendous mystery). The Kennedy assassination has developed into an immortal conversation, a critical exchange of ideas, opinions, and expressions, and we welcome this ultimate justification of our freedom of speech. Furthermore, we are enthused by any author's endeavor to contribute new information into this infamous puzzle.

Regrettably, though, there doesn't seem to be anything really new written on this subject for quite some time. What there seems to be, instead, are dozens and dozens of books written over the decades that tell the same story over and over again, just in different words. One author sourcing other works to twist the base theory into something he can call his own. But with 632-796—and the subsequent flood of documentation which then followed regarding Souetre—something very new indeed was injected into this course of inquest, and then it was seemingly rejected.

All we can ask is the most obvious question: why?

One answer might be that the experts in the field feel that 632-796 and what it proves is not particularly important. But how can a foreign assassin being secretly deported out of Dallas two days after Kennedy's death not be important?

The other possibility is that these experts haven't yet recognized the full importance of 632-796. Perhaps they don't believe Souetre could have been involved in Kennedy's assassination because they haven't discovered any plausible links to suggest this.

Well, we have discovered those links, as we shall reveal.

The Secret Army

"OAS outrages soon escalated to assassinations of
prominent government officials . . ."

— DOUGLAS PORCH
THE FRENCH SECRET SERVICES[1]

IN ORDER to fully understand the dire implications of an OAS member
in Dallas, Texas, on the day of John Kennedy's murder, we must first
understand exactly what the OAS was, not only in its relation to world
affairs in the early '60s but also in its relation to the president of the
United States in the same time period. And to understand this, we must
recount a snippet of French twentieth century history.

When Charles de Gaulle and his Fifth Republic took charge of France
in 1958, two crisis points awaited him: skyrocketing inflation and the
war in Algeria. This was a cyclical problem, however, as the war proved
to be the direct cause of the inflation. De Gaulle faired reasonably well
against the inflation by exercising a series of economic tweaks as well as
making charismatic appeals to the public to tighten their bootstraps and
live more frugally. The ploys worked, and even became popular, but that
still left the frustrating conflict in the North African country of Algeria,
which had long been part of the French Union—a victim of French
imperialism, in other words. War had broken out in 1954, causing
France to send in half a million troops in order to hold on to the country as part of their so-called protectorate. But even France was finally
having its doubts about its imperialistic ventures; after all, they'd been
crushed by Ho Chi Minh in Vietnam to tremendous embarrassment and
loss of life, and now it looked like the same thing might happen in
Algeria. When the former French government, the weak Fourth

Republic, had granted Morocco and Tunisia (two other French "protectorates") full independence, the French military grew uneasy to the point that France was drawing terribly close to a civil war. But when de Gaulle assumed the presidency in 1958, he defused the prospect by pledging to keep Algeria (and its newly discovered oil fields) in the firm grasp of France. This quelled the disgruntled French Army, but then de Gaulle began to feel some international pressures. By the late '50s, "imperialism" was a bad word, and more and more global sensibilities supported the notion that all countries should have the right of self-rule. Possibly as a countermove, then, de Gaulle, in 1960, granted full independence to yet another protectorate—the French Congo—but Algeria still remained a hot spot. Now de Gaulle was between a rock and a hard place. On one hand, he had international pressure to grant Algeria its independence, while on the other hand he had his own military to whom he'd promised that Algeria would always be under French control. Further pressure ensued, however, from none other than John F. Kennedy, to let Algeria be free.

Slowly but surely, de Gaulle manipulated his posture, first suggesting a loosening of French influence in Algeria, then suggesting peace talks, then hinting at a "partial" independence. Meanwhile, the war raged on (ten thousand French soldiers died in the conflict), and the native rebel factions couldn't have cared less about de Gaulle's plans for partial freedom. To the rebels, partial freedom meant partial oppression, and they'd had enough of that. Not to mention the public opinion of the French populace—once those casualty statistics started coming in, the citizens of France began to support a pullout. (They were as sick of seeing their sons come home in coffins as U.S. citizens were in the late '60s.)

This situation left de Gaulle with little choice but to lean toward a granting of total independence to Algeria, and once the French Army got wind of this, they saw it as the last straw. It was the military's support of de Gaulle that had awarded him the presidency in the first place, and now that same military felt as though it had been stabbed in the back.

Hence, the formation of the OAS—the Secret Army—headed by Algerian War veteran and public hero General Raoul Salan. Salan encouraged discontented French soldiers to join the cause of standing up to de Gaulle's betrayal. These were right-wing hardline nationalists, and their view was they'd been fighting and dying in Algeria since 1954 and if de Gaulle pulled out of Algeria, then the ten thousand French who died there would have died for nothing. Furthermore, the OAS believed France only weakened itself by letting go of its protectorates. They'd lost Indochina, Morocco, Tunisia, and the Congo, and now they were going to lose their last global conquest.

Salan's plan was to take a strong military stand against the de Gaulle government, which he hoped would result in the entire French military—in Algeria and in France, too—defecting to his cause and then overthrowing de Gaulle.

In April, 1961, the OAS made their move. Salan and his Secret Army Organization staged their coup and seized control of Algeria's capital, Algiers. But what Salan hoped for most—a rally of support from the rest of the French Army—never happened. De Gaulle's forces counterstruck, the capital was retaken, and Salan and his deserters were forced into hiding.

But the conflict wasn't over by any means.

The overthrow had failed, but Salan, a master of field tactics with three wars under his belt, would persevere in his efforts against the president he once supported but now despised. For the next year, the OAS waged a bloody terrorist war against forces loyal to de Gaulle, Algerian rebels, and Algerian collaborators alike. This terror campaign was highly effective, and it's important to consider this: Salan's men were the diehards of the Algerian conflict, the survivors, many of whom had been fighting in this strange land for years. They were the best trained, the most hardened by combat, the most familiar with the land and the culture, and the most committed to the cause. Many of the younger soldiers who initially came to Algeria to fight for their president traded their barracks for body bags in short order. They were easy pickings for the fine-honed killing skills of the OAS. Pandemonium ensued just as quickly; the OAS seemed to be able to wreak havoc and kill in grand style. They bombed buildings, pilfered weapons and supplies, funded themselves by robbing banks, and with expert snipers assassinated officials at will. They even had counter-insurgency experts, a psychological warfare unit, and their own highly effective intelligence network in league with undercover supporters back in France. Soon they were able to wage their terror campaign in Paris as well.

With the OAS, de Gaulle was in the weakest position of his political career. A nationwide military overthrow seemed just days away. Meanwhile, the French populace was scared and confused. How could their imposing war hero president be rendered so helpless against what the papers were calling a band of outlaws? Even worse, the OAS was beginning to successfully infiltrate the mainland army with its call to rid France of this traitor for a president who'd lied to his people and disgraced the country.

And then, Salan and his terrorists embarked on their most audacious endeavor.

They began planning to assassinate de Gaulle.[2]

SDECE and the French Mafia

THE OAS, in fact, made repeated assassination attempts against de
Gaulle, and some proved to be very close calls. Some found their way into
the French press; some didn't. De Gaulle, of course, preferred the latter as
he was very concerned with presenting an unperturbed public image; the
notion of former members of his own army trying to kill him was not a
sign of a president in control. But the crisis was growing on a daily basis,
and de Gaulle knew that he had to find a fast and effective solution if he
wanted to save his government and his life. He'd long despised the operations of intelligence agencies, the world's and his own.[2] But with the OAS
threatening to dismantle his Fifth Republic, even after multiple counter-
strikes, the tall, gaunt president eventually sought out his own version of
the CIA—SDECE.

The acronym is properly pronounced "steck," and it stands for *Service
de Documentation Exterieure et Contre-Espionage*, whose duties
included domestic security and intelligence, overseas intelligence, and
counterintelligence. Amongst other intelligence agencies, they were infamous for their brutality and inhuman practices. (In the earlier days of the
Algerian problem, SDECE feigned complicity with Algerian nationalist
chief Muhammad Ben Bella and promised him a safe flight back to
Algeria. When the plane reached an altitude of twenty thousand feet, they
threw him out.) [3] SDECE also had a reputation as masters of torture, and
some of their predecessors were the very same men who'd trained Ngo
Dinh Nhu's secret police in these nefarious skills. So when de Gaulle's

government seemed on the verge of coming apart, SDECE was given orders to stop the OAS. Two men in particular led the endeavor: Jacques Foccart, the French secretary for African affairs; and Roger Frey, the minister of the interior. (Whereas the CIA exists under the direction of the National Security Council, SDECE served as part of the French Ministry of the Interior.) De Gaulle instructed Frey and Foccart to simply solve the OAS problem. He didn't give them parameters, and he didn't tell them how to do it. Just do it, he charged them—at any cost.[4]

Frey and Foccart had their work cut out for them, as this operation was unlike anything they'd had to deal with before. This was a secret army of highly trained French soldiers they were trying to defeat, and the task was all the more difficult since the OAS engaged in terrorist tactics and used guerilla warfare techniques. This was not a force, in other words, that the French regular army could meet on the battlefield. By the fall of 1961, OAS special forces units were especially successful against national police units in Algiers, and the death-toll mounted. Add to that the growing success of OAS snipers, who were not only knocking off political officials in Algeria at will but had also assassinated the mayor of Evian in France, where peace talks were being conducted.[5] It was during this period that the OAS had gathered its greatest head of steam, and with their successes in the field, they began to gain more sympathizers for their cause: members of the French government, the French military, and even SDECE, which trebled the difficulty of the task as far as Frey and Foccart were concerned. Though the OAS could objectively be defined as an organization of ruthless mutineers, there were still some military and governmental components who saw them as heroes and sided with their cause, and furthermore, it's understandable that some French soldiers and intelligence operatives would be reluctant to fight against their own countrymen.

Now Foccart and Frey shared this conundrum with their president. Unable to trust even their own intelligence operatives, they began to recruit men they could trust, men with which SDECE had maintained a highly reliable and very discreet relationship since the end of World War II—the Mob.

The Marseille and/or Corsican Mob was the French equivalent to the U.S. Mafia, and it's important to note that many western intelligence agencies established working ties with the criminal underworld as World War II was ending. In fact, the United States had some indisputable kinships with the Mafia even before that; in 1942 and 1943, U.S. naval intelligence struck under-the-table deals with heroin kingpin Meyer Lansky and his even more powerful business partner Lucky Luciano. Via the agreements, Mafiosi snuffed out enemy agents and saboteurs from the New York harbor where sabotage was becoming a big problem. A year later, through the orders of Luciano, Sicilian mobsters related critical intelligence information and even served as operational guides, which hastened the success of the Allied invasion of Sicily. In return for this invaluable assistance, the U.S. military later released Luciano from prison and allowed him to return to his homeland. This release allowed Luciano and his associates such as Lanksy to build the foundation of a global heroin industry.[6]

Similar collusion between government authorities and mobsters took place in the city of Marseille. Located on the Mediterranean in southern France, Marseille has always been the country's most important seaport, and this fact would eventually make the city the most active manufacturing nexus of heroin. Shortly after World War II, threats of communist insurgence began popping up in Marseille, which SDECE regarded as a prime concern. But unlike the Nazis, this new enemy wore no uniform other than the indistinguishable garb of the common working man. So SDECE took an example from the U.S. Office of Naval Intelligence and began to strike bargains with the city's organized crime bosses. Mobsters proved to be very effective intelligence informants, and in short order, SDECE put a tight lid on communist rabble-rousers.

But nobody works for free.

In exchange for this vital information on communist activities, SDECE agreed to look the other way with regard to the Mob's criminal pursuits. This explains why Marseille's vast heroin laboratories were allowed to remain in operation for twenty years without any significant government intervention.[7]

And as if SDECE didn't have enough problems in the following decade with Vietnam, Morocco, Tunisia, and the French Congo, de Gaulle's orders to destroy the OAS had to have been their most trying task. The only viable solution for Frey and Foccart was to allow SDECE to yet again solicit the help of the underworld. It might be difficult for modern Americans to understand, but if you put yourself in France's place, it's much easier to see. The last major armed revolt in America was the Civil War over 130 years ago, but in France it was a different story. The French had tasted violent rebellions throughout their history, and with the OAS wreaking its havoc in the early '60s, France had another civil war hanging over its head. Frey, Foccart, and SDECE sought the help of Marseille's criminal syndicate to help save their nation.[8]

The mobsters were enlisted into a quasi-military unit known as SAC (*Service d'Action Civique*, sort of an undercover tactical unit); in professional parlance, though, they were referred to as *barbouzes* (spooks).[9]

Frey and Foccart were smart men; they knew that brute force could not defeat the OAS. Brains, not brawn, were the major ingredients for success. Hence, Frey and Foccart, using the handful of operatives in SDECE that could be trusted, dispatched the barbouzes to Algeria, to infiltrate the OAS from the inside and gather the intelligence data that SDECE needed. These men may have been thugs, criminals, and dope peddlers, but they were professionals in their own arena.

In fact, by one such OAS infiltration, the barbouzes foiled an assassination attempt against de Gaulle himself[10] and would later render further OAS efforts useless. It was all part of the job.

The Mysterious Souetre

"Next to de Gaulle . . .
the OAS hated Kennedy the most."

— *The Heroin Trail*[1]

JEAN RENE SOUETRE: a French Army deserter, an OAS member and traitor to the country he'd once devoted his life to, a man who voluntarily became an insurgent and a terrorist, and a killer who was in Dallas on the same day Kennedy was in Dallas. That's what Document 632-796 tells us about this man. But what else is known about Jean Rene Souetre?

Document 632-796's assertion that Souetre was a former captain in the French military who later joined the OAS is verified in CIA Document CSCI-3/776,742 with an alarming addition. This document (See Appendix B) states that in May 1963, an attempt was made in Lisbon, Portugal, by the OAS to enlist support of the CIA in their terrorist attempts against President de Gaulle. Bear in mind, by 1963 the OAS was fizzling out; most of its infrastructure was destroyed now by SDECE's barbouze campaign, and most of its best men, including its leaders, were in prison by that time. What little remained of the *Organization de l'Armee Secrete* was desperate now, and, as verified by this document, they even asked the CIA for assistance. And the document names as one of the solicitors none other than "Captain Jean Rene Souetre."

Souetre presented himself to a CIA representative as the OAS's "coordinator for external affairs," after which our mysterious captain suggested that the CIA and OAS might have a common interest in removing de Gaulle from power in France and was then bold enough to ask for "monetary or material support." Souetre was playing a wild hand, taking a shot, but there was little reason for the CIA to want to have anything to do with the OAS or their activities, and the CIA representative at this meeting told Souetre that "the U.S. had absolutely no intention of working with any person or group against the duly-constituted government of France." But before the CIA rep showed him the door, Souetre provided some curious and potentially critical information. "Souetre explained that he traveled on various passports, one of them being a U.S. passport."[2]

Known criminals, fugitives from justice, and especially documented terrorists can't get passports—not legally, that is. Where would Souetre procure such convincing false identification?

When at full strength, the OAS incorporated some of the best-trained members of their military occupational specialties. It wasn't just combat soldiers who joined the OAS, but also intelligence officers, logistical personnel, maintenance personnel, and intelligence personnel; and, as previously mentioned, there were even some SDECE operatives in the OAS. The only reason OAS killers were able to travel back and forth from Algeria to France was that they had this kind of infrastructure. Any effective military apparatus has the operational counterintelligence means to manufacture credible phony identification. It's perfectly feasible that Souetre obtained all the fake identification he needed from the OAS in order to do his job. It's also pertinent to mention that the type of fake ID which stands up best against thorough investigative scrutiny is one that effectively identifies the bearer as some other real person. Document 632-796 (and other official documents to follow) shows that Souetre used aliases such as Michel Roux and Michel Mertz, and we can prove that Roux and Mertz were definitely real people. It's reasonable to assume that Souetre was using passports in these names, and this is all a very important consideration when we recall that Souetre is said to have been in Dallas the same day Kennedy was shot.

But that's not all we know about Souetre based on this second document. We know that Souetre served under "Major Pierre Sergent," which further authenticates his claims because Sergent was one of the OAS diehards who continued attacks even after their leader, General Salan, had been captured. We know that Souetre was born in the "Gironde Department of France" on October 15, 1930 (which would make him thirty-three years old in 1963). We know that he escaped from a detention camp full of OAS captives in 1961 (at the same time SDECE barbouzes infiltrated an OAS detention camp and were able to glean information about an OAS plot to kill de Gaulle). Lastly, we learn that "he was alleged to have been involved in an assassination attempt against de Gaulle."[3]

If that's not curious enough, let's again snap back to 632-796, the precursor to all of these considerations. "In January, he [Souetre] received mail from a dentist living at 5803 Birmingham, Houston, Texas." You can bet that this dentist was investigated and interviewed, not only by the U.S. Justice Department but also by the private sector. After archivist Mary Ferrell's piecing together of parts of this infamous pre-declassified document, she spread the word to others in the Kennedy assassination research community, one being J. Gary Shaw, co-director of the JFK Assassination Information Center in Dallas and author of several intriguing books on the subject.[4] Upon the revelation, Shaw sought out this dentist and interviewed him over the phone on October 5, 1977. The dentist's full name was Larry M. Alderson who did indeed reside in Houston, Texas, just as 632-796 stated. The transcript of the interview, as well as a memorandum of the interview, can be found in their entirety in Appendix D, but we'll cite some choice selections here and expound on them.

From the outset, Shaw's interview verifies something hinted at in 632-796, which states that Alderson received mail from Souetre; hence some association between Souetre and Alderson exists. What link could there be between Souetre, a French terrorist and potential assassin, and Alderson, a Texas dentist?

Shaw's interview answers this all-important query right off the bat. It turns out that Souetre and Alderson were indeed friends—Alderson knew him "very well," he asserts, and as the interview progresses we learn how they became friends. "When I knew him," Alderson says, "I was a Security Officer with him in France and I lived with him." In other words, Alderson and Souetre were stationed in the same garrison together in France, at a joint post where U.S. military personnel served with French personnel. Afterwards, Alderson returned to civilian life in Texas but remained in touch with Souetre over the years, exchanging Christmas cards and presumably correspondence. But it wasn't any correspondence with Souetre that informed Alderson that Souetre had deserted the French military to join the OAS; it was Souetre's wife, with whom Alderson had also kept in touch. "But he [Souetre] very definitely left, I presume, his wife," Alderson told Shaw. Souetre's wife was a beautiful woman from a rich wine family in southern France. "I have not heard from her in, well, many years," Alderson said, but "she was the one that told me that he had left the French Army and had gone into the underground trying to save Algiers."

Alderson also gives us a description of Souetre: "He was good looking, tall, rather angular, last time I saw him. He had kind-of curly hair, dark brown, good looking guy, handsome guy."[5]

But Alderson was also interviewed the following day, on October 6; from a memorandum of the interview, Alderson tells us more:

- Souetre was approximately twenty-five years old in the early '50s.
- Souetre was a linguist who spoke excellent English with no trace of an accent; he also spoke Spanish and German.
- He was a sharp dresser and a ladies man.
- He was well acquainted with "all the French politicians."
- He stood six-foot-one, and weighed about 175 pounds.

That gives us a better picture of the man, physically and personally: a dedicated officer but not-so-dedicated husband; a proverbially tall, dark, and handsome "ladies man;" and a socially outgoing man who knew "all the French politicians."[6]

More important than any of this, however, is that when Shaw mentioned 632-796's statement that Souetre was in Dallas the same day Kennedy was shot and deported shortly thereafter, Alderson knew all about it.

FBI agents began tailing Alderson shortly after Kennedy was assassinated, and eventually they stopped the spook games and interviewed the doctor. Keep in mind, Shaw's interview took place in 1977, but this FBI interview took place "soon after the assassination." And they claimed that they contacted Alderson at that time "because of a four- or five-year-old Christmas card which he had sent to Souetre."[7]

This means that the FBI knew about Souetre being in Dallas on November 22, 1963, and his expulsion shortly thereafter—several months before CIA Document 632-796 revealed the fact that the French (in March of 1964) had queried the FBI about Souetre's deportation destination.

Naturally, what the FBI most wanted to know was if Alderson knew details of Souetre's expulsion from Dallas—the reason being that the FBI, shortly after Kennedy's murder, considered Souetre an assassination suspect. We know this because Alderson told Shaw: "They felt that Jean knew who or he himself had assassinated Kennedy."[8]

The FBI considered Souetre an assassination suspect, but, inexplicably, they didn't mention this to the Warren Commission. Furthermore, Alderson also tells us that he himself reported what he knew about Souetre. "I've never heard from the investigation," Alderson told Shaw, "except I contacted the, I guess, defunct Committee that doesn't exist anymore or, whether they do exist I really don't know, they've been through so much hassle the last year or so."[9]

The only committee that had been experiencing any hassle in this time period was the House Select Committee on Assassinations. True, it wasn't "defunct" in 1977, but anyone casually following its progress in the newspapers would surely have expected them to be when one considers the constant political objections to its existence due to its large budget and nonstop turmoil, infighting, and overall havoc among its members. "The Committee" never got back to him.

Document 632-796 reveals that on March 5, 1964, the French queried the legal attaché's office in Paris, and it also tells us that French intelligence (SDECE) had also queried the FBI in New York about Souetre. The FBI began to investigate at once.[10] Alderson told the FBI precisely when he knew Souetre (1953) and precisely where (Petette Malioun near Rheims, France). This document is dated March 6, 1964—the next day— and from there a slew of other FBI documents proceeds: investigating Alderson, investigating Souetre's aliases, investigating relative commercial air flights that might have deported Souetre. They don't tell us a whole lot as far as detail, but they do verify that while the Warren Commission was in session, the FBI was investigating Souetre.

Perhaps the FBI did report their knowledge of Souetre and his deportation to the Warren Commission; and if that's the case, then it was the Commission itself that suppressed the evidence. But who suppressed the evidence is immaterial. A terrorist was deported out of Dallas shortly after the most shocking assassination in U.S. history, and multiple elements of the U.S. government knew about it yet never reported it to the American people. If that's not suspicious enough, there's also clear evidence that some element of the U.S. government did the actual deporting.[11]

The only thing that could make this worse would be if the FBI knew about Souetre before Kennedy's assassination, which would support allegations that the FBI had received notice of a Kennedy assassination plot before Kennedy was killed.[12]

This would be a revelation of monumental proportion because it would prove that our Justice Department knew not only of a plot against Kennedy but also of an assassin who might be connected to the plot. It would prove that either the Justice Department participated in Kennedy's murder (which we do not assert) or that they had enough warning to prevent Kennedy's murder but bungled it either by dismissal or incompetence and then suppressed these facts in order to protect themselves. This is our position.

But in order to prove that accusation, we would have to prove that the FBI knew about Souetre before the assassination. In Henry Hurt's excellent book *Reasonable Doubt,* the author clearly spells this out: "There is no known evidence that the FBI contacted Alderson until after the receipt of the query from the French" (March 5, 1964).[13]

The only reason the FBI could have been investigating Alderson would be to discern Alderson's knowledge of Souetre. Hence, for the FBI to have investigated Alderson before Kennedy's assassination would prove they had concerns about Souetre before the fact. But despite the fact that Henry Hurt's superb book tells us that there is no known evidence to support this possibility, FBI Document 105-120510-2 proves that the FBI was indeed investigating Alderson on April 4, 1963 (See Appendix C), more than seven months before the assassination.[14]

The Quagmire of Paper

"You don't understand. The FBI is just one federal
department that has millions of classified documents
stored all over the country. When laws order us to
declassify and release thousands of documents a
year, the declass officers sometimes make mistakes.
It's too much work for too few employees; it's
impossible to read every line of every document up
for declassification and still do your job.
Sometimes we make mistakes. Sometimes we release
things that aren't supposed to be released."

— JUSTICE DEPARTMENT DECLASSIFICATION OFFICER[1]

HENRY HURT'S *Reasonable Doubt* is one of the most exhaustively
researched books ever written on Kennedy's murder, but by now the
book (published in 1985) is dated. Since 1992, a steady trickle of government files pertaining to Kennedy's death have been appearing at the
National Archives, and in October 1998, the long-awaited Assassination
Records Review Board released its 208-page report. The report sounds
hopeful at first, stating: "The review board's experience leaves little
doubt that the federal government needlessly and wastefully classified
and then withheld from public access countless important records that
did not require such treatment." Furthermore, an important Associated
Press article in *USA Today* sounds just as hopeful: "The government for
decades 'needlessly' and 'wastefully' withheld millions of records about
the assassination of President Kennedy, causing Americans to mistrust
their government."[2] But a few lines down, we're informed, "However,
the board was not charged with reopening the investigation, and while it

added to the millions of documents in the National Archives touching on the assassination, it did not address the question of who killed Kennedy." This is puzzling. What exactly was the purpose of the board? The article summarizes, "The records will be kept at the National Archives. Some still must be processed before the public can inspect them. Remaining blacked-out sections of some records will come to light at different dates between now and 2017." In other words, the ambiguities remain just as they always have with a federal records review board that doesn't release the records it reviews. Duffy and Ricci say it best in their book, *The Assassination of John F. Kennedy*:

> Critics of both the Warren Commission and the House Select Committee wonder if it is possible for a body representing the federal government to conduct an impartial investigation on an assassination in which agencies of that government appear to have played a role.[3]

Similarly, it is difficult for the federal government to police itself in the way it stores, classifies, and declassifies information. To date, it has been extremely difficult for Kennedy assassination investigators of any kind to assemble and analyze the pertinent information. For example, when Henry Hurt states in his excellent book that "[t]here is no known evidence that the FBI contacted Alderson until after the receipt of the query from the French," he does so only because the necessary documentation wasn't available to him. The more recently declassified FBI Document 105-120510-2 is dated April 8, 1963—long before Kennedy's death—and though parts of it remain redacted, we'll reproduce it for you on the next page (though a full copy of the document is included as Appendix C).

The redactions clearly indicate the classification officer's need to protect the identity of the informant, a trademark in multitudes of federal documents. The official term is "partial release." But we needn't worry about the redactions because what's not redacted tells us everything we need to know. This document proves beyond any doubt that the FBI knew about Souetre and was looking for him seven months before Kennedy's death. There is no other reason conceivable for the FBI tracking down Alderson, and it's also obvious how the FBI came to learn about our French terrorist Souetre and Alderson in the first place: the previously mentioned fact that they (the FBI) told Dr. Alderson that they were investigating a four- to five-year-old

```
United States government
Memorandum

TO:   DIRECTOR, FBI                  DATE: 4/8/63
(ATT: FOREIGN LIAISON UNIT)

FROM:     SAC, NEW YORK XXXXXXXXXXX Informant
SUBJECT:  ALDERSONS,
          5803 Burlingham, Houston, Texas
          IS - FRANCE
          Informant
     For the information of the Bureau and Houston, on
4/3/63 XXXXXXXXXXXXXXXXXXXXXXXXXXXXXXXXXXXXXXXXXX
XXXXXXXXXXXXXXXXXXXXXXXXXXXXXXXXXXXXXXXXXXXXXXX
     Houston is requested to identify the ALDER-
SONS, and when this information is forthcoming,
the Bureau is requested to advise what, if any,
information may be furnished to this source.


     2-Bureau (RM)
     2-Houston, (RM)
     1-New York, XXXXXXXXX
               Informant


     LHB:EG
     (5)
```

Christmas card which Alderson "had sent to Souetre and which had ended up in the post office dead letter files."[4]

Yet another FBI document (105-120510-1) from the director's office to the Foreign Liaison Unit is dated just one month later, and it clearly indicates a full-scale investigation of Alderson by the FBI. The Houston dentist is examined with such scrutiny that the FBI verifies not only Alderson's military service but also former places of employment, previous addresses, the schools he attended, and criminal background (which proved negative). The FBI even investigated Alderson's wife, mother, and father. An attachment to the same document, dated May 21, 1963, proves that this investigation could only be as a result of Alderson's previous acquaintance with Souetre because it states, "Our files contain no information indicating that Dr. Alderson and his wife have been outside the U.S. or have been engaged in any anti-France activity."[5] These documents prove that the FBI was deeply concerned about Souetre long before November 22, 1963. Without these valuable pieces of paper, we would never be able to positively establish that fact.

This shows clearly that the truth is buried in the documentation. Everything else consists of speculative links and secondhand testimony and various interpretations of vague, elusive hypotheses. The only way to find out what really happened to Kennedy is to find the official records that reveal it. Those records, obviously, are being withheld from us.

They could be located in hundreds of places. Every arm of the federal government has a variety of facilities in which they store records. Important documents could be hiding in the storehouses of the FBI, the CIA, the NSA, the Army, the Navy, the Air Force, the DEA, the DIA, the BFT, or one of the other seemingly countless government organizations. Even in this age of digitalization, high-tech databases, and storage-drives the size of a quarter that hold a million pages of text, the federal government still has billions of pages of documents that need to be properly categorized, cataloged, and stored. The FBI, for instance, has not one but at least three major record depositories: one in Washington D.C., one in Clarksburg, West Virginia, and another in Pocatello, Idaho (yet only a handful of classification officers to manage all those records). The U.S. Army Military Intelligence branch is actually connected to numerous intelligence-related branches such as INSCOM (Intelligence and Security Command), ASA (the Army Security Agency), and (AISA) Army Intelligence Support Activity. The same thing is true in the Navy: ONI (Office of Naval Intelligence), NSC (Naval Security Command), NSOG (Naval Security Operations Group), and NSGA (Naval Security Group Activity). There are so many departments with inner departments, each with its own additional department where it stores its records. Then there are a number of seemingly unidentifiable storage facilities, such as the Records Redeposition Repository, the Back-Processing Database (rumored to be part of the CIA), and the Federal Information Storage Unit. If someone is interested in a particular FBI document that's not in the National Archives, it may be somewhere else, even if it's not classified. In that case, you have to deal with one of the liaison units that exist between federal branches, such as the IGA (Inter-Agency Group Activity), which exists as an official conduit between the FBI and the National Security Council. Or perhaps a particular document has been stored by the DIS (Defense Investigative Service), which deals with NSC, FBI, CIA, and all military intelligence branches.

Our ultimate point is this: for decades, critical documents have been shotgunned all over the country, into various record vaults. No one really knows how much material is out there. And even if that could be officially discerned, who knows where it is?

And of all these billions of documents, many are classified for good reason. Certainly the public always has the right to know what its government is doing—and has done—but not if that same knowledge could circulate to foreign and domestic parties who don't have a right to know—namely enemies of the United States. This is the legitimate purpose of restricting certain information, and with equal legitimacy it protects the interests of our national security. Few would argue with this.

But on the other hand, this same legitimacy of information restriction has been purposefully perverted, contorted, and misused all for the purpose of circumventing the truth, and that official statement that we've all heard so often ("restricted in the interests of national security") has become a buzz-line for keeping America in the dark.

The Warren Commission lied in 1964, the House Select Committee on Assassinations deliberately ignored evidence in 1979, and the Assassination Records Review Board said in 1998 that critical Kennedy documents continue to be withheld from the public until 2017.

Here's another buzz-line, one that seems to have been forgotten lately: "A government of the people, by the people, for the people." What ever happened to that? This government isn't "by the people" when our elected officials continue to keep "the people" from knowing important truths. There's another word for that sort of thing: crypto-fascism. Decades have passed since John F. Kennedy was murdered, yet after all that time, "the people" are still being told by their elected officials that to release all pertinent documents relative to Kennedy's assassination would compromise our national security. America should not allow this continued abuse of power and subsequent cover-up. America should not have to wait until 2038, or even 2017, for the truth. America should not have to wait another day.

But America will wait. And who knows what further snow jobs will follow?

But, again, after all that time, perhaps time itself has worked to the advantage of the populace—sometimes by accident, but also by the sheer number of documents scheduled for legitimate declassification and release because the information they contain truly does not jeopardize our national security.

A legal scheduling procedure exists to release to the public thousands of classified government documents per year whose information is no longer considered sensitive in nature. Certain criteria are involved, particularly the amount of time that has passed since a given document's classification, and of course the specific nature of the information contained in that same given document. This means that people are assigned the task of making certain determinations about the documents slated for release. These are more often than not subjective determinations. In other words, for every government document that is declassified and released to the public, there is a person who must make a judgment as to that document's relevance to national security.

For this job to be executed without error, the person charged with the task would have to be a psychologist, a consummate historian, and an absolute expert in U.S. foreign policy. But most of the people who do this job are none of the above. They're typical people. They're clerks. They're office assistants. They're nine-to-five paper-pushers, and the majority of them surely do the best they can. But in all our previous criticism of shady federal government kangaroo commissions, committees, and review boards steadfastly manipulating the information that's released to us, it can be said that the sheer volume of documents works against them too. There's too much to keep track of and too much material in too many places for any body of government to remain fully aware of after more than thirty-five years. Let's look back at an excerpt of the epigraph for this chapter:

It's too much work for too few employees; it's impossible to read every line of every document up for declassification and still do your job. Sometimes we make mistakes. Sometimes we release things that aren't supposed to be released.

This is a statement made to us via a phone interview with an anonymous "classification officer" who works for an arm of the United States Justice Department. Which arm scarcely matters. His statement elucidates the overall problem: too much material for too few people. Hence, "Sometimes we release things that aren't supposed to be released." This is understandable, and naturally we asked the next logical question. Exactly who makes the determination about what's "supposed" to be released and what's not? The answer was, if anything, obscure. A particular chain of command, so to speak. It was made clear, though, that when a document was released that wasn't supposed to be released, the employee who released it definitely heard about it from the boss of the boss of the boss of the boss of the classification employee, in other words—a power in high places.

But this all makes perfect sense, really. One would assume that most records clerks in 2000 probably wouldn't even have been born in 1963, or if they had been, they would've been too young to understand how what was happening in the world back then could present a national security violation almost four decades later. Big Brother's document labyrinth is too big now even for Big Brother to keep a handle on. This might explain how so many Kennedy-assassination documents remain withheld from the minds of the U.S. population, but it can also explain how a few have slipped out—documents such as CIA Document 632-796, FBI Documents 105-120510-2 and 105-120510-1, and many of the other documents we will present to you in this book.

Regarding this instance and 632-796, Henry Hurt makes a critical point: "There is no reason to believe the matter would ever have come to light were it not for the routine query [regarding Souetre's presence in Dallas on the day Kennedy was murdered] from French intelligence. It seems highly unlikely that the CIA officer charged with deciding the release of secret papers in 1976 had even an inkling of the revelations contained in this particular document."[6] So, too, for FBI Document 105-120510-2, as well as others. In particular, 105-120510-2 plainly states at the bottom that it was "reviewed by FBI/JFK Task Force on 2/26/97" and the declassification order was to "Release In Part."[7] To augment Henry Hurt's cogent point, with regard to the FBI document that proves the FBI was investigating Souetre months before Kennedy's assassination, it's not very feasible that the FBI records examiner who released

105-120510-2 in early 1997 had any cognizance whatsoever as to the document's importance thirty-four years after it was written.

Sometimes, even when the government inadvertently releases a sensitive document, they can often quickly correct that error. Here's an example. When coauthor Brad O'Leary had directed his research chief, Tim McGinnis, to find specific DEA files regarding international heroin-trafficking in the early '60s, McGinnis went to the National Archives and, along with his assistant Brent Ruhkamp, found thirty-six boxes that weren't indexed. This left them with no choice but to go through each box and scan each document individually—a fairly painstaking task, given that they contained thousands of separate files. The process took days, but by the time they made it through twenty or so, they began to hit pay-dirt: they were getting into actual DEA records concerning Marseille, France, and the heroin labs there. They were able to narrow the approximate critical dates to two boxes of files, but by the time they were able to do this, it was closing time at the Archives. McGinnis and Ruhkamp had to leave, but not before putting those two boxes on reserve. They were primed and ready to return the next morning and begin photocopying the documents.

But when Ruhkamp returned the next morning to pull up the reserved boxes, he was told that there was a problem, a big problem. He was introduced to two high-level archivists who were responsible for that collection, and then he was told that he was accessing material that hadn't been properly cleared by the DEA for public consumption. Furthermore, he was told that none of the original thirty-six boxes should ever have been made accessible.

The DEA had made a big mistake, and neither McGinnis nor Ruhkamp ever got to see what was in those last two boxes. It only causes one to wonder: why would two boxes of forty-year-old DEA files be deemed too sensitive for release?

We have no choice but to wait till the year 2017 to find out.

At any rate, nearly two generations have passed since Kennedy's assassination. Most of the people who were in power then are dead now, hence these "mistakes" in document declassification and release. But these mistakes prove to be a veritable treasure trove to those who seek the truth.

14

Alias Michel Roux

*"Put not thine hand with the wicked to be an
unrighteous witness."*

— Exodus 23:1

THE LAST chapter may seem like a sidetrack, but it was necessary in order to lay the foundation for our ultimate case about the South Vietnamese government's involvement in Kennedy's assassination. The following information helps to shore up that foundation. Previously, we've discussed Jean Rene Souetre, his high-ranking affiliation with the French terrorist group known as the OAS (a group that routinely assassinated its opponents), and the fact that he was in Dallas, Texas, on the same afternoon that Kennedy was assassinated. We've further discussed how Souetre was then quickly and quietly flown out of the country by some element of the U.S. government less than two days later. We've provided—in their entirety—the official government documents that prove this, along with other documents and official interviews proving that Souetre was being investigated by the FBI seven months before Kennedy was killed. We've also proven, via the OAS's history, that this militant group had every political reason to want to kill Kennedy (it was Kennedy who urged de Gaulle to grant full independence to the country that OAS was fighting to keep dependent to France: Algeria). The OAS tried repeatedly to assassinate de Gaulle, their primary enemy. Kennedy was their secondary enemy, so it is entirely feasible that the OAS would try to assassinate him too. And who would be better qualified to achieve such a terrorist feat than the OAS, a band of highly trained insurgents, killers, and snipers?

88

But now let's look back again to the first line of information on 632-796:

8. Jean SOUETRE aka Michel ROUX aka Michel MERTZ

Here are two aliases for Souetre: two men with the first name Michel, one whose last name is Roux and another whose last name is Mertz. How the information of these aliases ever found their way onto a CIA document can only be guessed at, but it's logical to grant that this information came from "the SDECE man" who had queried the FBI about Souetre's deportation. SDECE would know better than anyone else any aliases of OAS members. Remember, in this time frame, SDECE had just soundly defeated the OAS movement via counterintelligence ploys in which they had recruited French mobsters—barbouzes—to infiltrate the OAS infrastructure. The OAS never saw it coming, and they fell apart as a result, slowly but surely watching their once-effective ranks dissipate due to French arrest and imprisonment. And something else to remember from our SDECE chapter: the OAS and their reign of terrorism seriously threatened the survivability of de Gaulle's government (not to mention the direct attempts on de Gaulle's life), so when de Gaulle ordered Frey and Foccart to end the OAS problem, it was considered a national priority. Utilizing SDECE, Frey, Foccart, and their underlings fulfilled their tasks (but with catastrophic ramifications, which we'll discuss later) and in the process gathered an incredible amount of intelligence information on the OAS members that they eventually captured. And we know that Souetre himself was one of those captured because, according to CIA Document CSCI-3/776,742, "Souetre . . . escaped from a detention camp in 1961." Not only did SDECE have full access to regular French military personnel records (this is important, since most of the OAS were formerly part of the French military) but also they gradually accrued new intelligence information on those same men after they had deserted and joined the OAS. SDECE did this via essentially standard means: confidential informants, wiretaps, surveillance teams, and the like.[1] (And let's not forget torture, one of SDECE's favorite operating procedures.) Another thing that helped immensely was the arrest of an OAS courier in September 1961 and the confiscation of a briefcase full of OAS personnel records.² Along with all of that, we have the barbouzes (a pool of Marseille mobsters) personally infiltrating the OAS and delivering still more intelligence and personnel data back to SDECE.

Therefore, it's perfectly logical that SDECE would have been able to identify aliases that were being used by many OAS men, including Souetre.

The next step is to investigate the aliases listed on 632-796, the first one being Michel Roux.

Michel is the French equivalent of "Michael," and Roux is a fairly common French surname. Now, as we've previously established that some elements of the FBI knew about Souetre prior to 632-796 (and prior to Kennedy's death), we can assume that most of the more standard elements did not. This is reasonable because immediately after 632-796 appeared—even on the same day, March 5, 1964—FBI and INS personnel in Texas began looking for any evidence of a Jean Rene Souetre, Michel Roux, or Michel Mertz being in Dallas on or near the assassination date, as well as any evidence of individuals by these names being deported. All three of these names came up blank.

This might lead to the suspicion that Souetre's aliases were made-up names. There's no documentary evidence at all to suggest that within this time frame the name Michel Mertz popped up anywhere during the Justice Department's investigation. But a few days later, the name Michel Roux did.

In an FBI teletype from Dallas to Washington D.C. on March 11, 1964, we learn that the investigation did indeed find evidence of a Frenchman named Michel Roux being in Texas on November 22, 1963. Like Souetre, he not only spoke French but also was fluent in English and German, and what's more, Michel Roux claimed to have been in the French Army and served in Algeria.

So did the FBI have their man? Regrettably, no. As it turns out, even in spite of the coincidences, Roux, a hotel clerk and restaurant-management student from Paris, was visiting American friends in late November, 1963. Where? Fort Worth, Texas—not far from Dallas.

A successful and respected businessman, Leon Gachman, and his family were entertaining Roux during the Frenchman's visit to Fort Worth. They had become friends a month previously when Gachman had made a business trip to Paris; Roux served as his tour guide. Later, Roux accepted Gachman's invitation to come to Fort Worth for a visit, hoping that Gachman could line up a job for him in the restaurant business. To make a fairly long story short, Roux spent the entirety of his trip with some or all of Gachman's family. On November 22, 1963, between 10 A.M. and noon, Roux attended classes with Leon Gachman's son, Arnold, amid a multitude of witnesses, and thirty minutes later when Kennedy was being murdered in Dallas, Roux and Arnold were having lunch at a Fort Worth café, surrounded by still more witnesses. It was in this café that Roux and Gachman's son heard about the assassination.[3]

But what of the similarities between Roux and what we know about Souetre?

1) Both men were multilingual. True, but so are millions of French. French schooling actively encourages students to learn other languages.

2) Both men were in the French Army and served in Algeria. True, but more than 500,000 men in the French Army served in Algeria.

3) Both men had dark hair. Hardly conclusive.

The physical difference alone clearly demonstrates that Michel Roux couldn't have been Souetre using a false name. In 1963, Souetre was thirty-three years old, while Roux was described by Gachman as being in his mid-twenties. Souetre was six-foot-one and 175 pounds in 1953; ten years later, Roux was five-foot-eight and between 140 and 150 pounds. Even if Souetre lost at least twenty-five pounds between 1953 and 1963, it's not likely that he could have also lost five inches of height.

In the end, however interesting the prospect might have been, we learn that Michel Roux, on a job lead from Leon Gachman, departed the United States on December 6, 1963 "at Laredo, Texas, for Mexico."[4] Now we know the most convincing reason Roux wasn't Souetre: Michel Roux was not expelled from the country within forty-eight hours after Kennedy's murder; instead he legally and verifiably left the country on December 6.

On March 13, 1964, eight days after the alarm bells went off over

632-796, the FBI, satisfied that Roux was clean, discontinued their investigation of him.[5]

So much for Michel Roux. More than likely Souetre chose this name as an alias simply because it was common.

But what of Souetre's second alias?

A Man Named Mertz

WITH ALL the government documents we've gotten our hands on over the last few years, particularly the slew of them that were hastily declassified and released between February 1997 and October 1998, we haven't found a trace of the name Mertz in any of them except in its citing as an alias for Jean Rene Souetre. It seems peculiar that our Justice Department could locate and fully investigate a real person named Michel Roux almost immediately after the name first appeared on 632-796 and then find nothing on a similarly common name such as Michel Mertz. Perhaps this means that there simply was no one named Mertz in Dallas on the day of or shortly after Kennedy's assassination.

But since the French—and in particular, the SDECE—had made the initial inquiry to U.S. authorities and were well aware of Souetre's aliases, isn't it logical to assume that SDECE searched their own files for anyone named Mertz and found nothing? However, just the opposite is true. SDECE not only had Mertz in their files; Mertz worked for SDECE.

We're not certain why a man like Souetre would want to use as an additional alias the name of a man as clearly innocuous as Michel Roux, but we can be comfortably sure why he would use Mertz as an alias.

Mertz and Souetre knew each other. More important, Mertz and Souetre were personal enemies. In fact, if either man could be considered more notorious, it would not be the OAS soldier Jean Rene Souetre. It would be Mertz.

Michel (Michael) Victor Mertz, like Souetre, was a member of the

French military, but this was ten years prior to Souetre's time of service, namely in World War II.

But before Mertz joined the French war effort in 1941, he was inducted into the German Army. Mertz was born in 1920 in the Moselle/Lorraine sector of northeastern France, not far from the French/German border. The entire French Army was destroyed in about a month's time by Hitler's blitzkrieg, and by June 1940, the government of France was headed by Henri Phillipe Pétain. Pétain was lionized because of his strategic brilliance in defeating the Germans in World War I at the Battle of Verdun, but now he was collaborating with the Germans, his country's historic enemy. He essentially handed his country over to them and urged the people of France to fight no more and to join the Nazi protectorate.

In short order, the German war machine began to recruit Frenchmen into their efforts of continental conquest. Michel Victor Mertz was one such young man, recruited at age twenty-one, a year after France's capitulation. This was no volunteer army, mind you. Frenchmen, as well as men in other countries overrun by the Germans, were "recruited" by intimidation and by force. Any resistance to Nazi will was met with threats against one's family.

But like many patriotic young Frenchmen at the time, Mertz got his fill fast, and he defected from the German military forces at first opportunity to join the *Françaises Libres*, the French Resistance movement, which vowed to continue to fight Hitler at all costs, in spite of its country's hasty armistice under the former hero Marshal Pétain.

This French Resistance was led by General Charles de Gaulle.

Mertz worked the Haute-Vienne and Limousin districts, a perimeter along the Vienne River, southwest of Paris. At the time, this was a highly strategic location. Its cottage industry of porcelain factories and brickworks was effectively converted into more war-worthy industries for the Nazis, and far more important, its major railways and junctures were just what Hitler needed to maintain his supply routes toward the end of the war.

Michel Mertz acclimated well to his new environment. It was here in the Limousin region that he learned his first real trade: killing. He learned it well. In fact, Mertz wreaked such havoc on the German Army traveling in and out of his territory that he quickly ascended in rank and was given his own unit to command. Very little is known of Mertz's technical and leadership skills as a field commander in France, but it's safe to assume that he rose to the task with considerable prowess and spilled a lot of German blood. Mertz and his unit of field killers became legendary throughout the French Resistance circles, and when the war was over and the flags of Hitler's Third Reich had been dragged through the dust, Michel Victor Mertz stood tall as a Resistance hero. He was awarded multiple medals for valor.

A man of Mertz's skill and insight wasn't overlooked. Shortly after World War II ended, the French intelligence apparatus promptly recruited him, after which he became a deep-cover field operative. Now that France was freed from Nazi domination, they immediately returned to their own designs of foreign domination. Vietnam was theirs again, handed back to them by their victorious allies, not to mention their other protectorate interests in Algeria, Morocco, and the Congo.

In other words, now that France had miraculously survived World War II and was having its previously empty pockets filled by U.S. rehabilitative aid from the Marshall Plan, they needed to get their hands back into that big imperialistic pie that they'd been dining on for nearly the last century. Two billion dollars in additional aid landed in their laps, care of President Harry S. Truman, to fight the Communists in Indochina, but funding for other imperialistic efforts was sparse to none. Hence, SDECE needed qualified undercover men to perform intelligence work in some of these other countries, and we know that Michel Victor Mertz was one of these men. One of his first postwar assignments was field duty in Morocco, where he posed as an officer in the French Army. Mertz performed well in the field, proving his potential to the shady crew who had originally recruited him. Other duties included field work in Germany and Turkey, where communist insurgencies were rearing their heads (Turkey in particular, which during the late '40s and early '50s was a major supplier of opium base for the French heroin syndicate).

There's nothing unusual about a French Resistance hero working for SDECE, since intelligence agencies frequently recruit operatives with military experience. (Lucien Conein, for instance, originally fought for the French Resistance too, then joined the U.S. Army, and after that was recruited by the CIA.) But Mertz's case in particular helps us see a lot of the gray that mediated between the black and white back in those days, because while still working as a SDECE operative, Mertz got into the business of smuggling heroin.

It's not known for sure what brought about his first indoctrination into the heroin business. It is known, though, that many SDECE agents were also involved in heroin smuggling and became rich through it. It's also known that Mertz married the daughter of a man named Charles Martel, a French brothel owner who later got into heroin smuggling with Mertz. Was it SDECE that got Mertz into this highly illicit business, or was it Martel?

It's safe to say that it was probably both. Nevertheless, by 1960, Mertz was no longer working actively for SDECE. Instead, he had become one of the most important smugglers of heroin from Marseille to the United States. In fact, Mertz worked personally with other men in the heroin-trafficking business who were also SDECE members from the old days.*

Mertz's system of trafficking processed heroin to U.S. Mafia connections was brilliant: he managed all of the problematic financial intricacies (payoffs, money-laundering, wire-transfers, coded Swiss bank accounts); he hired, trained, and supervised the actual trafficking personnel (Mertz even trafficked a fair volume of product himself); and he charted the actual smuggling channels (this latter aspect being of the utmost importance since it not only involved getting the heroin from Marseille to the United States but also involved the critical time-tabling and scheduling of delivery to the pickup men on the U.S. side). Mertz executed his duties flawlessly, and it's fair to say that his ultimate bosses—the Guerini Brothers, who by the early '60s were the criminal overlords of the Marseille Mob and its global heroin syndicate—were very pleased with Mertz. Mertz got rich in a hurry.

A great deal of his operation involved transporting French automobiles (mainly Citroens) from France to America via steamships. Inside these vehicles, Mertz's concealment experts would hide up to 220 pounds of pure heroin. The cars were then legally purchased on the U.S. side by more Guerini agents and delivered to the proper U.S. Mob affiliates. From there, these great caches of pure heroin were "stepped on" (diluted

---

*It's also interesting to point out that in the late '40s and early '50s the majority of opium that was processed into heroin in Marseille came from Turkey, and we know that somewhere in that time frame Mertz worked SDECE jobs in Turkey. But during the Eisenhower administration, the Turkey-to-Marseille opium supply was decimated by law-enforcement intervention. This created quite a problem for the Marseille Mob; without a reliable opium supplier, they couldn't run a reliable heroin business. Curiously, it was Ngo Dinh Nhu of South Vietnam who, in 1958, reopened the opium business in his own country and also became the number one supplier of opium to the Marseille Mob.

with inert additives such as baking soda or powdered milk) and then sold nationwide—at incredible profit—to America's multitude of heroin addicts. Mertz's operation would also hide hefty amounts of heroin in rebuilt car engines and large household appliances such as refrigerators. Mertz was so successful, in fact, that he would eventually deliver to America a half billion dollars worth of heroin.[2]

But then, in the early spring of 1961, Mertz took a short hiatus from his heroin-trafficking enterprise. His country needed him again, and Mertz was all too happy to comply. SDECE had another job for him.

16

Crisis in France

". . . an orgy of gratuitous cruelty and sadism."

— DOUGLAS PORCH
THE FRENCH SECRET SERVICES[1]

IT WAS on April 22, 1961, that the crisis in Algeria came to a head. This was when French general and war hero Raoul Salan, backed by his secret army of supporters called the OAS, initiated the first strike of its rebellion against what they viewed as the treachery of the man they'd once risked their lives for: President Charles de Gaulle. By force, they staged their coup attempt and took over the capital of Algeria. Even though the attempt failed, this was only the beginning for Salan and his OAS, and the beginning, too, of the reign of terror that would then commence, bringing de Gaulle and his government perilously close to total destruction. When de Gaulle called on his trusted deputies Roger Frey and Jacques Foccart to combat the crisis, SDECE seemed the perfect organization to confront the problem, but by then even the directors of SDECE didn't know who to trust in their own organization, since many SDECE operatives as well as French military officers sympathized with the OAS and its efforts.

So SDECE, left to its own devices to remedy the OAS problem, took it upon itself to call on former affiliates that they could trust. Men like Michel Victor Mertz who had worked for SDECE in earlier days but now worked for the Marseille heroin syndicate were just the kind of men they were looking for. It's even likely that de Gaulle himself authorized this enlistment of Marseille underworld types to solve his problem.[2] And when SDECE came calling, Mertz was all too happy to oblige. But this raises a particular question: why would a man like Michel Mertz temporarily leave his lucrative heroin-trafficking business and agree to be recalled into a dangerous SDECE operation? The answers are abundant. First there is an element of leverage. SDECE knew full well of Mertz's heroin dealings and had kept quiet about it for years. Plus, many of Mertz's underworld associates had previously worked for SDECE, too. SDECE had granted a serious favor to men such as this in the past—simply by allowing them to continue their heroin profiteering—and now SDECE needed a favor in return.[3] Another logical reason for Mertz's unhesitating willingness to answer another of SDECE's calls was simply because these old contacts had remained friends and accomplices with Mertz for years. But there's still another motive for Mertz's accommodation—the best motive of all.

Men like Mertz—and in fact the entire Guerini heroin syndicate—needed the current government to remain intact so that their own business would remain intact. If the OAS movement succeeded, then a new government would take power in France, and there was a high likelihood that that new government would not tolerate a global heroin network headquartered on its own soil. Clearly, it was SDECE and its place of power in the de Gaulle government that provided the clandestine protection of the Marseille Mob; this same protection is what allowed the vast heroin labs in Marseille to run full-tilt for two decades without any interference from local law-enforcement.[4]

It's also documented that many members of the Marseille Mob also worked for SDECE. Here are a few:

- Joseph Attia: a French heroin honcho for years, he was also an assassin for SDECE.

- Christian David: a name familiar to Kennedy assassination buffs, mainly through Nigel Turner's controversial documentary video *The Men Who Killed Kennedy*. David served prison time for heroin trafficking. He also was recruited as an agent for SDECE to help in their effort against communist Moroccan insurgent leaders. David, in fact, testified that he took the equivalent of $150,000 for his part in murdering a Moroccan leftist leader and burning and burying the body.

- Andre LaBay: served prison time for heroin smuggling, he also, through SDECE connections, was recruited into counterterrorist operations against the OAS.

- Ange Simonpieri: served prison time for heroin trafficking, he also worked for SDECE in the fight against the OAS.

- Roger Delouette: yet another man who served prison time for heroin trafficking and who also worked for SDECE in Algeria.

- Achille Cecchini: a major French heroin kingpin, he worked for SDECE and was a major heroin partner with Michel Mertz. Cecchini was a main import organizer of opium for the Guerini heroin enterprise.[5]

Together, as a coterie working for SDECE, men such as these engaged in what Douglas Porch's intensive book, *The French Secret Services*, calls "an orgy of gratuitous cruelty and sadism." They didn't fool around, in other words. These guys meant business.

By agreeing to fight against the OAS, Mertz and his colleagues were actually fighting to keep in place the business elements that had made them—and would continue to make them—very rich and powerful men. Mertz was fighting for his own turf. And he fought well.

Mertz was the spy to end all spies, with the ultimate undercover plan. SDECE sent him to Algiers with documents that officially identified him as a French Army parachute captain. From here he expeditiously insinuated himself into the midst of the OAS and soon effectively installed himself as a genuine sympathizer to the OAS cause. By the summer of 1961, Mertz had so effectively fooled his OAS enemies that they were actually sending him on field assignments, not only in Algeria but also in mainland France.

But Mertz's job, after all, wasn't just to credibly penetrate the OAS and become one of their trusted members. It was also to provide, whenever possible, intelligence information on the OAS and spirit that information back to SDECE. This was Mertz's most difficult, and dangerous, task. One slip-up could result in catastrophe. One infinitesimal mistake, and Mertz knew full well he could wind up with his throat cut from ear to ear.

But Mertz didn't make any mistakes. What he did instead was arrange for himself to be arrested with some other OAS officers, officers who trusted him implicitly. They never doubted Mertz's allegiance to their anti–de Gaulle cause. Upon their arrest—for promulgating printed OAS propaganda in Paris—Mertz allowed himself to be incarcerated in an OAS detention camp right along with these other OAS officers. This was in July of 1961, and from there, within this prison camp overloaded with OAS men, Mertz rose to his most useful posture for SDECE. He became the eyes and ears of his confidantes. He so successfully infiltrated himself into the body of the OAS's most trusted officers that he became privy to OAS tactical and strategic plans. One of those plans was an elaborate machination to assassinate Charles de Gaulle.

It's true the OAS had tried to kill de Gaulle a number of times before, but these attempts all failed and were essentially kept masked from the press and the French populace. The de Gaulle government still had a tight rein on the press, and they knew that they couldn't afford to let their population of voters know that this band of thugs known as the OAS had come close to killing their president on several occasions. (This sentiment would turn out to be wrong in the future—in fact it would be the most effective weapon for de Gaulle and his government.)

Mertz, in his successful infiltration of the other OAS elite imprisoned with him in the detention camp, learned of the secret army's plan to kill de Gaulle by blowing up his car on a standard route the president took home every day through a place called Pont-sur-Seine.

Through his inside contacts, Mertz managed to alert his SDECE bosses of the upcoming assassination attempt. Foccart and his underlings staged a scenario that enabled them to get Mertz out of the camp in a way that would not cause the real OAS officers to become suspicious. Then Mertz was able to relay all of the assassination details to SDECE, and immediately afterward, Mertz was put back into the detention camp to maintain his undercover credibility. Mertz, in fact, never blew his cover. In the meantime, SDECE was well prepared for the OAS attempt on de Gaulle's life. The plan was foiled, and the would-be assassins were arrested.

Mertz, again, was a hero. He'd received medals while in the French Resistance for killing Germans in World War II, and now he was credited with personally saving President de Gaulle's life via his equally heroic infiltration of the OAS.

But Mertz did more than just that. It was the "patriotic" efforts of these thugs, these barbouzes, these Marseille/Corsican gangsters that allowed SDECE to accumulate enough intelligence data on the OAS to arrest the organization's most powerful members. Among them, General Salan, their leader, was arrested and thrown in prison, and so were many of the OAS's other crucial founding members. Though it's not absolutely certain exactly how many OAS members were taken into custody due to the efforts of the barbouzes, it's historically suggested that the undercover operations of Mertz and his heroin-trafficking colleagues provided the intelligence information that soon put French authorities onto many of the six hundred OAS suspects who were then arrested and incarcerated. It's even more interesting to note that sixty-nine of these convicts were active assassins.[6]

Afterwards, Mertz was lauded by his SDECE superiors. He saved de Gaulle's life and brought invaluable intelligence information to SDECE that led to the arrests of hundreds of members of this secret terrorist community. What it boils down to is this: a coterie of heroin peddlers helped save de Gaulle's Fifth Republic.

Codename: QJ/WIN

"French sources indicate that Souetre is the name of
a former French army captain who escaped from a
detention camp in 1961."

— CIA Document
CSCI-3/776,742

IT'S NOT unusual for government intelligence agencies to recruit criminals and members of organized crime for certain tasks, especially unauthorized tasks that the agency could not become officially involved with. We've already cited instances of our own CIA engaging in such ploys. It's also well known that contacts for the CIA also recruited such infamous U.S. Mafia figures as John Roselli, Santos Trafficante Jr., and Sam Giancana to arrange at least one assassination attempt against Fidel Castro.[1] Furthermore, it's been reasonably proven that the CIA condoned the activities of, and even forged alliances with, anti-Soviet insurgents in Afghanistan who were marketing opium in order to finance their war against Russia.[2]

But is it a coincidence that Michel Mertz and Jean Rene Souetre happened to both be in an OAS detention camp in 1961? In fact, Souetre admitted knowing Mertz to a French reporter named Jacques Chambaz in 1983, and to one of coauthor O'Leary's researchers (Monique Lajournade) on June 9, 1999.[3]

Souetre, as we know from CIA Document CSCI-3/776,742, escaped from that camp. But we also know that Souetre, even after that escape, remained a high-ranking OAS officer. He was so trusted with OAS intelligence business that he was picked out as the one to approach the CIA for help in their continued anti–de Gaulle activities. Souetre was named as a participant in a previous assassination attempt on de Gaulle. But knowing, as we now do, that Souetre and Mertz knew each other (and that Mertz helped crush the OAS by successfully posing as one of their members), isn't it reasonably likely that Souetre was one of the men Mertz fooled? If they were both in that detention camp during the same time-frame—which appears likely—it's not hard to imagine where Mertz received the crucial information regarding another OAS attempt on de Gaulle's life: from Souetre, one of the men who'd been involved in an earlier attempt. And even if that's not the case, Mertz and Souetre were on opposite sides. Souetre was fighting for a return to French imperialism and an end to de Gaulle's government. Mertz was fighting for the survival of that government because survival guaranteed that his own wealth and power, as well as the power of the Marseille heroin trade, would remain intact.

Keeping that in mind, though, let's switch gears a bit. A number of very credible Kennedy-assassination sources have connected Jean Rene Souetre with a curious handful of capital letters: QJ/WIN.

This is undoubtedly a CIA cryptonym (a kind of codename).[4] More than one man can have the same "crypt," and sometimes the crypt doesn't refer to an individual at all, but a CIA operation. For example, in the 1960s, MH/CHAOS was not a person but an operation regarding antiwar protestors.[5] More appropriately, the crypt ZR/RIFLE was not the crypt for a CIA operative but for a CIA program which involved recruitment of foreign nationals and criminals for potential political assassinations abroad[6] (the same program in which the CIA contracted Florida Mafia don Santos Trafficante to provide snipers to kill Castro[7]). Usually, crypts of this structure denote particular people, either full-fledged CIA operatives, contract agents, assets, or suspects. (GP/FLOOR, for example, was the CIA's crypt for Lee Harvey Oswald during its post-assassination investigation.) [8]

And in the realm of the Kennedy assassination, the aforementioned CIA crypt QJ/WIN has popped up with some curious frequency. A number of experts in the conspiracy theory community believe that Jean Rene Souetre and QJ/WIN were the same man. And this same group has asserted that QJ/WIN was also a foreigner with U.S. Mob contacts who was specifically inducted into the CIA's executive-action program.[9]

We know that Souetre was at the very least a potential assassin; certainly his thorough combat training in the French military, his field experience in Algeria, and his further experience as a terrorist with the OAS might provide him with exactly the kind of skills the CIA would be looking for in possible recruits for their ZR/RIFLE program. Additionally, we know that Souetre came in direct contact with CIA operatives in Lisbon when he made his bid for CIA support for OAS efforts against de Gaulle. The above three facts might make a solid foundation for the case that Souetre was indeed QJ/WIN.

But the same files that inform us that Souetre contacted the CIA in a plea for support also document that the CIA representatives fully rebuffed Souetre. They sent him packing. And this makes sense because, as CIA Document CSCI-3/776,742 implies, the CIA had no conceivable reason to want to support any operations against de Gaulle or his government. The United States would have no reason whatever to support a de Gaulle overthrow by right-wing terrorists trying to keep Algeria under French rule, especially when it was Kennedy himself who urged de Gaulle to grant Algeria full independence and totally withdraw all French influence from the country.

If QJ/WIN wasn't Souetre, maybe it was Mertz, whose name was sometimes confused with Souetre's. After all, Mertz had undeniable ties with the U.S. Mafia, who were the very best customers of the heroin he smuggled. And though it can't be proven that Mertz himself had any direct contacts with the CIA, we do know that his ultimate employers—the Guerini Brothers, who controlled the entirety of the Marseille heroin syndicate—did have contact when the CIA recruited them for help in dispersing the communist dock strikes in Marseille in 1947 and 1950. However, this happened more than thirteen years prior to the assassination, and by then the CIA was long gone from Marseille. By this time, now well protected by SDECE, what feasible reason could there be for the Guerinis' enterprise to reestablish asset connections with the CIA, especially when the CIA's employer—the United States government—was among the world's harshest critics of the Marseille heroin market? Ultimately, the U.S. government under the Kennedy administration was a bitter enemy of the Marseille Mob because the Marseille Mob channeled heroin to the U.S. Mob, with whom the Kennedys were waging an all-out war. In fact, there's nothing that's cogent to support the notion that the CIA crypt QJ/WIN might have anything to do with Mertz or Souetre at all.

The inception of the reference seems to have bloomed from something seemingly unrelated but interesting nonetheless. It involves a seedy sort by the name of Thomas Eli Davis III who, along with Jack Ruby, smuggled weapons to Cuba.[10] Davis is also thought to have been a CIA contractor.[11] More interestingly, though, less than a month after Kennedy's death, Davis was imprisoned in Tangier and was detained by Moroccan authorities because he possessed a letter which referred to Lee Harvey Oswald and the Kennedy assassination. It is in Anthony Summers's superb book, *Conspiracy,* that we learn the most about this confusing episode. FBI files identified Davis as a bank robber with CIA ties who indeed knew Jack Ruby. Davis turns out to be another one of those figures who died by suspicious means after it was discerned that he might have information regarding the Kennedy assassination. (He was electrocuted while cutting a power cable.) But Davis's relation to the crypt QJ/WIN goes back to his short prison term in Tangier. Davis was released through the efforts of a CIA operative known as QJ/WIN. In 1975, the Senate Intelligence Committee verified that QJ/WIN was a CIA affiliate with criminal ties who was enlisted by the CIA somewhere in Europe.[12] This presents precious little evidence that QJ/WIN may have been Souetre or Mertz. Peter Dale Scott, in his own fascinating book, *Deep Politics and the Death of JFK,* makes a much better case that QJ/WIN may have been an agent affiliated with the ZR/RIFLE program named Charles Siragusa.[13]

But since many implications have cropped up in Kennedy assassination theory that Souetre and QJ/WIN were the same person, we felt it appropriate to touch on it here and to express our misgivings. We're not terribly concerned with the actual identity of this shadowy CIA cryptonym; what we are concerned with is the direct relevance of Souetre and/or Mertz regarding what took place in Dallas on November 22, 1963. We've already cited almost everything that is officially known about Jean Rene Souetre, so now we're focusing more sharply on Mertz—the name specified on 632-796 as an alias of Souetre's.

The fact that he knew Souetre—and that they were enemies—is vitally important, and we'll get more deeply into that later. But remember, it was Mertz who personally infiltrated the detention camp and gleaned the details of the next OAS assassination attempt on de Gaulle, and this expert undercover work provided SDECE with all the information it needed to foil that attempt. Not only was de Gaulle's life saved by this information, it in turn contributed more than anything else to the downfall of the OAS. Unlike previous assassination attempts, the one at Pont-sur-Seine was fully reported in detail by the French press, and when the populace read about it, they were absolutely appalled. Any sympathy they may have had for the OAS cause went right down the drain. Total support swung straight back to de Gaulle and his Fifth Republic, and the once-powerful OAS was ruined.

In the aftermath, SDECE found itself in the best graces of their president. But this left one tiny problem. Now that SDECE had successfully achieved their objective of neutralizing the OAS, they found themselves seriously indebted to Mertz and the other mobsters who'd taken part in the anti-OAS campaign.

During Mertz's undercover jaunt for SDECE, he had jeopardized his previous heroin contacts with the U.S. Mafia via his smuggling points in Montreal and New York City. As payment for the debt that was now owed, SDECE arranged for the French Ministry of the Interior to assume all expenses to move Mertz and his wife to Canada where he could then safely reestablish his old heroin connections in New York City with the U.S. Mafia.

Within a month, Mertz was getting rich again, and by January 1962 his contacts were sufficiently re-solidified. He was back in France running his end of the business again for the Guerini heroin syndicate, and business was booming.

By this point, Mertz had opened large Swiss bank accounts for himself to contain his immense profits. Bear in mind, this was a man officially living on a captain's retirement pay, yet Mertz, by 1969, owned a hunting lodge on over a thousand acres of prime land, as well as his own airfield, opulent condos in Paris and Metz, more expensive land in his home region of Moselle, a vacation house in Corsica, his own villa near Paris, and his own airplane.

Mertz was a millionaire a dozen times over, and we can see how SDECE repaid him for his service. They allowed him to maintain his lucrative trafficking enterprise, and they allowed the same for all of the other mobsters who would help fight the OAS. They helped by continuing to fully protect the Marseille heroin labs and their global distribution network from any law-enforcement interdiction for as long as possible. To do otherwise was to risk the most unthinkable catastrophe. If some other element of the French government—independent of SDECE—should start cracking down on the Marseille dope network and arresting its members, an awful lot of angry heroin peddlers would start talking about how SDECE had recruited organized crime figures for their government-sponsored operations (some of which involved the murder and torture of former French countrymen). This would not only destroy SDECE's reputation among the rest of the world's intelligence agencies but also cast an international shadow over the designs and intents of the government of France.

That's why SDECE bent over backward for as long as it could to protect the interests of the Marseille heroin industry. (It's also reasonable to suppose that some of that heroin cash found its way into the palms of certain SDECE officials in return for their continued cooperation.)

Meanwhile, on the U.S. side of things, our own Federal Bureau of Narcotics (the precursor to the DEA) began arresting many of Mertz's mules, and some of these men admitted that Mertz was the operation's ringleader. After that, the FBN immediately began to complain to French law-enforcement authorities that Michel Mertz headed a network that was smuggling over a quarter of a ton of heroin per year to the United States.[14]

Of course, SDECE had some considerable influence over these French law-enforcement authorities. For example, the Paris unit of the U.S. Bureau of Narcotics and Dangerous Drugs in Europe had never heard of Michel Mertz.[15] They'd been unable to find any information on Mertz, a man whose military records would certainly be on file. Clearly, SDECE withheld those records and other far more important records too. Any documented record of Mertz's existence simply and conveniently vanished.

To make the longer story short, the Federal Bureau of Narcotics complained about Mertz to French authorities for four years and nothing was done. During that time, Mertz and his Marseille Mob cronies (Cecchini in particular) continued to move huge volumes of heroin to the United States.[16] All the while, the French continued to spin their wheels. They refused to do anything about Mertz, even with heaps of evidence dropped into their laps.

But when de Gaulle resigned in 1969 (he died a year later), the next French president, George Pompidou, clipped SDECE's wings by installing a new director with no political connections at all. Therefore, SDECE's power to protect the Marseille Mob dwindled considerably, or at least it dwindled enough that SDECE could no longer keep Mertz and men like him immune to arrest.

Eventually, after years of insistence from the FBN, Mertz was arrested and tried for heroin trafficking. Mertz received a five-year prison term—a pretty light sentence considering that for almost a decade he had distributed tons of refined heroin to the United States. In most countries, the United States included, conviction for trafficking a volume of heroin as large as this would instantly result in a life sentence without hope of parole. Mertz's primary business partner, Achille Cecchini, received the same sentence but never served a day of prison time because a "court-appointed" physician declared him to be too sick to survive in a prison environment. But evidently he wasn't too sick to frequent Mob-owned night clubs in Marseille and continue to consort with post-Guerini heroin kingpins.[17]

And as for Mertz? He was released from prison after serving only eight months of his five-year sentence,[18] and by now, it's pretty easy to figure out why.

18

Kernels of Truth

". . . he was approached by Antoine Guerini and offered the 'contract' to kill President Kennedy . . ."

— FBI DOCUMENT
62-109060-82601

IN THE mid-1980s, journalist Steve Rivele stumbled upon an informational tip that came close to breaking the walls of Kennedy assassination theory down.

It's not quite clear how, but Rivele, during the course of his research, was led to an imprisoned Marseille mobster named Christian David. David was a French heroin smuggler who worked for none other than Antoine Guerini, the godfather of the Marseille heroin syndicate. According to Rivele, David slowly began to reveal what he claimed to know about the Kennedy assassination in return for Rivele's help in procuring a lawyer for David, to keep him from being sent back to France where he was wanted for murder.

David details a fascinating story indeed, linked to professional assassins, the U.S. Mafia, and the Marseille Mob, links that the authors of this book strongly support. To Rivele, David claimed to have been approached by Antoine Guerini, in May or June of 1963, and asked to undertake the contract on President Kennedy's life. Specifically, David was asked to assemble a "hit-team" for the job. But David told Rivele that he turned the offer down because it was far too risky; killing Kennedy on U.S. soil presented far too many organizational and operational problems for David to view with even a sliver of optimism. Hence, someone else took Guerini up on his chancy offer—exactly who that was

110

isn't clear—but David, over the following years, got wind of the details, because his own associates knew the members of the hit-team that were finally dispatched to kill Kennedy.

David claimed that four rifle shots were fired at Kennedy. Two were discharged from behind Kennedy—one shot hit Kennedy in the back, and the other hit Governor Connally. A third shot was fired from in front of the car—the position of the grassy knoll—which caused Kennedy's fatal head wound, while a fourth shot came from behind, which missed. David also claimed that the man who fired the grassy knoll shot was a member of the Marseille underworld named Lucien Sarti, who frequently disguised himself in local military and police uniforms when on a murder contract. Initially, this is very interesting because it seems to back up the popular Oliver Stone theory that the fatal headshot was indeed fired from behind the wooden fence on the grassy knoll by someone wearing a Dallas police uniform.[2]

A second gunman implicated was a Marseille criminal named Sauveur Pironti, and the third gunman was yet another Marseille man named Joseph Bocognani.[3] According to Rivele, David went on to explain that these three men, after the contract was sealed, took a plane from Marseille to somewhere in the vicinity of Mexico City roughly a month before Kennedy's assassination. The three hired killers stayed in Mexico City for about two weeks; then they were transported by automobile to Brownsville, Texas, where they used Italian passports to cross the Mexican/U.S. border. From Brownsville, they were picked up by a member or members of the Chicago Mafia (Sam Giancana ran the Chicago Mafia at this point in time) and then transported to a "safe house" in Dallas, Texas. Now in Dallas, the three assassins took time to tactically assess the area in Dallas that Kennedy would be driving through; they surveyed the area thoroughly and took photographs of key locations.

After the assassination, Sarti, Pironti, and Bocognani were flown privately from Dallas to Montreal, Canada, after which they were flown back to their headquarters in Marseille.[4]

Speculatively, these assassination links to the Marseille Mob seem far more sound than the more popular theories that accuse the CIA and the military/industrial complex. What Christian David revealed to Rivele even directly implicates druglord and Mafia don Carlos Marcello as a participant.[5] (Further evidence supporting Marcello's involvement is discussed in the Afterword.)

When one combines the speculative links herein, plus the harrowing information that David delivered, it's no surprise that the wealth of Kennedy assassination research was shaken in a big way—but not for long.

After examining David's information, Rivele wisely challenged it. He asked David for some corroboration, given that David's testimony would be pounced on critically—David was admittedly a criminal, murderer, and heroin peddler. So David gave Rivele the name of another man, another Marseille heroin networker named Michel Nicoli. Nicoli was now a government informant and part of the U.S. Witness Protection Program; Nicoli was being granted immunity for his own crimes in exchange for testifying in heroin trials for the Drug Enforcement Administration. It is documented that Nicoli was considered by the FBI and the DEA as a highly reliable information source. (And after all, he would have no reason to lie now that he was in the Witness Protection Program; the U.S. government was now his keeper and protector.) Rivele claims that Nicoli accurately corroborated David's story, after which Rivele reported his knowledge to U.S. authorities. But this is where Rivele's revelations begin to lose steam.

On February 8, 1988, Nicoli was officially interviewed about the matter by Michael Tobin, a high-ranking operative with the DEA's Heroin Investigations Section, and FBI Supervisory Special Agent Donald Pierce. The official summary of their interview states that:

> Nicoli confirmed some of the allegations made by David but only in general terms . . . . Nicoli further advised that in the latter part of 1965, he, Christian David, Roger Bocognani, Lucien Sarti, Sauveur Loule Pironti . . . were in a coffee shop in Buenos Aires. There was general conversation but something was said by someone other than he or David that made him think they [Bocognani and/or Sarti] were involved in the killing of President Kennedy.

Still sounds interesting, right? But now let's read why the DEA and FBI lost their interest in Nicoli's corroboration:

> As best as Nicoli can remember he thought 'they' [meaning Sarti, Bocognani, and Pironti] said something about going through Mexico, in 1963, into the U.S., and they did something.[6]

They did something? If these three "hitmen" had perpetrated the assassination of a president, isn't it likely that Nicoli would have remembered it? Wouldn't he have been able to recall something more detailed than "they did something"?

It's not hard to see why U.S. authorities chose to waste no further time investigating. Nicoli's admission that "they did something" is not much in the way of rock-solid corroboration. Nicoli's reputation as a reliable informant probably dropped several notches that day. But there still was something to go on, wasn't there? Why not investigate the three assassins Christian David claimed were recruited to kill Kennedy?

Sarti, Bocognani, and Pironti were indeed investigated shortly after this information was aired on British television. It turns out that none of these men had any confirmed reputations as assassins. They were all, instead, smalltime Marseille hoods, dope bagmen, punks. Furthermore, two of them were teenagers at the time of Kennedy's murder.

How believable is it that a man as smart and powerful as heroin lord Antoine Guerini would contract French teenagers to undertake one of the riskiest political assassinations in history? We're supposed to believe that these French teenagers successfully staked out Dealey Plaza, credibly disguised themselves as Dallas cops, and pulled off a perfectly executed triangulated crossfire to kill Kennedy? Not likely.

In addition, after being investigated, all three were verifiably proven by government authorities to have been nowhere near Dallas, Texas, on November 22, 1963. Sarti was a dockworker; Pironti had been drafted and was swabbing decks on a French mine sweeper; and Bocognani was in jail.[7]

And after more scrutiny, we find a few more holes in David's credibility. Another FBI summary document[8] cites that David told Rivele that French intelligence had hired David in 1961 to assassinate Petrice Lumumba, a militant leader in the Belgian Congo. David also claimed that the CIA hired Lucien Sarti for the same job. But even a cursory examination of events reduces these claims to folly.

On December 2, 1960, Lumumba was imprisoned by opposition forces, and he was executed a month and a half later, on January 17, 1961.[9] Why would French intelligence and the CIA send assassins to kill a man who was already in prison and sentenced to death? David claims to have been contracted for this job in 1961, but Lumumba was only alive for seventeen days of that year.

David's attorney, Henri Juramy, adds still more foolishness to the conversation. Juramy claims to possess a handwritten letter in which David has revealed every iota of what he knows of the Kennedy assassination. This letter is supposedly sealed and locked away, and David's instruction to Juramy is that the letter remain unopened, we're told, until David is released from prison.

A simple subpoena might remedy this problem, and we can only question Mr. Juramy's skills as a lawyer, for if there was any genuinely new information in this secret letter, Juramy could easily have used it to make a plea-bargain or early-release agreement for his client.

It's pretty clear now what really happened with regard to David's "earth-shattering" revelations. By mixing lies with a sprinkle of truth, David's story to Rivele sounded genuine at first hearing, and from there David clearly took advantage of Rivele's investigative talent and interest, sending Rivele on a wild goose chase. Why would David do this? By baiting Rivele with truth-tinged lies, David had nothing to lose and everything to gain in his desperate desire to have his deportation back to France canceled. And by claiming to have knowledge of Kennedy's assassination, U.S. authorities might easily have granted him that. In U.S. prisons, David need not fear for his life, but that was not the case in French prisons where there were surely quite a few contracts on David's head.

Now Christian David's lies have been exposed, but what of the kernels of truth he peppered them with? We believe that David was indeed telling the truth when he implicated Marseille godfather Antoine Guerini of hiring assassins to kill Kennedy. David would have little to worry about in the way of retribution by revealing Guerini's involvement. (Guerini died in 1967, and his brother was imprisoned; the Marseille heroin syndicate was then taken over by Guerini's enemies who would be overjoyed to see their nemeses' involvement revealed to the world.) But the idea of Guerini's involvement presents an undeniable intersection of logic, motive, and opportunity. Guerini's connections to U.S. Mafia kingpins Carlos Marcello, Santos Trafficante, and Sam Giancana are equally undeniable.

But Guerini had an even more vital link that dramatically affected his own power and profit, as well as the power and profit of the U.S. Mafia honchos, and that link was Ngo Dinh Nhu of South Vietnam.

19

The Real Conspiracy

"[President Johnson] indicated that he thought the conspiracy was international . . ."

— WALTER CRONKITE[1]

CONSPIRACY IS a word that seethes with intrigue and mystery. By definition, it is an agreement to perform an illegal, treacherous, or evil act—combining or acting together, as if by evil designs. By most people's definition, a premeditated effort by multiple parties to assassinate a chief of state would qualify as evil, and few would disagree that organized crime fits the bill as well. If ever there was an "evil design," this is it. But we're talking about something much more concrete: business.

The more popular assassination theories cite business profit—and the jeopardy thereof—as the cause of Kennedy's murder. When told effectively, for instance, it's a convincing conjecture: Kennedy was killed via a conspiracy between the CIA, the Mob, and the military-industrial complex because to all three of the aforementioned, Kennedy remaining alive threatened their business interests. Kennedy threatened the CIA because he fired the agency's director Allen Dulles and Director of Plans Richard Bissell (who helped engineer the Bay of Pigs Invasion) as well as other CIA-connected potentates.[2] (And isn't it a bit odd that Dulles would later be appointed to the Warren Commission?)

But the authors of this book find it hard to swallow that any organized congregation of the Central Intelligence Agency—whose job was to serve the president—would conspire on any significant scale to kill him. A rogue cell? A handful of dissenting operatives working in collusion? Maybe. But the idea of major members of the CIA working in tandem to kill Kennedy simply doesn't wash. If any president made the CIA look

115

like a disorganized band of idiots, it wasn't Kennedy, it was Johnson, whose confidence in the very same agency helped lead to the worst military failures and the highest U.S. casualties in the Vietnam War. If the CIA were the masterminds of covert activities during that war, it's reasonable to point out that they didn't do a very good job. No matter how hard any assassination researcher stretches the links and the possible motives, the CIA just doesn't fit. These men were stalwart patriots serving their country and their president. There's little genuine evidence to suggest otherwise.

We contend that the same is true with regard to the so-called military-industrial complex. The military conspired to kill Kennedy simply because they wanted to prolong a war? The military proves its value and ensures its survival by winning wars quickly, not by drawing them out. Besides, there is hard documentation against the idea that Kennedy was going to pull out of the war. And why would a bunch of soldiers want to kill Kennedy just to keep some businessmen rich from combat-hardware contracts? As intricate and intriguing as it sounds, the notion is really farcical and simplistic when you look at it objectively. War-based economies are regressive; they're sinkholes for tax-dollars and fertilizer for inflation and public unrest. Throughout history, regressive economies have caused revolutions. There were no spoils to be gained by America in the Vietnam War. Certainly the military and the CIA knew this, and the only gain for both of them was to see to it that the war ended as quickly as possible. But for over ten years now we've been force-fed the idea that these parties wanted to continue a war that could only lead to— and did lead to—popular dissatisfaction, outrage, and rebellion on a national level. It's a conflict of logic for either party to want to continue the war in Vietnam.

The U.S. Mob, though, is another story. We've heard that the Mob killed Kennedy because Kennedy blew the Bay of Pigs Invasion, which cost the Mob gambling profits. We've heard that the Mob killed Kennedy in retaliation for Bobby Kennedy's use of his attorney general's office to harass them. But in truth, Bobby's assaults on the Mob didn't produce any major prison sentences of Mafia kingpins. Sure, the Mob hated Kennedy and Bobby and would have loved to see them both out of the picture. They considered the Kennedys to be the ultimate traitors because their father—Joseph Kennedy—was a mobster himself, building the family fortune from bootleg liquor. And it's true too that the Mob

NHU AND DIEM

President Ngo Dinh Diem (left, with Eisenhower; credit: National Archives) and his brother Ngo Dinh Nhu (right, front; credit: AP Wideworld Photo): the two most powerful men in South Vietnam. Diem openly defied Kennedy's policy wishes, while Nhu used his secret police to kill, beat, torture, and incarcerate the pacifistic Buddhist majority. Nhu also ran South Vietnam's opium network and provided an endless stream of product to the Marseille heroin syndicate in France, which was later sold to the U.S. Mafia.

On November 2, 1963, Nhu and Diem were murdered in a coup d'etat actively supported by Kennedy and his chief State Department advisors. Three weeks after Diem and Nhu were assassinated, President Kennedy was assassinated.

MADAME NHU

The notorious "First Lady of South Vietnam," Madame Nhu publicly celebrated the deaths of Buddhist monks, viciously criticized President Kennedy, and even threatened revenge after Nhu and Diem were assassinated. (AP Wideworld Photo)

Appendix A

~~SECRET~~

HAZ-22592
1 Apr 64

" Jean JOUETRE's expulsion from U.S.

CIA HISTORICAL REVIEW PROGRAM
RELEASE IN FULL 1995

-2-

1964

8. Jean JOUETRE aka Michel ROUX aka Michel MERTZ - On 5 March, Mr.
Papich advised that the French had hit the Legal Attache in Paris
and also the STECE man had queried the Bureau in New York City concerning subject stating that he had been expelled from the U.S. at
Fort Worth or Dallas 48 hours after the assassination.* He was in
Fort Worth on the morning of 22 November and in Dallas in the afternoon. The French believe that he was expelled to either Mexico or
Canada. In January he received mail from a dentist named Alderson
living at 5003 Birmingham, Houston, Texas. Subject is believed to
be identical with a Captain who is a deserter from the French Army
and an activist in the OAS. The French are concerned because of
De Gaulle's planned visit to Mexico. They would like to know the
reason for his expulsion from the U.S. and his destination. Bureau
files are negative and they are checking in Texas and with INS. They
would like a check of our files with indications of what may be passed
to the French. Mr. Papich was given a copy of CSCI-3/776,742 previously
furnished the Bureau and CSDB-3/655,207 together with a photograph of
Captain JOUETRE. WR/3/Dublis; CI/SIG; CI/OPS/Evans

* of President Kennedy

Document Number 632-796

for FOIA Review on JUN 1976

[text rotated/inverted:] 22. JAN 20 3 SS.HANT

~~SECRET~~

SIG/RID

DOC 632-796

CIA Document 632-796, the shocking truth that not only was a trained foreign killer in Dalla
Texas, during the same time that Kennedy was shot but that this same killer was secretly flow
out of the United States by some element of Robert Kennedy's justice department.

SOUETRE

French terrorist Jean Rene Souetre, suspected of at least one assassination attempt on French President Charles de Gaulle. CIA Document 632-976 names Souetre as the man secretly flown out of Dallas two days after Kennedy's assassination. But was it really Souetre or an old enemy using Souetre's name? (National Archives)

PAVLOTSKY

KGB Colonel Ilya Semyonovitch Pavlotsy. Pavlotsky was the ranking member of the KGB's own investigation into Kennedy's death. "Kennedy was shot by a professional assassin hired by French and South Vietnamese agents," Pavlotsky attests. (Associated Television News)

TRAFFICANTE

Santos Trafficante: Florida Mob and heroin boss and friend of Carlos Marcello. Trafficante stated several times that he'd partaken in Kennedy's assassination. He was shot to death the day before he was set to testify. He is also known to have traveled to Saigon to negotiate deals for opium base from Vietnam on behalf of Antoine Guerini, Marseille's heroin overlord. (AP Wideworld Photo)

MARCELLO

Mafia chief Carlos Marcello. Little-known FBI documents cite that not only did Marcello know Jack Ruby, he also personally met Lee Harvey Oswald.

In 1989, Marcello confessed to federal detention officers that he was involved in Kennedy's assassination. (AP Wideworld Photo)

OSWALD

Lee Harvey Oswald: a bad rifle shot and a man so incompetent that the Soviet KGB immediately rejected him for potential recruitment as an agent. According to investigator Edward Becker, Mafia kingpin Carlos Marcello said that he'd secured Oswald as the "lone nut" to "take the fall." (National Archives)

Oswald's "Uncle Dutz," Charles Murret (no photo available), was a bookmaker for Marcello and employed Oswald as a number bag-man out of Felix's Oyster House in New Orleans.

RUBY

Jack Ruby. The Warren Commission insisted that no evidence existed to link Ruby to organized crime in spite of a mountain of such evidence. Ruby worked for Joe Civello, who ran Marcello's Mafia operations in Dallas. When Ruby murdered Oswald, did he do so under orders from Carlos Marcello? (National Archives)

REPRODUCED AT THE NATIONAL ARCHIVES

TRANSLATION FROM DUTCH

Assassination of Pres. John F. Kennedy

Dutch Aerogram to the FBI from a man who signs himself "a Hollander," but gives no name.

Amsterdam, Holland
(No date in the text)

Information on the murder of the President. Follow the tracks of Mrs. Diem and her daughter and the so-called millionaire where daughter Diem was photographed. That millionaire lived also in Texas. I believe if you follow carefully all those people and all (their) acquaintances, you will learn more. I hope so now.

"a Hollander"

COPIES DESTROYED

44 DEC 21 1972

Translated By
Edward P. Arbez : del
December 6, 1963

7·9 DEC 18 1963

62- 109060 -
NOT RECORDED
20 DEC 16 1963

THE "A Hollander" DOCUMENT

An interesting portion of FBI Document 62-109060, dated December 6, 1963. This anonymous letter to the FBI accuses South Vietnam of complicity in the Kennedy assassination. Several more FBI documents do the same. (National Archives)

LODGE

Ambassador Henry Cabot Lodge said, "We are launched on a course from which there is no respectable turning back: the overthrow of the Diem government." (National Archives)

LANSDALE

Old school CIA field operative Edward Lansdale told Daniel Ellsberg that Kennedy discussed the possibility of killing Diem. The insinuation was that Kennedy was asking Lansdale to assassinate Diem, just as Lansdale was working on post-Bay of Pigs operations to assassinate Fidel Castro. (© Bettman/Corbis)

PRESIDENT JOHNSON

Kennedy's successor, Lyndon Johnson (seen here with CIA Director Richard Helms). Johnson told many people that the South Vietnamese were involved in Kennedy's murder— an act of retribution for Kennedy's involvement in Diem's murder. (National Archives) helped get Kennedy elected in 1960 by tinkering with the late vote count in Illinois. But these are not good enough reasons by themselves for the Mob to undertake the riskiest and most complex hit in history. They had too much to lose by taking such a chance.

The Kennedys were a gadfly to the Mob, an annoyance like a mosquito buzzing around one's picnic, and this is certainly more grist for the motive. But we contend that the U.S. Mafia had a much more potent reason for partaking in a conspiracy to kill Kennedy: heroin.

More than any other reason for the Mob to want Kennedy dead was that he threatened the U.S. Mafia's biggest cash cow: the security of their multibillion-dollar heroin enterprise. Since the 1930s, the Mob's most lucrative endeavor was heroin. Each year the profits rose and rose, as did America's number of hopeless addicts who would do anything to pay for the product. And these profits made the New York Stock Exchange look paltry by comparison. By the late '50s, heroin distribution was the Mob's biggest winner, and also its biggest purveyor of underworld power. Gambling, prostitution, protection—all those tried-and-true Mafia enterprises took a backseat to heroin sales.

Chronologically, the conspiracy to kill Kennedy may well have been preceded by Kennedy's own conspiracy to overthrow South Vietnam President Ngo Dinh Diem, and we see the seeds of this plot meticulously well planted by a host of key Kennedy administration figures. For those stalwart readers who still don't believe that the United States supported the overthrow of an allied nation, we provide a few more documented verifications.

More than a year before the actual overthrow, Kennedy asked the U.S. Embassy in Saigon to prepare a classified appraisal, from their point of view, of what Diem and Nhu were doing for South Vietnam, their good points and bad points, how their efforts were succeeding against the Communists, and how well U.S. interests were being served. By now, it's needless to say that the list of good points is essentially nonexistent. But there's an abundance of bad points, and we can read them quite plainly in this special memorandum, dated August 16, 1962. Originally classified "secret," the memorandum was prepared by Joseph A. Mendenhall, the political counselor for the American Embassy in Saigon from August 1959 to July 1962. This was a year before Henry Cabot Lodge was installed as ambassador there. The list itself was Mendenhall's swan song in which he collected all that he'd seen and learned during his time in

Saigon and put it all down on paper for Kennedy. The subject line of this critical six-page memo reads: "Viet-Nam-Assessment and Recommendations." (It was declassified by the National Archives on January 21, 2003.) In this respect, Mendenhall was considered one of America's foremost experts on the political and social climate in Saigon; he probably had more firsthand knowledge of the subject than anyone else in the United States government. Here's what he had to say to Kennedy through Kennedy aide, Deputy Assistant Secretary Edward E. Rice: "President Diem and his weaknesses represent the basic underlying reason for the trend against us in the war." And, "There is no chance of changing Diem and Nhu's political ways or methods of organization and governing. Diem is too old and set in his mandarinal ways. Both he and Nhu are convinced they know Viet-Nam better than anyone else, and thus infrequently accept advice. Both likewise so basically distrust almost everyone outside the family that they are completely disinclined to change their 'divide and rule' method of governing." That's the assessment of the U.S.'s best political analyst in the field, his professional view of the effectiveness of Diem and Nhu as leaders of a free nation in a war against communist aggression. So what was Mendenhall's recommendation on the subject to Kennedy? "Conclusion: that we cannot win the war with the Diem-Nhu methods, and we cannot change those methods no matter how much pressure we put on them. Recommendation: Get rid of Diem, Mr. and Mrs. Diem and the rest of the Ngo family."

That's some recommendation. Mr. Mendenhall could hardly have been more to the point. Get rid of Diem. And that's exactly what Kennedy would do little more than a year later.

Here's more documentation:

In the period from August to November 1, the United States Government approved and encouraged the plot to overthrow the South Vietnamese Government. The United States, in a series of public actions, rebuffed the Diem regime and, through suspension of aid, encouraged the coup leaders to move against the government. The United States maintained secret contact with the plotting generals throughout the planning and execution of the coup and sought to advise them on alternate coup plans. Immediately after the coup, the United States advised the victorious generals on the formation of a new government and accorded it prompt recognition.[3]

That's from Senator J.W. Fulbright, chairman of the Senate Committee on Foreign Relations.

Here's another:

For the military coup d'etat against Ngo Dinh Diem, the U.S. must accept its full share of responsibility. Beginning in August of 1963 we variously authorized, sanctioned and encouraged the coup efforts of the Vietnamese generals and ordered full support for a successor government. In October we cut off aid to Diem in a direct rebuff, giving a green light to the generals. We maintained clandestine contact with them throughout the planning and execution of the coup and sought to review their operational plans and proposed new government. Thus, as the nine-year rule of Diem came to a bloody end, our complicity in this overthrow heightened our responsibilities and our commitment in an essentially leaderless Vietnam.[4]

That's Senator Mike Gravel, commenting on a U.S. foreign policy study. Not to belabor the point, but on November 24, 1998, still more verification of Kennedy's complicity was discovered when thirty-seven previously classified presidential audio tapes were suddenly released to the public, and on one of these tapes Kennedy himself says, "We must bear a good deal of responsibility for it [the coup]."[5]

What else was recorded on these staff-meeting tapes? On October 29, 1963, between 4:25 and 5:15 P.M., CIA division director William Colby explained to Kennedy that the number of anti-Diem forces and pro-Diem forces in Saigon were about equal (approximately ten thousand men per side). Bobby reacted to this information with discouragement and said, "Diem has sufficient forces to protect himself." Then Colby agreed. So what we've got here is a CIA boss advising not only Kennedy to cancel the coup but also Kennedy's own brother and attorney general. What does President Kennedy say in response? "I'm sure that's the way it is with every coup. It always looks balanced, until somebody acts."

It's hard to conceive of a more irresponsible presidential response to official advice. Later, in the same Cabinet Room meeting, Bobby continued to try to talk Kennedy into canceling or postponing the coup.

I just don't see that this makes any sense, on the face of it. We're putting the whole future of the country—and, really, Southeast Asia—in the hand of somebody we don't know very well [Big Minh] .... If [the coup's] a failure, I would think Diem's gonna tell us to get out of the country .... He's gonna have enough, with his intelligence, to know that there's been these contacts and these conversations [between the CIA's Lucien Conein and the coup generals] and he's gonna capture people. They're gonna say the United States was behind that. I would think that we're just going down a road to disaster.

Secretary of State Dean Rusk and General Maxwell Taylor agreed. But after being assured by Lodge that the coup had a good chance of succeeding, Kennedy went ahead with his authorization of the coup. (All of the above information, and more, regarding the recently released White House tapes can be found in Ken Hughes' article "The Tale of the Tapes: Kennedy and the Fall of Diem; Three Weeks Before His Own Assassination, President Kennedy Launched a Coverup in the Assassination of the President of South Vietnam," which ran in the *Boston Globe* on October 24, 1999.)

Kennedy's chief targets in the coup, of course, were President Diem and his brother Nhu—the two men whose activities against the Buddhists hotly threatened Kennedy's reputation nationally and internationally. But if anything, Diem's entire family could be likened to an octopus where even the smallest remaining tentacle could thwart the plan.

One of these tentacles was Diem's sister-in-law, known historically as Madame Nhu and colloquially as "The Dragon Lady" and "The First Lady of Vietnam." So vocal was this woman, and so controversial, that reporters would frequently refer to her as Diem's wife, when actually she was the wife of Diem's brother and chief of staff Ngo Dinh Nhu, who was also the director of the civil guard, the secret police, and South Vietnam's intelligence and counterintelligence networks.

Madame Nhu's maiden name was Tran Le Xuan; she was born into a Buddhist family made rich through its collaboration with the French. Her father, Chuong, was an esteemed lawyer; her mother was part of the Vietnamese royal family—something close to an Asian version of the Kennedys. All the fineries of life were lavished upon Madame Nhu since the day she'd been born, and, like her mother, she stepped out in high style while the rest of the nation squirmed in poverty and the grip of French repression. Known far more for her beauty than her intelligence, Le Xuan never excelled in her studies and finally flunked out of her costly private high school, never even learning to write in Vietnamese. Nevertheless, she served as the prize of the Tran family, who groomed her to marry into aristocracy and wealth. In fact, it was Le Xuan's mother, Madame Chuong, who may have taken this endeavor to some shocking extremes. Madame Chuong reportedly engaged in many illicit sexual affairs with younger men—the cream of the aristocratic crop, so to speak. Was she trying out potential future suitors for her charming daughter? This may well have been the case because Ngo Dinh Nhu, a French-educated intellectual from a rich family, was one of Madame Chuong's many sideline lovers.

In 1943, the lissome Le Xuan converted to Catholicism and married the dashing and handsome Nhu in a grandiose ceremony. She produced four children for Nhu in short order, while she and her husband sat out the French-Vietminh war surrounded by servants and luxury at the Ngo family's palatial mountain estate in Dalat. But in 1955, they moved at once to the even grander Presidential Palace once Diem became chief of state through the election rigged by the CIA. Nhu immediately took to his brother's side, helping him forge a new nation by repressing Buddhists, misappropriationing U.S. aid, and eventually turning the local opium market into an enormous profit machine through his deal with the Marseille heroin syndicate.

But Madame Nhu, with her effervescent personality, was not content to sit around the palace while her husband and Diem ran the country. Instead, she set out to earn her nickname. She formed her own female militia, and she erected memorial statues in memory of the Trung Sisters (the Vietnamese heroines from the first century A.D.). However, the statues bore a suspicious resemblance to Madame Nhu herself. Off and on, she would stoke the fires of her public notoriety by launching such pro-Catholic moralistic causes as banning beauty pageants and closing down bars (even though she herself was a big drinker and prided herself on her beauty). She supported referendums to ban abortion, contraception, adultery, and divorce. The liberal Vietnamese populace responded to Madame Nhu's mandates with outrage, since her own brother, Tran Van Khiem, was a known party animal about town, philandering with the local girls, dropping big money in the casinos, and using his powerful family name to wring protection money out of Saigon shopkeepers. Indeed, Madame Nhu earned her nickname as The Dragon Lady, but she was also The Queen of Double-Standards. And the U.S. was not incognizant of her activities. The women behind men in political power are often sources of power themselves, and while we know by many archived records that

Kennedy and his advisors were looking closely at Diem and Nhu since they took over in Saigon, we know by similar records that Madame Nhu herself was under Kennedy's microscope. Foreign Service Dispatch #255, dated December 22, 1961, from the Saigon Embassy to the State Department, is a five-page memo, classified confidential, that is devoted entirely to Madame Nhu's new "social purification" laws, namely a national proposal entitled Bill No. 60. Here are a couple of lines from the summary: "The National Assembly has just received a proposed bill, No. 60, to purify society by forbidding certain 'foreign-introduced' vices such as smoking and drinking by minors, dancing, boxing, holding animal fights or beauty contests, engaging in slander, furthering sorcery, divulging information about the private lives of another, participating in prostitution or practicing birth control." The "foreign-introduced" comment is obviously a slam at the American presence in the country. Never mind that all of these vices were well in place long before the U.S. support and advisory personnel arrived in South Vietnam (less than two thousand of them at this early date). Interestingly, Bill No. 60's strident summary doesn't mention widespread opium use or South Vietnam's notable role in channeling morphine base to the French heroin syndicate, nor does it mention Nhu's Gestapo-like secret police with its reference to banning the practice of "divulging information about the private lives of another." We doubt that this bill meant to dissolve Nhu's 100,000-member force of undercover whistle-blowers whose job it was to identify citizens with anything but a positive opinion of the Diem government. The title of this bill is "To Strengthen Society." The actual function of this internal political action, however, is best synopsized by Joseph A. Mendenhall (the counsel of Embassy for Political Affairs) and his own advisors in Saigon:

By its various provisions it risks alienating some of the younger progressive elements in Vietnamese society, particularly young military personnel, it will be accused of striking hardest at non-Catholics [the Buddhist majority, in other words] . . . . The bill's appearance is thus an untimely and unfortunate development.

This legislation was initiated by South Vietnam's National Assembly (akin to the U.S. House of Representatives), but Mendenhall points out that, "The bill is actually the work of Madame Ngo Dinh Nhu." In the end, via the document's credence, we discover its true purpose, to alienate certain groups whose support, particularly that of the young officers, is badly needed . . . . Even if by unlikely chance the Assembly should reject or emasculate the bill or the President [Diem] refrain from promulgating it, much of the damage would already have been done by its presentation.

What this means in a nutshell is that Madame Nhu deliberately drafted this public law because she knew that the public reaction to it would be highly negative toward America in general and help actively sway the South Vietnamese military against America in particular. Bear in mind, this is the same woman who laughingly referred to Buddhist self-immolations as "barbeques" and referred to their protests against the Diem government as the workings of people "intoxicated" with communism. This is the same woman who said, "Let them burn, and we shall all clap our hands." But more than anything else, Madame Nhu—insisting on keeping her nose in political affairs—viewed her greatest contribution to her nation as the constant indictment of the United States, the same body that was propping up her own government against the Vietcong with money, material, and men.[6]

Indeed, Madame Nhu launched a trash campaign on America from the day she stepped into the Presidential Palace. But for the most part, her scathing criticisms of the U.S. never got further than the government-controlled newspapers in South Vietnam, at least not until the Buddhist repression. Once Buddhist monks began burning themselves to death in the summer of 1963 out of protest to the Diem regime, the outrage began to hit the international papers, and with it Madame Nhu's caustic anti-U.S. statements.

Suddenly, to Kennedy and his State Department, Madame Nhu was as harmful to Kennedy's 1964 reelection prospects as Diem and Nhu. In the meantime, and to make matters worse, Madame Nhu was asking for permission to enter the United States and embark on a speaking tour. This went over like a lead balloon with the Kennedy Oval Office. At first the tactic was to simply deny her entrance, but with that came the high price of her heightened criticisms to the international wire services in Saigon. This would only skewer Kennedy more. But then someone got an idea.

By June, if not earlier, the White House began seriously considering the possibility of a Diem coup, seeded by information from NSC advisor Michael Forrestal's meeting with South Vietnam's ambassador to the

United States, Tran Van Chuong (Chuong was Madame Nhu's father). Chuong told Forrestal in the Spring of 1963 that Diem's repressive regime could not possibly win the war and suggested that the only solution was a violent overthrow of Diem.[7] That clearly got the Kennedy minds ticking, and soon thereafter, the Kennedy White House began to conspire with anti-Diem generals expressly for that purpose. But Madame Nhu presented an obvious obstacle to the plan. Being the most vocal member of the Diem triumvirate, her death during a coup might raise suspicions among Kennedy's detractors, especially those detractors who knew of his direct involvement with post–Bay of Pigs endeavors to kill Castro.[8]

By late-summer 1963, Kennedy, Lodge, McNamara, the Bundys, and the rest of the State Department knew that South Vietnam's mutinous generals were going to make a coup attempt. The White House knew that because the White House helped set it up and gave the generals the green light. But one thing the White House didn't know was the exact date that the coup would commence. At that time, Kennedy and his State Department only knew that it would take place sometime in the autumn of 1963. Is it mere coincidence, then, that the United States, after previously refusing permission for Madame Nhu to enter the U.S., suddenly granted that permission for the autumn of 1963?

On October 7, 1963, the caustically anti-American Madame Nhu was allowed to come to the United States and commence with her vociferous and hypercritical speaking tour, where she would appear at major colleges such as Georgetown, Princeton, Howard University, North Carolina State, and many others, to whip up support for her husband and Diem (and continue to criticize the Kennedy administration). Additionally, she made several radio interviews and even appeared on television shows such as *Meet the Press, The Today Show,* and David Susskind's *Open End.* The White House knew they would have to take it on the chin for a little while, but they also knew that once the coup had taken place, anything Madame Nhu had to say would be completely eclipsed in front page coverage. And that's exactly what happened.

Once Diem and her husband were dead, Madame exploded to the U.S. journalists, but by then no one cared. The Dragon Lady's hostile barbs and threats at the U.S. were ignored as the press focused their attention on the coup. Shortly thereafter, she was booted out of the country, leaving a colossal unpaid bill at the Beverly Wilshire Hotel. She went to Paris, then to Rome to reunite with her children, and for all the years since then, she's kept strangely quiet about the entire ordeal of her husband and brother-in-law's murder, living in seclusion in an obscure villa reportedly owned by the Catholic Church. In fact, after the coup, she never uttered a further objection.

Hence, part one of the plan worked. But there were several other parts that needed to be tied up, and one of them was Madame Nhu's father, Tran Van Chuong, South Vietnam's ambassador to the United States.

Kennedy was in dire need of Chuong's support for a coup (we know that Chuong himself had already suggested it to National Security Council advisor Michael Forrestal in a classified meeting). There is no absolute proof, but an abundance of rumors suggest that President Kennedy personally met with Ambassador Chuong in August and asked him to resign his post as ambassador, for the good of his country. Regardless, Ambassador Chuong did indeed resign his post shortly after this meeting was rumored to have taken place. And after that, Chuong went on a speaking tour himself, to counter his daughter's criticisms of the United States.*

The final obstacle was Diem's oldest and most influential brother, Archbishop Thuc, the Vatican's prelate of South Vietnam. To call Archbishop Thuc a radical would be putting it lightly (later in his life, he would be excommunicated from the Catholic Church, not once but twice, for heretical activities[10]), and to call him corrupt would be putting it politely (Thuc extorted U.S.-aid-founded kick-backs from provincial chiefs).[11]

It's one thing for political tyrants to be killed during a coup d'etat, but Archbishop Thuc was the cornerstone of the Diem family, and he was loved by Catholics and equally hated by the pro-Buddhist insurgents. If Thuc had remained in South Vietnam during the coup, he most assuredly would have been murdered along with his brothers. And if that had happened, Kennedy would have been running an even further risk if it were ever discovered that his own government had spurred the overthrow with intelligence, cash, and weapons. This could link Kennedy—a world-famous Catholic—to a political maneuver that had resulted in the murder of a Catholic archbishop, which would not go over well with American Catholics.

---

*Incidentally, decades later, Chuong and his wife were murdered in their home in Washington D.C., and the accused murderer was their son, Madame Nhu's brother, Tran Van Khiem. Khiem was never officially charged nor tried, but instead he was committed to St. Elizabeth's mental hospital. He always maintained his innocence, however, and argued that his parents were killed because of what they knew about the Kennedy assassination.[9]

It's not difficult to imagine what Kennedy discussed with the Pope during his abrupt visit to the Vatican in early July. Suddenly it was decided that Thuc would be recalled to Rome to attend an ecumenical meeting during the time period that the coup was projected to occur. Another coincidence?

Diem had a fourth brother—a harmless brother—tucked away at an emissary post in England. Kennedy needn't worry about him, and we've already cited what happened to Diem's fifth brother, Can, the political overseer of Central Vietnam: after the coup commenced, Can was murdered by Minh's troops after being promised protection by Lodge.

This is irrefutable evidence of a conspiracy on the part of the Kennedy White House to support a coup d'etat against the government of South Vietnam and the assassination of President Diem. More than anything else, we contend, this was the rich ground in which a counter-conspiracy was planted, the conspiracy that led to President Kennedy's own assassination.

Shadow Men

"They [the FBI] felt that Jean [Souetre] knew who or
he himself had assassinated Kennedy."

— DR. LAWRENCE ALDERSON[1]

NOW THAT we've reasserted Kennedy's own conspiracy against an
allied chief of state, let's trace back to Chapter Seventeen and the tag-
names directly connected to what we believe is the most important
Kennedy assassination document to yet see the light of day: CIA
Document 632-796.

Jean Rene Souetre was an OAS terrorist and a man who may have
used as an alias the name of a World War II French Resistance combat
veteran who later became a major heroin mule for the Guerini/Marseille
international heroin syndicate. Due to that evidence, we know that
Souetre was in Dallas, Texas, on the afternoon of Kennedy's assassination. We also know that within forty-eight hours after that assassination,
Souetre was picked up by some arm of the United States Justice
Department and then secretly expelled from our country.[2]

Souetre had the most solid of motives for wanting Kennedy dead. He'd
deserted the French Army in Algeria to join the rebellious right-wing
OAS. The OAS was an organization that hated Kennedy for his pressure
on French President Charles de Gaulle to grant Algeria full independence
from the French Union. Additionally, assassination was part of the OAS's
operational protocol; they assassinated droves of police, military, and
government officials during their terror campaign, and snipers were frequently employed to do the job. Furthermore, the OAS made repeated
assassination attempts against de Gaulle, and we know that our own CIA
cited Souetre as being involved in at least one of those attempts.[3] Hence,

Souetre proves to be a man with the motive, the means, the training, and the skill to credibly undertake the endeavor to kill Kennedy.

But we also know that Souetre and Mertz personally knew each other at one time (the late-'50s to early-'60s) because Souetre admitted it in interviews in 1983 and 1999.[4] As a terrorist, it makes perfect operational sense for Souetre to have used the name of his enemy Michel Mertz when traveling for illicit purposes. He'd be leaving a trail that could link back not to himself but to a man he despised. But there's one very important possibility that Document 632-796 doesn't consider. Maybe Jean Rene Souetre wasn't the man whom the U.S. Justice Department secretly expelled from Dallas shortly after Kennedy's murder—maybe it was Mertz, using Souetre's name as an alias.

There are three reasons that we raise this point for consideration. One, Michel Victor Mertz had just as much training, skill, and combat experience as Souetre—if not more. Mertz was a hero for the French Resistance; for two years he was killing Germans in German-occupied territory. The French Resistance were guerilla warriors whose primary methods of warfare against the Germans were sabotage and assassination. It was commonplace for triangulations of French Resistance snipers to be utilized against German officers in the field. And this is the kind of life Mertz led when he commanded his own elite Resistance unit during World War II. In other words, Mertz clearly had the combat-hardened skill necessary to assassinate a president.

Secondly, he also had the equally solid motive for wanting Kennedy dead. Kennedy and his Justice Department were waging all-out war on the U.S. Mafia, particularly organized crime chieftains Carlos Marcello, Sam Giancana, and Santos Trafficante, all of whom ran vast heroin distribution networks in the U.S. and all of whom got their product from Antoine Guerini's Marseille-based heroin enterprise. And we know that Mertz worked directly for that same enterprise. Kennedy's attack on U.S. Mob bosses threatened the stability of the U.S. heroin market, which in turn threatened the stability of Guerini's Marseille heroin market. Almost all of the heroin bought by U.S. addicts came from Marseille after it was processed from the opium base provided by Nhu. Hence, Guerini and his syndicate had a lot to lose if Kennedy was allowed to maintain his war on the U.S. Mob.

Mertz had a lot to lose too: his livelihood, his way of life, and his power. The third and most significant reason that we speculate Mertz was using Souetre's name in Dallas rather than vice-versa is based on something purely objective. The real Jean Rene Souetre was identified and located by French journalist Jacques Chambaz in 1983. Souetre not only admitted to knowing Michel Victor Mertz in the past, he implied that they were long-time adversaries, and, even more importantly, he asserted that Mertz sometimes used Souetre's name when he traveled.[5]

21

Souetre Speaks

*"One cannot say that Mertz was a war hero, he was
really a murderer."*

— JEAN RENE SOUETRE

IT'S CURIOUS to look deeper into the contingent of Frenchmen who keep popping up, first with regard to the Diem assassination, and secondly with regard to the Kennedy assassination. As for the former, we must remember that, by blood, Diem, Nhu, and Madame Nhu were Vietnamese, but culturally they were French. They were raised in French culture, were educated in France, and were fluent in the French language. The same goes for many of the insurgent generals who clamored to overthrow and kill Diem when the United States gave them the green light. Indeed, the major reason that these same generals trusted CIA operative Lucien Conein was because he, too, was by birth a Frenchman and acclimated to the language and customs (and this would explain Conein's claim that he was very familiar with not just the insurgent generals but also most of the Corsican gangsters living in Saigon. Defense secretary McNamara, in recently released White House audio tapes, even referred to Conein as "an unstable Frenchman"). On the Kennedy assassination side, we've got two more Frenchmen named in CIA Document 632-796 (Mertz and Souetre), French president Charles de Gaulle (who personally awarded Mertz a medal after World War II and whose life was potentially saved by Mertz's infiltration of an OAS detention camp), various French SDECE men who immunized Mertz from serious heroin-trafficking charges for years, and even U.S. Mafia kingpin Carlos Marcello, who was actually born in Tunisia (a French protectorate) and raised in the French Quarter of New Orleans. And overshadowing all of that is the international heroin syndicate, headquartered in Marseille,

France, and run by the French Guerini brothers. Their link to the majority of their opium base was through Nhu and his French middleman, Rock Francisci.

But there's another Frenchman involved who, like Rock Francisci, spent most of his time in Southeast Asia. His name is Matthew Franchini. Outwardly he has been described as a principled merchant and a respectable hotelier (he owned the famous Continental Hotel in Saigon). In truth, however, Franchini was the mastermind behind the secure shipping of Rock Francisci's opium from Saigon to the heroin labs in Marseille.[1] Why is this important? Because Matthew Franchini provides a valuable link in the Marseille Mob's chain-of-command, so to speak, not to mention the chain-of-command of the entire global heroin syndicate. Franchini supplied Marseille with base morphine—product that was flown freely into Saigon by Rock Francisci (on flights protected by Nhu). It was then Franchini who saw to the product's safe delivery to Marseille, no doubt protected by the same shady SDECE figures who protected Mertz himself. One principal character who was very concerned about the security of that supply line actually came to Saigon to meet with other heroin bosses from around the world, and that man was none other than Florida's own Santos Trafficante.[2]

Most of the actual sources on Matthew Franchini are anonymous U.S. Embassy sources and the like, but there is one person who can tell us about Franchini and who is willing to be identified—Jean Rene Souetre.

In the spring of 1999, coauthor O'Leary engaged the services of French researcher Monique Lajournade, who was able to locate Souetre, still working as a public relations director at the Casino de Divonne in Divonne les Bains, France. On June 9, 1999, Souetre was all too happy to be interviewed, and here's what he said about Matthew Franchini:

He was a Corsican. I know that they have been involved in heroin traffic, and that it was the Corsican *milieu* [the Mob] who were dealing with that. Mertz had been in contact with them, and it's quite possible that they were his [heroin] suppliers.

Finally, a man in the know attests to what we've been claiming all along.

Souetre also helps to dispel any suspicions that Mertz and Souetre were the same man. Of this, Souetre says:

Yes, it was quite amusing, because we were both parachute captains. We had the same type of physical behavior, obviously, because of the training. One gets similar attitudes. But there is also the question of age, and Mertz must've been ten years older than me, and he was in the *maquis* [the Resistance] during the Second World War. But really, if you knew him, you could see it wasn't possible.

We don't doubt that. Indeed, Mertz was ten years older. (He was born in 1920, Souetre in 1930.) In fact, when Mertz was commanding French Resistance guerilla warriors against Germans in the field, Souetre was only thirteen.

Now let's see what else Souetre has to say about Mertz:

Q: When did you meet Mertz?
Souetre: It was during the OAS period; he was one of the barbouzes who had infiltrated the OAS, pretending to be an active OAS supporter. His job was to infiltrate our organization and to expose and denounce the networks. So I had the opportunity to meet him. It was in the late-'50s and into '61 before I got arrested. And I did maybe meet him after that. I can't remember.

Because of Mertz, quite a few members of the OAS got arrested. He wasn't really known by anybody. He used to introduce himself as a paratrooper captain to become friendly with the members of the organization, making himself available. At that period we didn't have the time to check the origins and the previous activities of newcomers. He really did cause injury to the organization.

Later, once one found out about him, I think he got transferred somewhere else. Usually one doesn't keep an agent when he starts to become unreliable. French Secret Services were interested in his services for two reasons: first to protect de Gaulle who was traveling a lot and was supposed to go to Mexico and South America. Like in every secret service, one tries to locate people who could be dangerous. I think Mertz had been used like that at the beginning. But he also certainly could've been put in touch with the people who were preparing the assassination of Kennedy. Mertz could have been used to inform the French Secret Services about this, and to falsely implicate the OAS.

Q: What do you think about the idea of Mertz using your name?
Souetre: I think it's completely possible that Mertz was in the United

States, at the time of Kennedy's murder, using my name.

Q: In 1984, in a short interview you gave to Jacques Chambaz for the *Quotidien de Paris*, you mentioned that Mertz was one of your enemies. Is that how you regarded Mertz, as an enemy?

Souetre: Mertz penetrated the OAS with the sole aim of harming it. He was the agent of a service who was fighting us; therefore he was our enemy.

Q: Do you think he was part of the assassination of Kennedy?

Souetre: What I find very strange is the fact that he was there in Dallas the day of the crime and under my identity. What was he doing there that day? It's obvious that he knew that something was going to happen, and that by implicating Captain Souetre he could blame the CNR [*Comité Nationale de la Résistance*].

Q: The CNR?

Souetre: That's the later name of the OAS. At that period of time, the CNR was developing positive relations with some members of the Pentagon, like right-wing members who were very strong anti-Communists and who were finding in those relations with the CNR some common ideas. As there was this possibility of help from the Americans, from certain Americans, it is obvious that the French services [SDECE] working for de Gaulle had to stop those relations by any means, and one of them was to make us look like misfits, insane people. The French services would do anything to stop these relations between us and the Americans.

Q: What do you know about Mertz and his service in World War II, and the notion that he was a war hero?

Souetre: A war hero? Mertz had been taken in the German army as the *malgré-nous,* those Lorraine Alsacians who were mobilized by the Wehrmacht. There Mertz must not have done a lot. He is supposed to have deserted to join the Resistance, but this was the Resistance led by Commandant Gandoin, a pro-Communist resistance in the area of Tulle in the Creuse. This was toward the end of the war, during a period when Communists started coming back in the picture. They killed all the right-wing people who in the future could have been hostile to the rise of communism in this area. Following the information that we got on Mertz, we knew that he was part of it, that he took part in those rudimentary murders. One cannot say that Mertz was a war hero; he was really just a murderer and it is as a murderer that he was used.

Q: Didn't his infiltrations in the OAS allow him to foil an OAS assassination attempt against de Gaulle?

Souetre: I don't know. It's possible.

Q: While working for the Marseille heroin syndicate he was also part of the SDECE?

Souetre: He always belonged to an organization. He was part of a lesser known secret service of barbouzes under the command of M. Sanguinetti who was anti-OAS and who used people like Mertz to infiltrate the OAS . . . . The barbouzes were really ready for everything and were used that way by Sanguinetti who always supported Mertz and helped him out in difficult situations.

Q: Do you know anything about the suspicion that Mertz, because of his affiliation to the barbouzes, was allowed to continue transporting heroin without fear of arrest?

Souetre: When Mertz got arrested, he didn't stay in jail long, as Sanguinetti once again took him out so that he could continue with his misdeeds.

Q: CIA Document 632-796 states that one of these three men (yourself, Mertz, or Roux) were in Dallas the day Kennedy was killed. Did you ever know a man called Roux?

Souetre: I cannot remember anybody with that name. I'm convinced that the man who was in Dallas that day was Mertz under my identity for all the reasons I mentioned before.

Q: Can you comment on Mertz's drug contacts and how they might relate to southeast Asia?

Souetre: You know, it was a very unclear and secret milieu, a little bit of drugs, Mafia, bordellos—everything gets into everything. You find everywhere a little bit of the same. The Mafia perpetuated drug traffic, and the barbouzes that Mertz was connected to certainly had contact with people in South Vietnam. The supply of opium during that period was mainly southeast Asia.

Q: CIA Document #CSCI-3/776 claims that as an OAS captain you approached the CIA in Lisbon and asked them for help in anti–de Gaulle operations. Is this true?

Souetre: No, they were not for operations against de Gaulle. It is true that I was in touch with the CIA in Lisbon, with the CIA agent responsible for western Europe. We, the CNR, had contact with him, but it was with the aim of setting up a radio program

. . . which would have been mainly anti-Communist. We were looking for help, financial support from the States to set up this radio operation. But it never worked out mainly because of the Kennedy assassination. After that there were U.S. budget cuts for things like that.

Q: What do you think about all that's going on with respect to Kennedy's assassination today?

Souetre: What shocks me most is to see that Mertz was never interrogated. First, he was on the crime's location, then he got expelled by the FBI, exfiltrated to Canada. One doesn't get rid of a suspect like that so quickly. One tries to get information from him. What was he doing there? Apparently there has been no proper investigation. Consequently, Mertz was able to continue with his illegal activities. I find it quite strange that the U.S. authorities—who were able to find me so easily—never pursued Mertz for proper questioning. When they approached me, I proved to them that I wasn't the one in Dallas, that I had never been to the United States. So who else could it be? I'm convinced that Mertz was there that day. Why aren't they? From there, as one information leads to another, they should have interrogated Mertz; he was the one getting his orders from Sanguinetti, transmitting the information. He could have been interrogated and said what he knew, at least his relations with the Mafia, through his connections, what he had done on the drug traffic level and so on. He never got interrogated or worried. Instead, he died in a luxurious castle in France with lots of money. I can tell you that as a French military officer, one doesn't earn much money.

I ask myself why. Why was Mertz protected from the Americans by the French services? Could it be that the French services were afraid the Americans would discover the truth?

I got really scared when I heard that Americans wanted to interview me. They approached me in a very strange way, telling me: "We're preparing a book," they said, "a book on OAS." I told them: "Listen, I can actually tell you what happened, what I know about the OAS." So the Americans arrived here, and I was expecting them because I could visualize myself being carried in to the U.S. to be interrogated about the OAS. Really. You know in those channels one has means to make people disappear. So I had taken my precautions . . . .

So the Americans arrived, introduced themselves, and told me they were preparing this book on OAS; and their first question was "What where you doing in Dallas the day of Kennedy's assassination?" "Why did you come here?" I demanded. "I wasn't there and . . . I don't have anything to say."

They left like we say, one hand in the front, one hand in the back. Later I discovered that they were from the CIA.

Why me, but not Mertz? I find it really curious that he was never interrogated.

At any rate, the French services could have known about the preparation of the assassination but wouldn't have given the information to the U.S. authorities. Or maybe they did transmit the information, and it was then hidden.

Then Souetre comments more on Mertz's ability to masquerade as Souetre:

Souetre: It would be easy for Mertz, due to Sanguinetti's assistance. First of all, to get papers you had to have them made, and only an Information Service [*Service de Renseignement*] or *officine* could do that. And to be able to move around the way he did and especially with his police records, he must have had very important support from a very high level. All the facts show us that the French services, the parallel organizations, the barbouzes and so on, were involved in this area, which justifies the presence of Mertz in Dallas the day of the crime.

But it seems very odd to me that the Americans never tried to dig further. It has now been five years that Mertz has been dead. They had plenty of time to go to the French police with a rogatory commission. I had a rogatory commission who came to interrogate me. They could have done the same with Mertz. I told them what I'm telling you now.

Q: You're convinced that Mertz was protected by higher levels?

Souetre: He was very, very protected. He was always helped out of difficult situations by his employers. I can't give you any scoop. I can only send you a photocopy of his police record. It's very strange to see that after everything he did . . . .

Q: How did you get those police records?

Souetre: I can tell you that I got immediately interested in Mertz when I saw the direction events were taking. I told myself you'd better find out as many things as possible on this guy. Somebody like that had the perfect profile of a gangster. And it makes sense. He married . . . this woman, Miss Martel, who was part of a more involved Mafia. If you own a bordello network in Canada you need certain protections, at least self-protections against enemies. I'm convinced Martel was . . . connected with the Mafia. The Mafia could have even been participating in his activities. Mertz's wife won't speak . . . . She doesn't need any money because she has enough. One cannot ask to buy her husband's archives. Those people usually don't leave any records. Especially if Mertz got trained in a barbouze school, one is taught not to leave anything, never leave notes, never keep anything. Only if you want to blackmail your employer. But in this case the employer was a little bit too strong; to blackmail M. Sanguinetti seemed difficult. Sanguinetti, of course, will never speak.

Q: As for Mertz's drug trafficking, do you think I could find something in the press?

Souetre: From that period, it's possible; but I'm not sure exactly when it was. I don't have any proof of that because they're only rumors that were going on in our circle, but there was supposed to have been connections between the French services from the DGSE [*Direction Générale de la Sécurité Extérieure*] to get money to finance their operations by using drug traffic in the United States. And Mertz particularly could have used the American military services that got sent back to the States to transport in their baggage significant quantities of drugs. I think that at that period the case has been discovered by the narcotic office in the States and that there must have been some echoes in the press. But this is not something that has been exploited. Here too, it wasn't in the interest of the French to make noise about that. Now the Americans and especially those at the narcotic office should have information about that in their archives.

Q: And this is the occasion in which Mertz got arrested?

Souetre: He got arrested, and then he was freed very quickly, because of the help of Sanguinetti. If the Americans asked the French police to arrest Mertz, it's quite credible that Sanguinetti would be able to get Mertz released quickly. That you might be able to find in the press of the period.

That's the end of the interview, and you can see that Mr. Souetre was very forthcoming with a lot of corroborating information. (Sanguinetti—first name Alexandre—was the right-hand man of French Interior Minister Roger Frey, whose name you'll recall from Chapters Eleven and Fourteen. Frey was de Gaulle's fix-it man, and Sanguinetti was the one assigned to do the fixing. He was the liaison officer between SDECE and the government, similar to a top U.S. national security advisor.) We can expect Souetre to be careful with his words, though. Who wouldn't be, considering his adventures in the past? For instance, he never tells us that he believes that Mertz was one of Kennedy's murderers; instead, he tells us that he believes Mertz—a murderer—was in Dallas during one of the most monumental murders in United States history. Souetre also tells us that Mertz could easily have known about preparations for Kennedy's assassination in advance via his underworld contacts. Souetre was also quite guarded about the ultimate sources of his information, as we would expect from a man of his clandestine experience. Equally, we can only expect him to protect himself considering that his name is on CIA Document 632-796, right along with Mertz's. This is why Souetre, probably through his own covert channels, procured Mertz's official arrest record (see Appendix P) and biographical profile. The arrest record proves that Mertz spent thirty years vigorously breaking the law, and this file details his long string of infractions: assault and battery, burglary, harboring illegal weapons, homicide, flight to avoid prosecution, inciting riot, forgery, threatening to murder police. Plus we see record of abundant court fines and jail time, not to mention a five-year prison sentence for trafficking heroin to the United States and Canada.

Ultimately, the next best thing to find would be a picture of Mertz himself. Mertz died in 1995, so wouldn't there be a picture of him—the war hero—in any obituary notices? And what about photos previous to his death? Most national war heroes have been photographed countless times. But extensive research in many French archives could produce not a single photograph of Mertz.

Could it be that higher powers have expunged photographs of this man in an effort to conceal the truth? Working for Antoine Guerini's powerful international heroin syndicate (which was fueled by a steady supply of Ngo Dinh Nhu's opium base), Mertz had every motive and utility, and could easily have used his French Secret Service contacts to masquerade as OAS soldier Jean Rene Souetre. Isn't it reasonable that certain French officials, knowing the truth about Mertz, could have destroyed all photographs of him?

But what about French trial records? It was in this area that Souetre pointed our researcher, Monique Lajournade, in the right direction for more information about Mertz.

While searching for early-'70s newspaper articles that might mention Mertz's original arrest, Lajournade tracked down some names of people in French judiciary circles, people who might help her find some actual French criminal records on Mertz. Just as Souetre hinted in the interview, almost no such information remained accessible in French archives. However, with a little luck and a lot of investigating, she was able to find exactly what we were all looking for: genuine documentation of Mertz's criminal activities in general and his heroin-smuggling in particular, all in the form of the actual preliminary court records of Mertz's trial in Paris. (See Appendices O-1 and O-2.)

This court hearing, which took place on July 5, 1971, officially charged Mertz (as well as other French heroin kingpins, including Achille Cecchini) with violations of the national legislation on narcotics crimes. The charges and intent to prosecute were made by the 16th Division of the Tribunal of Major Crimes (the French equivalent of a U.S. federal court). This official record proves in black and white what previous writers could only allege through hearsay: that Michel (Michael) Victor Mertz was indeed a career criminal who trafficked vast amounts of heroin to the United States and received payments from operators in the Marseille Mob. Finally, after more than a decade of reaping huge profits from the Marseille-based heroin trade, Metz was caught, charged, and convicted. This obscure French court record proves it.

While Lajournade was making important progress in her investigations in France, two more of coauthor O'Leary's researchers, Tim McGinnis and Brett Ruhkamp, may have made the strangest discovery of all. After more than a year of requisitioning documents from the National Archives, and having almost no luck at all with DEA and old Federal Bureau of Narcotics files, in June 2000 they finally did receive permission to examine one box of files. One of those files was an extensive Justice Department report to the U.S. commissioner of narcotics, and the topic of the report involved French heroin operations in the early '60s, a time when Mertz's involvement was in full swing. (See Appendix

Q for a look at the cover sheet.) The report details the supply of Laotian opium base from South Vietnam to the Marseille heroin labs, and it clearly implicates all of Mertz's powerful criminal associates (Francisci, Simonpieri, Venturi, Cecchini, the Guerinis, etc.). Yet Mertz's name isn't mentioned at all.

Keep in mind, this report was produced during a time when French and U.S. law-enforcement organizations worked closely together in the war on drugs. Furthermore, Mertz's complicity with all of the men mentioned in this report is verified by extensive French records.

Did some element of the U.S. government expunge all mention of Mertz, the same element, perhaps, that saw to his escape from Dallas, Texas, two days after Kennedy's murder?

22

Brother Bobby's Cover-Up

"Johnson theorized that 'Kennedy might have been killed to avenge South Vietnam's president Diem's death, three weeks earlier.'"

— ANTHONY SUMMERS[1]

DUE TO the facts provided in CIA Document 632-796, we know beyond a reasonable doubt that someone (most likely Mertz) was secretly deported from Dallas, Texas, two days after Kennedy's murder. (It couldn't have been Souetre because Souetre, years later, was questioned by U.S. authorities and cleared.) But what's more important from the standpoint of a cover-up isn't who was deported so much as the circumstances surrounding the deportation. Certainly the Warren Commission would have a serious interest in such an occurrence if in fact the Warren Commission was not part of the cover-up. But thirty-seven years of history proves that the Warren Commission was anything but on the level. Additionally, one would think that the presence of a man suspected of OAS connections in Dallas on the same day Kennedy was killed might be cause for some alarm on the part of the U.S. Justice Department. One would think that those same Justice Department authorities would immediately arrest this man, or at least detain him for questioning. Furthermore, we would expect those same authorities to report his presence to the proper channels, including the Warren Commission, which was officially formed five days later with Executive Order 11130. But neither the expulsion nor "Souetre's" presence in Dallas was ever reported to the Commission. (Or perhaps it was, and this crucial evidence was ignored, as the Warren Commission clearly ignored an abundance of information and testimony that would contradict its conclusion that Kennedy was killed by a lone assailant named Lee Harvey Oswald.)

141

Instead, the Justice Department saw fit to secretly fly this terrorist out of the country, as quickly and as quietly as possible, and they never said a word about it thereafter.

It's clear who bears responsibility for this: the office of the United States attorney general, Robert F. Kennedy.

We know that Bobby Kennedy used the power of his office to cover up a great many things during his short-lived career, and all of these cover-ups were directly related to his brother, the president. We know that he covered up the chain of custody of Kennedy's evidence-vital brain and autopsy photographs, and we know that he went out of his way to conceal his and his brother's direct involvement with post–Bay of Pigs plans to overthrow and assassinate Fidel Castro,[2] all to protect the Kennedy family name, and especially the president's.

And now it seems all too clear that we have yet another Bobby Kennedy cover-up. Given the serious import of an anti-Kennedy terrorist present in Dallas on the day of the assassination and then the bizarre order to deport him shortly thereafter, where could such an order have come from? Who would have the sheer clout to order such an obvious violation of law-enforcement protocol? Only the man at the very top.

To support this allegation, we know that INS (Immigration and Naturalization Service) operatives received high priority orders from Washington to intercept a French national in Dallas shortly after Kennedy's murder.[3] Again, there's only one person in the Justice Department who would have the power to see that such an unorthodox instruction was carried out.

That said, isn't it also odd that immediately after Kennedy's funeral, French President de Gaulle began spouting to the newspapers and to advisers that he believed Kennedy was killed as the result of a conspiracy on the part of the Dallas Police Department? It's true, and it's clearly cited in an FBI document that wasn't declassified until 1993.[4] This seems curiously inappropriate if not downright uncouth.

During the immediate aftermath of a tragic event which shocked the world and when most other chiefs of state were pouring in their condolences to the United States government and its people, Charles de Gaulle—a long-time friend and ally—was going out of his way to stamp a ludicrous smear on President Kennedy's death by perpetuating this crass and unfounded rumor.

It almost seems as if de Gaulle were scrambling for a means of distraction at the precise moment when U.S. analytical bodies would be trying to mount a critical focus on the massive task of investigating the president's death. Why would de Gaulle do this? Furthermore, why would Bobby Kennedy order a potential assassin of his brother deported instead of arrested?

These two facts present some absolutely incredible assaults on logic unless one considers a very logical clandestine motive which, we suggest, leads back to Saigon and Diem's elite Presidential Palace.

As much as Bobby Kennedy loved and looked up to his brother, after November 22, 1963, John F. Kennedy was dead, and there was no bringing him back. As attorney general, his ultimate task was to see to the absolute protection of the president via his Secret Service.

After this colossal failure, Bobby had nothing left to protect except his brother's name in the history books, his family's name, and his own future political hopes. And this was a job he wouldn't screw up. Bobby knew that a comprehensive federal investigation of his brother's death would almost certainly lead to facts that might blemish the Kennedy legacy. Further investigation might disclose that Sam Giancana, at the reported request of father Joseph Kennedy, had engineered the Illinois voting fraud that had won Kennedy the 1960 presidential election.

No, the American public probably wouldn't take that information very well, nor would they take too kindly to learning that their beloved president had pursued secret efforts to overthrow and kill Fidel Castro before and after the Bay of Pigs Invasion and had many more attempts on the drawing board.[5] More to the point, how well would the American people take it if they ever learned that Kennedy had encouraged and aided a coup d'etat that had resulted in the assassination of South Vietnam's president, a U.S. ally?

Indeed, if the U.S. voters in mid-'60s America ever found out that the man they elected president was on one hand claiming to fight the threat of communism by sending half a billion U.S. tax dollars per year (plus fifteen thousand men) to support the Diem government but on the other hand supporting a secret military conspiracy to destroy Diem, those voters would probably neither be inclined to reelect Kennedy in 1964 nor to vote for Bobby Kennedy in 1968.

With Kennedy in his grave, the logical family consensus would have been to cut their losses and preserve what they still had left: a reputation of dignity and integrity.

This could certainly explain why a French terrorist sniper was quickly and secretly flown out of Dallas two days after the assassination, especially if that man was Michel Mertz. Isn't it also highly likely that, after the fact, the French Secret Service realized their colossal oversight and then admitted to de Gaulle, *Hey, we've got a big problem here. It turns out that one of the men who killed Kennedy was a Marseille heroin distributor who also helped us bust the OAS and save your life?* This could explain de Gaulle's bizarre blaming of the Dallas Police Department.

If information such as this had been revealed to the world—and especially to America—in 1963 or 1964, the public reaction would surely have been catastrophic. It would have destroyed not only any further political endeavors for Bobby Kennedy but also the public's perception of the Kennedy family in general and the iconic memory of the president in particular. It would have also destroyed U.S. trust and credibility abroad and forever stamp the United States as a government that is willing to overthrow and murder chiefs of state who don't go along with U.S. policy demands.

Saigon

The FBI, in several files, indexed Madame Nhu
and the Government of South Vietnam as JFK-
Assassination suspects.[1]

KENNEDY AND his State Department clique had done a picture-perfect job of covering their own tracks of involvement in the abortive Bay of Pigs Invasion and subsequent White House plans to assassinate Castro. One must consider how effectively the American people were hand-fed White House lies so many decades ago.

For decades, history books have clearly given the impression that the Bay of Pigs Invasion was President Eisenhower's baby and young altruistic John F. Kennedy inherited this evil scheme by an unavoidable default. We've been told that Kennedy wanted nothing to do with it but was forced to condone the operation because too many government machinations were already in place. Over time, of course, we've learned otherwise, and books and news articles continue to flow, demonstrating how deeply Kennedy was involved.

But back in 1963, the American people didn't have a clue that Kennedy, immediately after his inauguration, zealously supported a U.S. initiative to overthrow Castro, nor did they have a clue that Kennedy eagerly authorized the CIA to maintain anti-Castro political action and sabotage in Cuba.[2] The American people didn't have a clue that even after the Bay of Pigs failure, the Kennedy administration enthusiastically called for still more plans to overthrow Cuba and to fabricate events which would legitimize to the public a full-scale U.S. invasion[3], nor did they have a clue that the Kennedy administration approved of CIA plans to recruit U.S. Mafia figures such as Sam Giancana and John Roselli to assassinate Castro.[4]

If anything, Kennedy seemed to have a one-track mind and policy regarding foreign powers that didn't agree with him: covert overthrow. First Castro's Cuba, then Diem's South Vietnam. No, the American public in 1963 didn't hear about that.

Another thing they didn't hear about was that seventeen days after Kennedy's assassination, the FBI received correspondence from an anonymous source in the Netherlands that asserted that Madame Nhu and the government of South Vietnam were responsible for Kennedy's assassination.[5] The FBI also heard from a professional seaman named Erich Lintrop, who asserted that he'd intercepted information from the Turkish military, that the murder of John F. Kennedy was contracted by Madame Nhu and the government of South Vietnam.[6] A third informant, a German man identifying himself as KG3, asserted the same thing.[7]

The FBI fully investigated all three of these contacts, all shortly after Kennedy's murder, but never made this curious information public.

Of course, critics will be shouting that three separate sourced but unsubstantiated reports to the FBI about South Vietnamese involvement in the Kennedy assassination don't amount to a hill of beans in the long run. We agree. But that hill of beans starts to look like a mountain of suspicion when one begins to examine it in context.

Let's look at the timing. Three weeks after the assassinations in Vietnam, Kennedy is killed in Dallas. As previously mentioned, Madame Nhu was on a controversial speaking tour in the United States when the coup took place. She was in Los Angeles at the time, and when she learned that a coup was underway in Saigon, she immediately called a press conference and verbally blasted the United States. During that press conference, she said this:

> Such a cruel injustice against a faithful ally cannot go unnoticed, and those who indulge in it will have to pay for it. I did not believe them; but if the news is true, if really my family has been treacherously killed with either the official or unofficial blessing of the American government, I can predict to you all that the story in Vietnam is only the beginning.[8]

Sounds like a threat, doesn't it? And what a strange thing to say. This woman, after all, was in the United States to rally desperately needed public support for her government. So much for that.

What she said not only creates a suspicion that she and her government knew in advance of a U.S.-sponsored coup, it implies a threat of revenge against the culprits. Three weeks after Madame Nhu made this threat, Kennedy was shot to death. It's an odd coincidence, but practically speaking, how feasible is it that Madame Nhu, on her own now, along with family members and scattered remnants of Diem's regime back in Saigon, might have been able to orchestrate a retaliatory hit on Kennedy in three weeks?

It's not feasible. The conspiratorial operation that led to Kennedy's assassination must have taken, at the least, months to implement and execute. To organize a retaliatory strike against Kennedy in three weeks would have been close to impossible when one considers the necessary recruitment, logistics, transportation of men and material, and overall tactical and strategic planning. If it's not impossible, it's certainly unlikely.

It's much more plausible, instead, to presume that they all knew full well that Kennedy and his State Department were planning and approving the Diem coup far in advance.

If this weren't true, why did Nhu stockpile arms and ammunition in secret locations well in advance of the actual coup? We've already discerned that CIA efforts had disclosed these locations to General Minh and his rebels, but that's beside the point. All that proves is that the CIA was a more proficient intelligence operation in Saigon than Nhu's secret police. The fact that they were stockpiling arms and ammunition in secret locations strongly suggests that he did suspect in advance that an overthrow was in the wings.

We attest that no suspicion was involved at all. Nhu and Diem knew in advance that Minh and his generals were planning an overthrow. In fact, this proposal is incontestable.

Stanley Karnow, the renowned journalist and Vietnam War correspondent, informs us that Nhu's counterintelligence operatives had effectively placed electronic eavesdropping devices in Saigon's U.S. Embassy.[9]

Based on the clear fact now that the U.S. Embassy in Saigon was bugged, we can conclude that each and every conversation between Ambassador

Lodge and CIA spook Lucien Conein were overhead verbatim by Nhu and his counterintelligence people. Lodge and Conein (as well as Lodge and many other persons attached to the U.S. mission) clearly discussed White House support of the coup within the confines of the embassy.

It's only logical that Nhu and Diem knew what was in store for them, and it's equally logical that Nhu and Diem would take defensive measures. To put it more plainly, Nhu's weapons stockpiles and bugs in the U.S. Embassy make it all too clear that Nhu and President Diem knew that Kennedy was trying to have them ousted and even killed.

There's more evidence from the tape recording systems in Kennedy's own White House. We've previously cited the November 24, 1998, release of thirty-seven audio tapes of key meetings between Kennedy and his staff in the White House and Cabinet Room. White House tapes from October 25, 1963, reveal discussions between Kennedy and CIA Director John McCone. It's well known that McCone and his deputy, William Colby, strongly urged Kennedy to call off the coup. Here's another reason why: McCone had serious reason to believe that General Paul Harkins (the senior U.S. military officer in Vietnam) had secretly betrayed the coup plot to Diem. "In other words, Diem might have proof that Kennedy was plotting to overthrow him."[10] It's common knowledge that Harkins considered Diem a personal friend, and it's common knowledge that Harkins adamantly opposed an overthrow. And now the head of the CIA (who had access to the best and most accurate intelligence sources in the world) implies that he has reason to believe that Harkins, accidentally or intentionally, notified Diem that a coup was coming. It's hard to deny the credibility of the source.

This information only reinforces the idea that Diem and Nhu were well aware that Kennedy was plotting against them. We also know that Diem's fear of a coup goes back much further, to almost two years before the actual event. Powerful men are often paranoid, and Diem had reason to be. In a secret Department of State Policy Planning Council telegram, dated December 22, 1961 (subject: "Diem's Fears of Coup and Command Arrangements"), Kennedy undersecretary Averell Harriman is being notified by the chief of the U.S. Army's Military Assistance Advisory Group in Saigon that Diem was misusing his own U.S.-backed field units because he was scared to death of the possibility of an overthrow. Here's a quote from this long-classified document:

In brief, Diem is hobbling the ability of his armed forces to fight the Viet Cong in order to minimize the chances of a coup against himself. He does this by a variety of means including interference in the chain of command and tight control of field units.

From there the telegram gets more specific. In short, Diem was forbidding his counter-guerilla operations units to go out deeper into the field (the only place they could be effective). Instead, he ordered them to keep closer to him. Further, "Diem's practices, intended to guard him against a military coup, thus help create frustrations driving the military to stage one. The vicious circle needs to be broken."

How must Kennedy have responded to this information?

A month previously, on November 29, 1961, there's an equally interesting Department of State memorandum from assistant secretary Roger Hilsman to premier White House advisor McGeorge Bundy. It too is classified "secret," and its subject line reads "Coup Plotting in South Vietnam." Again, this is close to two years before the date of the actual coup, but the memo informs us that there's some very disturbing talk amongst some of South Vietnam's most crucial generals. Here's the opening line: "Two reliable reports indicate that top South Vietnamese leaders may be plotting a coup against President Diem." Later it reads,

On November 24, Maj. Gen. Duong Van Minh, Commanding General of the Army Field Command, was unprecedentedly critical of the Diem government in his comments to the US Army Attaché. He referred to Diem's re-organizational moves within the military establishment as being highly inadequate and nothing more than 'shams' to fool the Americans.

We can bet that this one got President Kennedy thinking about the future. There's more: "Gen. Minh stated that the situation was extremely grave, that the next few months could well be decisive, and urged the US to take a firm stand with Diem," and "Some military and civilian officials may have also concluded that the Saigon press attacks have weakened US support of Diem . . . . Their estimate of US intentions could strongly influence a decision to undertake a coup."

General Big Minh's urging "the US to take a firm stand with Diem" was clearly a success. If Minh was trying to manipulate Kennedy, he did an excellent job. These statements were his way of saying *Diem's ruining our country with oppression, corruption, and exploitation, and he's making a fool of you and the United States in the process. Help us get rid of this guy.* Big Minh got his wish, in spades.

Knowing all of this, it makes sense that Diem would try to strike first. But one thing we know that was never disclosed in Saigon's U.S. Embassy was the actual date of the coup. The insurgent generals never said exactly when the coup would occur. We also know that several go-dates for the coup were called off—which Nhu and Diem must have known, thanks to their bugs. Moreover, we know that Diem, on November 1, 1963, met with Lodge at 10 A.M. and mentioned rumors of a coup but just as quickly dismissed them (clearly having too much faith in his brother Nhu's plans to thwart their adversaries). Diem even promised to meet again soon with Lodge and finally clear up their differences.[11] Lodge merely nodded this off, but it's clear to see what was happening here. Lodge placated Diem because he knew that Diem would soon be overthrown, and Diem placated Lodge because he knew that Kennedy would soon be dead.

The only problem with Diem's plan, though, was that the coup took place a little sooner than Diem counted on. We contend that Diem and Nhu (along with their colleagues in the Marseille and U.S. Mafias) already had a plan underway to assassinate John F. Kennedy. But Diem and Nhu were assassinated themselves before their plan could be enacted.

How could Diem and Nhu not have known that plans against their own lives were already in place, with bugs in the U.S. Embassy and with Nhu's 100,000-man intelligence agency? To suggest that these men didn't know is preposterous. Nhu and Diem were very smart men. They'd outsmarted their enemies for nine years straight, against highly unfavorable odds, and had survived in their place of power. They gambled that they would do the same thing again. But they gambled wrong.

South Vietnam's involvement in Kennedy's assassination is actually much more plausible than theories about Russian involvement, a lone gunman, or involvement by the so-called military-industrial complex. The potential of a Diem overthrow was a thousand times more threatening to certain powers than Kennedy's potential meddling with oil-depletion allowances and profits of a few companies such as Bell

Helicopter and General Dynamics. We simply don't believe that Kennedy was killed by rich Texas oil men and several industrialists. We simply don't believe that Kennedy was killed by the CIA because the CIA was mad at him over the failure of the Bay of Pigs Invasion. And we simply don't believe that a solitary incompetent like Lee Harvey Oswald could pull off the most difficult assassination in history with an obsolete, inaccurate rifle.

We believe, instead, that Kennedy's assassination was a premeditated conspiracy between the U.S. Mafia, the Marseille Mafia, and the highest echelons of the South Vietnamese government.

24

Suspicions of LBJ and the KGB

"He [Kennedy] murdered Diem,
and then he got it himself."

— LYNDON B. JOHNSON

SO WHAT have we got? We've got proof that the Kennedy administration supported the coup against South Vietnam's President Diem in an effort that they went to painstaking efforts to keep secret from the American people.

We've got proof that Diem and his brother, Nhu, were well aware of Kennedy's plot against them and further proof that the deaths of Diem and Nhu had the potential to cripple the global heroin syndicate.

Next, we've got three classified FBI file surveys naming Madame Nhu and the government of South Vietnam as Kennedy assassination suspects.

We've got Madame Nhu herself publicly declaring to the *New York Times:*

[I]f really my family has been treacherously killed with either the official or unofficial blessing of the American government, I can predict to you all that the story in Vietnam is only the beginning.

Moreover, here's a little-known fact: Kennedy's successor, Lyndon Johnson, repeatedly asserted that the South Vietnamese were part of the conspiracy that killed Kennedy. One source for this is Johnson's vice president, Hubert Humphrey. Humphrey tells us in his autobiography that President Johnson said, "We had a hand in killing him [Diem]. Now it's happening here."[1]

We've also got quite a few other published references citing Johnson's assertions.[2, 3, 4, 5] In his superb 1999 release, *Sons & Brothers,* official

Kennedy Library scholar Richard D. Mahoney reveals that Johnson said the same thing—but even more pointedly—to Kennedy aide Ralph Dungan just days after Kennedy's burial. Johnson took Dungan into the Oval Office and said, "I want to tell you why Kennedy died. Divine retribution. He murdered Diem and then he got it himself."[6]

This claim is backed up in James P. Duffy and Vincent L. Ricci's highly informative book, *The Assassination of John F. Kennedy*:

> During his years in the White House, Johnson is variously reported to have voiced the opinion that responsibility for the assassination belonged to . . . supporters of South Vietnam president Ngo Dinh Diem . . . .[7]

As we detail more fully in the Afterword, the Soviet KGB was immediately ordered by Khrushchev to make its own intensive investigation into who killed John F. Kennedy.[8]

The truth is, Khrushchev and his Soviet Union were absolutely terrified when they learned of Kennedy's assassination. As our ideological/political counterparts (and technically, as our enemies, with whom we were in a race to produce the most nuclear warheads), Khrushchev and his KGB knew full well that Oswald—the man named as Kennedy's assassin—had tried to defect, and even though the KGB had completely rejected him as an agent of any KGB use at all, Oswald's journey to the Soviet Union could be easily verified by U.S. intelligence sources. Khrushchev was hard-pressed to prove to the United States that Russia had not recruited Oswald for KGB activity and that Russia was not involved in any manner with Kennedy's murder. If this weren't the case, why did Khrushchev have the entire Oswald KGB file personally delivered to United States Secretary of State Dean Rusk on the day of Kennedy's funeral? We know this is true because it's documented in FBI Agency File 62-109060-4321.[9] Furthermore, we know, as a result of its own investigation, that the KGB concluded that Lee Harvey Oswald simply didn't have what it takes to pull off an assassination.

In a late-1998 interview, General Nikolai Leonov, the KGB operative who actually met Oswald at the Soviet Embassy in Mexico (and who later became KGB chief of operations and chief of the KGB analysis unit), positively confirmed Oswald's total lack of capability. To this day he still questions not only Oswald's emotional stability but also his abilities as a marksman. In the aforementioned interview, he said that it's "absolute nonsense" to think that Oswald could have killed Kennedy.

"When I met him, in September [1963] he was absolutely unfit for that sort of task," Leonov assures us, emphasizing that the prospect of Oswald killing Kennedy is "Absolutely impossible!"[10]

Another famous Russian who has an opinion is former president of the Soviet Union and Nobel Prize winner Mikhail Gorbachev. Gorbachev, whose name will go down in history for democratizing—and breaking up—the Soviet Union, as well as executing the *glasnost* policy, never spoke publicly about the Kennedy assassination until recently. In a 1998 interview from the Associated Television documentary, *The Secret KGB/JFK Assassination Files,* which aired nationally in 1999, Gorbachev answered questions about the assassination.

When asked specifically if he believed the Warren Commission's assessment that Lee Harvey Oswald was a lone gunman, Gorbachev answered:

You want me to answer the question, which the entire U.S. couldn't solve for so many years after conducting extensive investigations. Well, I think I have great doubt that it reflects what really happened at that time . . . . I have serious doubts that the Warren Commission presented a true picture of what happened. I don't believe it.[11]

Lastly, Colonel Ilya Semyonovitch Pavlotsky, the highest ranking officer in the KGB's investigative unit, concurs with Leonov: "My group, the special section for analysis, concluded that President Kennedy was not killed by Oswald. There was a lot of differences in opinion in the KGB but one thing we all agreed was that Oswald was too incompetent to have pulled this off."

But then Pavlotsky tells us something even more shocking, much of which supports the foundation for this book:

Kennedy was shot by a professional assassin hired by French and South Vietnamese agents. Our unit knew that the Americans helped overthrow and murder South Vietnam President Ngo Dinh Diem, who they had kept in power to fight the communists. Diem's brother Ngo Dinh Nhu was also killed, and this cut off the supply of opium that Nhu had been helping the Corsican Mafia smuggle to Marseille. The Corsicans then turned the opium into heroin and shipped it to the United States where American gangsters sold the drugs. Our group found that the Corsicans hired French hitman Michel Mertz, sometimes known as Jean Rene Souetre, to carry out the assassination with the cooperation of the American Mafia bosses.[12]

Conclusion

"[W]e must bear a good deal of
responsibility for it [the coup]. I should
never have given my consent to it."

— JOHN F. KENNEDY[1]

MOTIVE, MEANS, and opportunity—for almost forty years these three words have provided the investigative cornerstones in the effort to solve the mystery of who killed President Kennedy and why. The same thing is true in any murder investigation; after the physical evidence has been secured, marked, and assessed, the investigators then turn to speculating about the most likely suspects, weighing their motives, means, and opportunity to commit the crime.

We feel that the concerted efforts of the three parties—Guerini's Marseille Mob, the chieftains of the U.S. Mafia, and Diem and Nhu—demonstrate as much or more motive, means, and opportunity to execute Kennedy than any of the more publicized theories.

As we've stated, the three parties all had identical and/or intersecting motives for wanting Kennedy dead. Kennedy's brother was waging all-out war on the U.S. Mafia, and if Kennedy's efforts to oust Diem and Nhu succeeded, then the U.S. Mafia would suffer doubly because their steady supply of heroin would be interrupted and potentially destroyed. Likewise, Diem's and Nhu's deaths or displacement would not only threaten to destroy the Marseille/Corsican Mob's hold on the global heroin syndicate, it would leave the network in chaos and completely decentralize one of the most powerful organized crime efforts in the world. Thirdly, if a U.S.-backed coup succeeded, the opium profits enjoyed by Diem and Nhu would be terminated and, more important, so would their lives. And let's

156

not forget the complete ramifications of Kennedy's bungling of the Bay of Pigs Invasion; not only did the U.S. Mafia lose its gambling enterprise in Cuba, but so did the Marseille Mob.[2]

Diem's and Nhu's access to easily procured opium provided their own initial means to generate an assassination. The U.S. Mafia's ability to provide a fall guy and to transport foreign killers in and out of the country with a high likelihood of success demonstrates their own means, not to mention the dozens of Dallas police officers either on the Mafia's payroll or under some means of Mafia influence. Lastly, Antoine Guerini and his Marseille Mob had the perfect means to provide trained killers for the job, and Michel Victor Mertz's documented association with Guerini is a factor of importance that can't be denied.

Given this, all three parties, with all their organizational parts in place, clearly had the opportunity to kill Kennedy, and we believe that they seized that opportunity and succeeded.

Ultimately, of course, no book written on the Kennedy assassination will ever be more than a writer's hypothesis. Too many witnesses have died. Too much evidence has been destroyed, altered, or tampered with. Too many lies and too much disinformation, even from our own government, have been generated and force-fed to the public for too long. And too many truths have been forever swept away.

We hope that the reader finds our account to be as compelling as we do and finds that the objective facts (some which have not been revealed before, others of which we believe have been ignored or purposely nudged aside because of the light they might shine in their disclosure) sufficiently support our suspicions. We hope that it urges you to contemplate the tragedy of November 22, 1963, beyond the corrupted Warren Commission Report and beyond what our government at large still insists after all these years.

Afterword

IN OUR vast and varied research for this book, we the authors came across a number of fascinating facts that have, as of yet, never been fully explored by other assassination theorists. As an additional bonus to our readers and a service to the ongoing discussion of the Kennedy assassination, we decided to include these further segments that aren't necessarily connected to the core elements of our book but are interesting nonetheless and worth including.

Nosenko and the KGB

There is a camp of assassination theory loyalists who always have and always will believe that Kennedy was killed via a plot constructed by the Soviet Union and Premier Nikita Khrushchev. The basis of this theory is the claim that notorious Soviet defector Yuri Nosenko wasn't really a defector at all but a KGB plant sent to throw suspicion off of Moscow with regard to Kennedy's assassination. Nosenko, these theorists claim, had previously established his trustworthiness to the CIA by selling them intelligence data while serving a high post in the KGB. Two months after Kennedy was killed, Nosenko informed the CIA that he wanted to defect and that the time had to be now because his superiors were onto him.

Chief among the items of information that Nosenko then turned over to his U.S. rescuers was his claim that he had been the supervisor of Lee Harvey Oswald's KGB file. He claimed that, even though the KGB had a file on Oswald, they never expressed any interest in him for recruitment purposes,

159

never used him for any operation—covert or otherwise—and immediately dismissed him as a flake. All of this led the CIA to logically deduce that Oswald was not affiliated with the KGB when he killed Kennedy and that the Soviet Union, therefore, had no hand at all in the assassination.[2]

All of this information is essentially true, yet the Soviet theory group contests that it was all a trick and that Nosenko's information on Oswald was actually disinformation, a lie to divert suspicion from the Soviets. It was later discovered that Nosenko had lied about several things pertaining to his KGB status. And if he lied about those things, the Soviet theory group believes, then he was also lying about the KGB's lack of interest in Oswald, implying that Oswald killed Kennedy as part of a Khrushchev/Soviet plot.

Since 1995, a number of U.S. government documents have been declassified and released in full, and the most revealing of these documents (FBI Record #124-10144-10086) tells us that the Soviets turned over their entire KGB consular file on Oswald to the U.S. government two days after the assassination. Soviet Ambassador Anatoli Dobynin personally presented the file to Secretary of State Dean Rusk immediately after Kennedy's funeral. The information in that file revealed much of the same information that Nosenko told the CIA months later. Hence, when Nosenko related that the KGB had no interest in Oswald and dismissed him as a flake, he was telling the truth. Since that time, and since the fall of the Soviet Union, other high KGB men have testified similarly. Colonel Oleg Maximovich Nechiporenko, a member of the First Chief Directorate of the KGB, in his book, *Passport to Assassination,* excerpted a memo from the chairman of the KGB himself, Vladimir Semichastny, wherein the chairman verifies no interest in Oswald on the part of the KGB.[3] In October of 1998, another big KGB fish, Oleg Kalugin, made further verifications. At the time of the Kennedy assassination, Kalugin was working undercover for the KGB as a student at Columbia University, and he attests that Nosenko did lie about some of his credentials but was indeed in charge of the KGB's Oswald file, and that Oswald was quickly dismissed as unusable for any KGB interests. The main reason the KGB monitored Oswald was to determine whether or not he was a plant.[4] No one is disputing that the Soviets observed Oswald for recruitment possibilities when he first came to Russia, but we also know now that he was quickly rejected and deemed useless by the KGB who referred to him as a "neurotic maniac who was disloyal to his own country and everything else."[5]

From the aforementioned document, we also learn a few more things that prove the Soviets weren't involved in Kennedy's assassination. Indeed, they were very worried that the U.S. might suspect them of complicity (both the United States and the Soviet Union put their armed forces on a major alert only hours after Kennedy's death).[6] The Soviets were so concerned, in fact, of a potential misunderstanding that might lead to a nuclear war that they launched their own investigation[7]—first, to ensure that no KGB rogue cells were involved, and second, to ascertain what exactly did happen in Dallas on November 22.

Countless times, we've heard the reports that FBI snipers have tried repeatedly to replicate the shooting prowess Oswald needed to have performed if he indeed were the lone gunman—and these FBI snipers couldn't do it. KGB and military snipers in Russia performed the same test too, and equally failed.[8]

Colonel Boris Ivanov, chief of the KGB office in New York—and one of the men who ordered the KGB initial investigations in the first place—concluded that "Kennedy's death had obviously been planned by an organized group rather than being the act of one individual assassin."[9]

This documentation shows us the real reason for Russia's shock over Kennedy's death. The "Soviet Union would have preferred to have had Kennedy at the helm of the American Government" because he had "a mutual understanding with the Soviet Union, and had tried seriously to improve relations between the United States and Russia."[10] The man the Soviets were most worried about was Kennedy's successor, Lyndon Johnson. Nikolai Fedorenko, the permanent representative to the Soviet Mission to the United Nations, said that "little or nothing is known by the Soviet government concerning President Lyndon Johnson and, as a result, the Soviet Government did not know what policies President Johnson would follow in the future regarding the Soviet Union."[11]

In fact, it was Ivanov who later ordered a complete KGB investigation on Johnson.[12]

A Barndoor with a Bass Fiddle: Oswald's Shooting Skills

We can say with certainty that men such as Michel Mertz and Jean Rene Souetre were qualified killers, both with skills formed and hardened in real combat. Mertz earned medals of valor in World War II with the French Resistance, a militia that often assassinated German officers and

Vichy politicians with highly trained sniper units. And though fighting for a completely different cause, the OAS was operationally similar in that its militia movement was underground; the OAS frequently used long-range snipers to assassinate its enemies.

But what about Lee Harvey Oswald? Compared to men like Mertz and Souetre, Oswald was a veritable creampuff. He never fought in a war, never experienced combat, never really excelled in anything while in the Marine Corps. He was mocked by the other soldiers in his outfit, was repeatedly court-martialed and fined for negligence and misconduct, and was let out of the service two years early with an undesirable discharge.[13]

However, many Kennedy-assassination texts lead the reader to believe that Oswald was a terrific shot on the rifle range. Gerald Posner, author of the controversial *Case Closed*, tells us that in December 1956, Oswald scored a "212, two points over the score required for a 'sharpshooter' qualification, the second highest in the Marine Corps." And, in May 1959, Oswald "managed to score 191, enough to qualify as a 'marksman.'"[14]

Sharpshooter. Marksman. These words clearly denote expertise with firearms, right? Not at all, as they relate to Oswald's military rifle training. In truth, Oswald never qualified with high scores on the Marine rifle range, and his accuracy dropped as time went by.[15] In fact, during Oswald's last rifle qualification in the Marines, his firing was so poor that he scored only one point above flunking.[16]

There's a considerable difference between the word "marksman" in military terms and "marksman" in layman's terms. Marksman is actually the lowest qualification standard in the military. In the U.S. military, if you don't qualify as marksman on the basic-training rifle range, you fail. You either get discharged from the military or you repeat basic training. When coauthor Seymour served in the military, he qualified as "expert" with an M1911A1 .45 pistol (an above average military qualification) and as "sharpshooter" with the M-16 rifle (an average qualification by military standards). "Technically," Seymour says, "my worst shooting performance with a rifle was several points higher than Oswald's best performance. And these were stationary targets, not moving targets. Yet I can tell you that even with a weapon superior to the Mannlicher-Carcano, even with a semi-automatic rifle instead of a bolt-action, there's no way I could hit a human head in a moving car at the same range. No one with my or Oswald's shooting abilities could do that."

Yet so many writers continue to contort the truth to fit their own the-ories. Posner tells his readers that sharpshooter was "the second highest in the Marine Corps," but it's what Posner doesn't tell his readers that bothers us. Because sharpshooter lies in the mid-range of only three qual-ification categories, it only means average.

Posner also writes that this sharpshooter qualification "indicated that from the standing position, he [Oswald] could hit a ten-inch bull's-eye, from a minimum distance of 200 yards, eight times out of ten,"[17] and he sources this claim as coming from the Warren Commission testimony,[18] the same investigative body that has been suspected of lying for more than three decades.

The Warren Commission testimony is, after all, one man's opinion, and we challenge that opinion. In a December 1998 interview, Vietnam War veteran and former combat sniper Randy Martin told us that he underwent the same type of basic rifle qualification as Oswald before going on to sniper school (as a sniper in the field, he scored ten long-range "kills"): "Hitting a ten-inch target eight times out of ten at a min-imum of 200 yards on a stationary range far exceeds a sharpshooter qualification, even with an unlimited time-limit. As far as good military range shooting goes, Oswald's scores pretty much show a guy who couldn't hit a barn door with a bass fiddle."[19] This information is from a source that's not connected with the tainted Warren Commission, and it's a little more timely than Posner's information from 1964.

By now, of course, it's essentially undeniable that the rifle-work that killed John F. Kennedy and injured John Connally was not the work of an average rifleman—trained FBI snipers could not perform the same shooting feat that Posner and others tell us Oswald achieved.[20]

Further, the 6.5 Mannlicher-Carcano was a carbine, not a sniper rifle. It was a light infantry weapon with a short barrel designed for short-range, controllable hits on the battlefield. In fact, the rifle that was retrieved by police on the sixth floor of the schoolbook depository was a variant of a weapon that was taken out of active service in 1918 because its 6.5-millimeter round was determined to be insufficient for modern battlefield purposes.[21] It would make no sense for Oswald to choose the 6.5 Mannlicher-Carcano to kill Kennedy. It wouldn't do.

In 1963, Oswald could have purchased one of dozens of more accurate rifles from Dallas gun shops for close to the same price. Instead, Warren Commission loyalists tell us that Oswald mail-ordered an inferior weapon for the job, not even bothering to mention the further testimony that the Mannlicher-Carcano found in the book depository had misaligned sites, a faulty bolt action, and was not designed for use with a scope. In fact, Army experts asserted that using a scope with this weapon would make it even less accurate in the shooting conditions of Dealey Plaza, because after the weapon is fired once, the bolt must be cycled for the next shot, and in doing this, the scope is taken far off target.[22]

Lee Harvey Oswald clearly had neither the skill nor the equipment to do what the Warren Commission and the lone-gunman theorists claim he did.

The President's Brain Is Missing

In spite of our criticism of the Assassination Records Review Board, we're happy that they did at least see to the release of a lot of new assassination files. One file in particular contains testimony that addresses a puzzle which has intrigued the pubic for over thirty-five years. When doctors examined Kennedy's body at Parkland Hospital in Dallas, they reported that one-fifth to one-quarter of Kennedy's brain had been blown out by the gunshot wound to his head. Hence, most of Kennedy's brain was still in his skull when his body left Dallas. But once the body arrived at Bethesda Naval Hospital, the first thing a number of witnesses noticed was that all of Kennedy's brain was gone. The skull was empty when just hours before it had still contained at least seventy-five percent of his brain.[23]

But the Assassination Records Review Board provides an answer. In his October 1998 *Newsweek* article, Gerald Posner states: "The panel also seems to put one of the more gruesome mysteries of the murder to rest," and then informs us that the ARRB procured a piece of testimony which revealed that one of Kennedy's physicians, Admiral George Burkley, took Kennedy's brain out of the Bethesda facility in a bucket.[24]

Why did Admiral Burkley do this? To give the brain to Bobby Kennedy, Posner tells us. But immediately thereafter he tells us that the brain has never been located and was "presumably" buried with Kennedy's body. Unfortunately, this doesn't settle anything. Admiral Burkley is deceased now, but if he were alive today, it would be perfectly appropriate if not judicially mandatory to prosecute him for obstruction of justice and hiding evidence crucial to a monumental homicide. A ballistic and histologic examination of Kennedy's brain could have proven from which direction Kennedy's fatal head shot came and further shed critical light on the continuing controversy over whether Oswald was the lone gunman in the Texas Schoolbook Depository or additional snipers attacked Kennedy (or if Oswald himself was even involved at all).

A much better description of the events surrounding the disappearance of Kennedy's brain can be found in Gus Russo's 1998 *Live by the Sword*. In this intensively researched book, author Russo scrutinizes the chain of custody of the president's brain in far more detail than has ever been done before. Russo affirms that the brain was indeed given to Admiral Burkley, who then placed it in a Secret Service vault, under Secret Service custody. The brain, now preserved in a jar, sat in this vault for two and a half years until Bobby Kennedy ordered Admiral Burkley to deliver it to his brother's secretary, Evelyn Lincoln. Bobby Kennedy insisted on retaining full control of the brain and other "gross" autopsy materials, none of which could be released for examination without his written authorization.

From there, this "gross material" was placed in a trunk, and what happened to these items afterward remains officially unspecified. Many of the persons directly related to these materials stonewalled author Russo when interviewed.[25]

We'll probably never know where the brain really is, and most of the people who do know (such as Bobby Kennedy, Evelyn Lincoln, and George Burkley) are all dead. But an investigation into this issue in the late 1990s uncovered still more information indicating a government cover-up. Not one but two brains were examined.

A Tale of Two Brains

Detractors contend that nobody cares about the Kennedy assassination anymore. If so, why the influx of revelatory newspaper articles in late 1998? The headline of a *Washington Post* article published on November 10, 1998, reads:

Archive Photos Not of JFK's Brain, Concludes Aide to Review Board

The article goes on to explain how one of the staff researchers of the Assassination Records Review Board uncovered evidence which indicated that two different brains were examined with regard to the autopsy on Kennedy's brain. In fact, this Assassination Records Review Board analyst states in this *Washington Post* article, "I am 90 to 95 percent certain that the photographs in the Archives are not of President Kennedy's brain."[26]

This statement, and the shocking information in the article, is based on the analyst's dissection of witness testimony by several doctors who examined Kennedy's brain, a naval photographer, and even an FBI agent.

We've already explained that the Assassination Records Review Board was not charged with the responsibility of specifically seeking out Kennedy-related documents that might shed new light on the assassination. The board was only charged with seeing to the release of Kennedy-related documents over a certain timetable. But the board's potential for fact-finding was severely hampered by bureaucratic handcuffs and a bizarre set of instructions.

Douglas Horne, the board's chief analyst for military records, is at least one member of the board's staff who needs to be commended. This is the same man whose findings were originally reported in the aforementioned *Washington Post* article.

Horne, after making his own discoveries during his examination duties with the board, wrote an exhaustive thirty-page memorandum detailing the very high likelihood that two separate brains were examined by doctors following Kennedy's death. One brain was Kennedy's. The other was a substitute brain.

Here's a sample of what Horne has to say in his memorandum:

A review of HSCA records, coupled with attempts by ARRB staff to clarify the record of President Kennedy's autopsy . . . has revealed a pattern of circumstantial evidence indicating that two brains may have been examined subsequent to the completion of the autopsy on the body of John F. Kennedy . . . . The implications of two such events having taken place (and specifically, in such a manner that one of the two examinations must have been of a brain which was *not* President Kennedy's but which was knowingly represented as such) are of obvious importance, and would be difficult to overstate.

What Horne reveals is that approximately one week after Kennedy was buried, a second examination of his brain was performed.

How could this be possible?

Through painstaking research and investigation, Horne determined that Kennedy's brain was initially examined by doctors on the day of Kennedy's death and was examined again on the morning of Monday, November 25, 1963, whereupon it was immediately turned over to Admiral Burkley, at Burkley's official insistence.

Then between November 27 and December 2, 1963, another brain—said to be Kennedy's—was examined. But the brain, according to witnesses, was different. The first brain was sectioned (surgically sliced for analysis); the second brain wasn't. And the second brain—clearly not Kennedy's—was the brain whose examination results were reported to the Warren Commission. Why?

Horne expertly projects the most obvious answer:

The most likely motive for conducting a second ("late") brain examination would have been to suppress the true nature of the President's head wound(s) by recording a different pattern of damage (in a different specimen).

Furthermore, Horne explains that this information:

strongly suggests that the brain photographs in the Archives are *not* images of the brain of President John F. Kennedy. [27]

Horne's not a crackpot or some run-of-the-mill Kennedy assassination researcher—he's a professional government analyst. And the memorandum he wrote regarding official examinations of two different brains is based on an impartial, professional, and highly focused analysis of testimony, witness interviews, and cold hard facts.

But this is not the only new information Horne's studies provide. In another memorandum based on his findings for the Assassination Records Review Board, Horne describes an equal likelihood that not only were two brains examined, but two different Kennedy autopsy reports were written:

Further study of the record has revealed numerous indicia which support the possibility that the original autopsy protocol transmitted by the Burkley inventory . . . was a different (earlier) report than the autopsy protocol published by the Warren Commission. [28]

And:

> This statement . . . if not made in error, is circumstantial evidence of a
> different autopsy report than is in evidence today.[29]

Mr. Horne should be congratulated for going the extra mile in his
duties with the Assassination Records Review Board by providing these
very important analyses of his findings.

Ultimately, and with regard to Kennedy autopsy records in general, the
Assassination Records Review Board wrote this preamble on July 31, 1998:

> Forensic autopsies are indispensable to properly conducted homicide
> investigations. Ideally, a doctor who performs a forensic autopsy of
> a gunshot wound victim [such as President Kennedy] considers all
> ballistic evidence, speaks with the doctors who treated the victim
> before his death, examines thoroughly the clothing the victim wore
> at the time of the shooting, conducts a thorough and conscientious
> autopsy, and creates a detailed, specific, and fully documented
> account of the cause of death. In cases where a suspect is subse-
> quently tried in court for the homicide, the doctor who performed
> the autopsy generally is cross-examined and challenged on even the
> most minute of issues related to the cause of death. The autopsy and
> court records become public evidence that can be fully examined and
> evaluated by forensics experts.[30]
>
> One of the many tragedies of the assassination of President
> Kennedy has been the incompleteness of the autopsy record and the
> suspicion caused by the shroud of secrecy that has surrounded the
> records that do exist. Although the professionals who participated in
> the creation and the handling of the medical evidence may well have
> had the best of intentions in not publicly disclosing information—pro-
> tecting the privacy and the sensibilities of the President's family—the
> legacy of such secrecy ultimately has caused distrust and suspicion.
> These are now serious and legitimate reasons for questioning not only
> the completeness of the autopsy records, but the lack of prompt and
> complete analysis of the records by the Warren Commission.[31]

How could this happen in one of the most important murder investigations in history?

Some Things Never Change: The Autopsy Pix

For years, we've been hearing speculative controversy over the Kennedy autopsy photographs. We've heard that they were destroyed; we've heard that they were altered; we've heard that they were switched; we've heard that they were completely forged. And now, thanks to Douglas Horne's expert research, we've heard that the photographs of Kennedy's brain are actually photographs of someone else's. (And isn't it curious to wonder just where the government goes when it needs a spare brain?)

In fact, the controversy surrounding Kennedy's autopsy photos is something that simply doesn't go away (and we can presume that there is a reason). The previously cited Assassination Records Review Board summary takes a bold step toward suggesting the purpose behind the subterfuge the American people have had to swallow over the last thirty-five-plus years. Unfortunately, the average citizen interested in reading this and other ARRB reports must essentially be led through a bureaucratic labyrinth to gain access.

But as much as we've criticized the ARRB in general, we have to commend them for their initial objective of identifying Kennedy-related documents and releasing them to the public.

But even in recent years, with the help of ARRB or without it, we're still seeing nationwide news articles about the Kennedy assassination dilemma. If no one's interested in Kennedy's murder anymore, then consider this late-1998 Associated Press article entitled "New Photos Renew Dispute about JFK Autopsy":

New testimony released Friday about the autopsy on President John F. Kennedy says a second set of pictures was taken of Kennedy's wounds but those photographs were never made public.[32]

Few homicide investigators would argue that the most effective tool in discerning the mechanics of a murder is the autopsy evidence. In the case of a death by gunshots, the autopsy photographs become an absolutely essential component of the investigation.

But from the very start, we've got witness after witness, and expert after expert, insisting that there was some serious monkey business with regard to Kennedy's autopsy photographs.

After three decades, though, these points of objection begin to sound like a broken record; they become fuel for pro–Warren Commission authors like Gerald Posner who takes a nonchalant attitude toward a premeditated activity that any judge in the country would deem as withholding evidence. Posner asserts that all of the Kennedy X-rays and autopsy photos weren't released because the Kennedy family refused to release them.[33]

But the Kennedy family can't refuse to release them because they're not owned by the Kennedy family. The photos are owned by the taxpayers of the United States. Yet thirty-five years later, in late-1998, we learn that this "second set" of autopsy photos "were never made public."

Saundra K. Spencer, a technician who worked at the Naval Photographic Center at the time of Kennedy's death, testified that the archive photographs of Kennedy's autopsy were different from the photographs that she had helped process.[34] This strongly suggests that these additional photos were deliberately withheld from public knowledge. When some body of influence—any body of influence at all—seeks to prevent the public from making a total assessment of an incident it has a right to know about, it's called a cover-up. But Posner even uses this new revelation to obscure the truth. Because the photographs Ms. Spencer helped process showed "no blood or opening cavities," Posner tells us in his October 1998 Newsweek article: "This suggests that the Kennedys merely wanted sanitized images for possible public release."[35]

Again, what the Kennedys "merely wanted" doesn't matter. Ms. Spencer's observations are actually very alarming. She saw autopsy photos with "no opening cavities." How can there be "no opening cavities" on a human skull that's been hit by a rifle bullet unless that human skull has been surgically altered? It's long been suspected that Kennedy's head wounds were deliberately altered to support the Warren Commission Report's assertion that only one person—Oswald—shot Kennedy. Now we've got more professional testimony to back this suspicion up, but Posner dismisses it as the stuff of "conspiracy buff" fantasy.

Posner does the same with the even more crucial information he wrote about in the same article—Admiral Burkley commandeering Kennedy's brain. Posner writes: "Indeed, [Kennedy] family feeling, not official misconduct, seems to be a more plausible explanation for the questions that surround Dallas."

If a military officer taking possession of the president's brain doesn't qualify as official misconduct, then we have to seriously question Mr. Posner's perceptions of due process. Posner, in fact, in his book and in his *Newsweek* article, continuously refers to Kennedy assassination researchers as "enthusiasts" and "buffs"—essentially belittling the effort to find out what really happened to President Kennedy. He continues to legitimize the idea that somehow the wishes of the Kennedy family are more important than the taxpaying public's right to view the whole truth.

But Posner's book is rife with jabs at researchers whose findings disagree with his own; in fact, Posner devotes an entire chapter of his long-winded book to trashing researchers with whom he takes exception.[36] Of Henry Hurt's *Reasonable Doubt,* Posner says, "Hurt laid out the intricate details of a plot involving Oswald, the CIA, and anti-Castro Cubans, based largely on the unverified word of Robert Easterling, a person committed to a mental institution."[37]

In truth, Hurt's finely written book is not by any means "largely" based on the "unverified word" of Easterling. What it's based on, instead, is excellent research that demonstrates some very interesting connections and presents a convincing, thought-provoking theory. Hurt makes no bones about Easterling's overall unreliability: "Robert Wilfred Easterling is . . . a diagnosed psychotic and schizophrenic."[38] It's clear to anyone who reads Hurt's book that the oddity of Easterling's testimony is included only for its parts that verify relative events—not the "unverified word" that Posner tells his readers. Even more vehemently, Posner attacks author Mark Lane, accusing Lane of "Using only the evidence that buttressed his arguments . . . ." More Posner citings brazenly state that Lane's efforts were motivated by financial gain and self-promotion.[39]

However, others have similar criticism for Posner. Here's an example: "Posner lists anything that makes a silly choice look plausible and ignores or distorts inconvenient evidence." That's from Professor James H. Fetzer, editor of the 1998 landmark, *Assassination Science.*[40] This is a book composed of hard scientific facts written by multiple experts with indisputable credentials, focusing on the hardcore ballistic, photographic, and overall scientific evidence that Posner either cleverly skirts or, in our opinion, contorts to better prop up his own theory.

Posner's book, in fact, is so full of gaping holes, ignored facts and testimony, and preposterous interpretations that the godfather of Kennedy assassination research, Harold Weisberg (former Senate investigator and author of the very first book to popularly point out the errors in the Warren

Commission Report), saw fit to write an entire book—*Case Open*—to counter the questionable data in Posner's *Case Closed*. Weisberg's wonderful book highlights distorted, suppressed, and omitted evidence; omitted sources; and misleading claims to readers. Anyone who has read Posner's *Case Closed* should read Weisberg's *Case Open*.[41]

It's our opinion that if there's anyone who uses "only the evidence that buttresse[s] his arguments," it's Mr. Posner. Posner paints an all too simplistic picture of Saundra Spencer's observations about additional Kennedy autopsy photos and Admiral Burkley's whisking away of Kennedy's brain without ever objectively acknowledging their potential significance in a cover-up.

Mob Men

The U.S. Mafia has always figured into the most popularly regarded hypotheses about President Kennedy's murder, and these hypotheses are backed by a profusion of evidence. Chief among the suspects are Jack Ruby, Sam Giancana, Santos Trafficante, and, in particular, Carlos Marcello.

As for Ruby—Oswald's killer—the Warren Commission insists that no evidence exists to link Ruby to organized criminal activity[42] though many credible Kennedy assassination researchers have uncovered mountains of evidence that prove the very opposite.[43]

In the summer of 1999, coauthor Brad O'Leary met with Bill Bonanno in Santa Monica. Bonanno wrote the acclaimed *Bound by Honor*, an exemplary account of his life in the Mob. Bonanno is the son of the legendary Joe Bonanno, one of the most powerful Mafiosi of the '60s. Bonanno told O'Leary the story, which would later be published in *Bound by Honor*, that Mob families outside of the Marcello/Trafficante/Giancana circles immediately knew that the Mob was involved in Kennedy's assassination when Jack Ruby was seen on television killing Lee Harvey Oswald. "Jack Ruby was known to everyone in our world," Bonanno says in his book. When Bonanno made some calls, he was eventually able to contact an associate of Santos Trafficante (the Florida don) who told him that it was all a "local matter," meaning that it did not involve outside families and that outside families would be insulated against any problems that might arise. Of Ruby, Bonanno says, "He belonged to Sam Giancana like a pinkie ring." Bonanno's book also verifies something theorists have long believed: certain members of the Dallas Police Department were on the payroll of Louisiana/Dallas don Carlos Marcello, Officer J.D. Tippit in particular. "The cop Tippit was supposed to take him [Oswald] out, but Oswald got him. That was why they used Ruby," Bonanno was told on November 25, 1963, by Trafficante contact Smitty D'Angelo.[44]

Further, according to author John H. Davis, one of Jack Ruby's primary duties in Dallas was to ingratiate and eventually enlist corruptible Dallas police officers into Mob favor; he'd give the cops cash and set them up with prostitutes. Ruby, in fact, was on a first name basis with dozens of Dallas cops, bribing them for his boss, kingpin Carlos Marcello. Most interesting of all is that on the night before the assassination a number of U.S. Secret Service men were drinking at a Dallas bar. Specifically, these Secret Service agents were part of Kennedy's personal protection team.[45] When Ruby got wind of that, he immediately sent over some of his strippers to the bar to entice the agents into staying longer—and get them good and drunk.

But even more important than Ruby are the men he knew and worked for: Santos Trafficante, Sam Giancana, and Carlos Marcello. These three men weren't simply involved in organized crime; they were organized crime, the dons of their cities. And the three of them together helped form a nationwide syndicate of narcotics distribution, money laundering, prostitution, gambling, and any other kind of conceivable activity that might constitute racketeering. Trafficante was the Mob boss of Florida; Giancana, the boss of Chicago; and Marcello, the boss of New Orleans and Dallas. They were all connected, and they have all long been suspected of complicity in the Kennedy assassination.

Sam Giancana, for instance, worked with the CIA, utilizing his heavy Cuban contacts in at least one assassination attempt on Castro.[46] Several of Giancana's relatives asserted that he was principal in Kennedy's assassination.[47] Giancana had any number of motives for wanting Kennedy dead, the most interesting of which is the long-held contention that it was Giancana and his powerful Chicago Mafia network that falsified the late-return votes in Illinois that were instrumental in pushing Kennedy over the top in the 1960 presidential election[48] (which he only won by a paper-thin margin of 118,000 votes). The sense of betrayal Giancana must have felt is easy to perceive: after helping Kennedy win the election, Giancana, and other Mob bosses, were then relentlessly attacked by Kennedy's brother, Attorney General Robert Kennedy. Bobby Kennedy

went out of his way to make Giancana's life difficult by ordering constant FBI surveillance on him to the extent that other underworld figures
and friends were afraid to go anywhere near him.[49] (It's interesting to
note that Giancana was murdered while under police protection immediately before he was slated to testify to the Senate Intelligence
Committee in 1975.)[50]

Santos Trafficante was also involved with the CIA in plots to assassinate Castro.[51] Trafficante reportedly made a number of verbal references
that he was involved in the plot to kill Kennedy.[52] Even more interesting,
six days after Kennedy's death, a memorandum was transmitted from the
CIA to Lyndon Johnson's national security aide Mac Bundy, verifying
that when Trafficante was incarcerated by Castro in 1959, he was visited
in prison by none other than Jack Ruby.[53] This clearly establishes a solid
link between Ruby and organized crime in general, and Trafficante in
particular (something the Warren Commission, which was formed by
Johnson, claimed to have never found evidence of). On his deathbed,
Trafficante reportedly admitted to his attorney—Frank Ragano—that he
had been involved in Kennedy's murder along with his associate and
friend Carlos Marcello.[54]

Marcello's Confession

Marcello too, perhaps more than any of the other Mafia honchos, had
been suspected of active involvement in the Kennedy assassination since
the moment the assassination occurred. Charles Marcello was the head
of America's oldest crime family. He was a genius and a maniacal murderer. And with his friends Santos Trafficante and Sam Giancana, he ruled
the lucrative underworld and all of its profits from heroin proliferation
and innumerable other racketeering enterprises. Marcello, Trafficante,
and Giancana were the oligarchs of organized crime. All three of these
men hated Kennedy and had a motive for wanting him dead: Kennedy's
younger brother Bobby was using his Justice Department (his Federal
Bureau of Investigation, his Federal Bureau of Narcotics, and his Office
of the Attorney General) in a steadfast attempt to destroy the Mafia and
burn its remains to the ground.

It's most curious, however, that the Attorney General would launch such
a relentless campaign against organized crime when he must have known
that the untold wealth and power of his own family were derived from an

identical source. The Kennedy family fortune was founded in the distribution of bootleg liquor during a time when possession, consumption, and distribution of alcoholic beverages was illegal in America due to the Volstead Act of 1919. This was the work of the Kennedys' famous patriarch, Joseph, who made a fortune in bootlegging by allying himself with business partners directly connected to such organized crime figures as Meyer Lansky, Dutch Schultz, and Lucky Luciano.

Nevertheless, Bobby waged an all-out war on the Mafia, and the Mob boss he attacked more thoroughly than any other was Carlos Marcello.

Born in North Africa of Sicilian parents, Marcello had immigrated to Louisiana in 1910 when he was less than a year old. The family worked a farm near New Orleans, and young Carlos (his birth name was Calogero Minacore) was raised in an environment of hard work and honest values. When Carlos was old enough, it became his responsibility to transport the family farm's wares—by horse and wagon—to the crowded marketplaces in New Orleans. These markets, however, were controlled by the Mafia, and it didn't take long before young Carlos had bumped shoulders with enough local hoods and criminals to see that there were more interesting ways to make money than farming.

Soon, he'd become a street hood himself now that he'd discovered this exciting new world of extortion, theft, gambling, and police and political corruption. This was Carlos's training ground, and he learned well. By his late teens Carlos was burglarizing homes and stores and robbing banks; later, he gravitated toward slot machines, illegal liquor, gambling, and narcotics. And by the time he was thirty-seven years old, Carlos Marcello was the undisputed boss of the New Orleans Mafia.[55]

No one dared contest Marcello because by then he owned the necessary police and politicians and, by his careful manipulation of greed and fear, had become the most powerful boss of the oldest Mafia family in the United States.

Marcello was a bullish man—short, stocky, thick-necked—and the manner in which he managed organized crime befit his looks. A dropout at age fourteen, his command of the English language had developed little past street-level diction and a lexicon of slang. But beneath the thug's bearing, Marcello displayed a startling flair for mathematics and a business sense worthy of Wall Street. His power ranged beyond Louisiana, well into Oklahoma, Arkansas, and Texas, with certain operations stretching even as far as California and Central America. Marcello was the Al Capone of the south; in fact, he even hired Al Capone's personal chef as his own.[56]

Marcello's private headquarters existed at a remote tavern near the swamps, part of his vast estate composed of thousands of acres. It was at this tavern every Sunday that the kingpin of Louisiana would sit down to business with his local chieftains who oversaw his enormous operations: bookmaking, prostitution, the numbers racket, gambling, and heroin distribution. Corrupt politicians were also in attendance, as were local sheriffs on the take and even mayors and high-ranking police officials.

Choosing to erect his estate on swampland served a dual purpose. Marcello loved the dense beauty of the land: the sound of the bayou, the spires of cypress and ash draped with Spanish moss, the herons and gulls lifting off into the sun. But this tract of land also served as a body dump of the first order. When collectors held back or associates "dropped dime," Marcello would simply order them strangled as he watched, after which the perpetrator's body would be dissolved in barrels of corrosives and the ichorish remains emptied into the swamp.[57]

But the most interesting bit of Marcello's history involves one of his direct references to John and Bobby Kennedy. Here is a brief synopsis, based on revelations from John H. Davis's *Mafia Kingfish*, the best and most comprehensive study ever written on Carlos Marcello.

In 1962, at a farmhouse on the estate, Marcello met with a pair of associates, Edward Becker and Carlo Roppolo, concerning a distribution deal for engine lubricants. Becker made the mistake of offhandedly referring to Attorney General Bobby Kennedy, after which Marcello instantly flew into a tirade. "Take the stone out of my shoe!" he bellowed, referring to Bobby, and then reasoned that the only way to get Bobby off the Mob's back was to kill his brother. Marcello knew that killing the attorney general would only induce the president to attack the Mob harder. But if the president were to die, Bobby would be immediately dismissed as attorney general by Johnson, who hated him.[*]

---

[*]There were other potential reasons Marcello felt sure of this. For over a decade, Johnson had been receiving campaign contributions from Jack Halfen, a financier who was also a bag-man for Marcello, which makes it likely that those contributions originated as ill-gotten gains from Marcello's rackets. It would later be speculated that this conspicuous link might explain why Lyndon Johnson, as a U.S. senator, had vigorously assisted in terminating any anti-racketeering legislation that might have depreciated Marcello's profits in the Texas Mafia regions. Many would also later speculate that these connections might have influenced Johnson in the manner in which he chose to have John F. Kennedy's assassination investigated, namely the Warren Commission.[58]

This is an easy thing for Marcello to say, but even the Mafia couldn't pull off a presidential assassination on its own. The only way to do it, Marcello had told Becker that night, would be to hire assassins not connected to the U.S. Mafia and then set up a "nut" as the fall guy—the same way they did it back in Sicily.[59]

Marcello was adamant about this, perhaps even pathological. The merest mention of the name Kennedy would cause him to explode into an insane rage. All sense of reason was lost, all rationality dissipated like vapor and transformed the keen, calculating genius of the New Orleans underworld into a fist-pounding, red-faced maniac a few heartbeats short of a stroke. It wasn't just Robert Kennedy's targeting of the Mob in general; Marcello's hatred bore a personal tint. In fact, it was Kennedy who had caused the greatest embarrassment of Marcello's life.

In April 1961, Bobby Kennedy had Marcello kidnapped, under the guise of deportation, and flew him to Guatemala City where a forged birth certificate in Marcello's name had been conveniently "found." Marcello was denied the right to call his counsel and not allowed to contact his family or even get to money or a change of clothes. Instead, he was peremptorily handcuffed by INS agents, thrown onto an empty plane, and dumped off at a military airport in Guatemala City without a dime.[60]

It wasn't until months later, after spending much time in the jungle, that Marcello was flown back to Louisiana by a Mob-linked pilot named David Ferrie,[61] only to find over $800,000 in tax liens waiting for him, compliments of Kennedy's IRS.

So Marcello's hatred of Bobby Kennedy is all too easy to understand. Though Bobby assaulted the U.S. Mafia bosses, he singled out Marcello, which humiliated him on a nationwide scale. If there's one thing you don't do to a Mafia chieftain, it's embarrass him in front of his peers. These Mafiosi all saw themselves as men of respect; it was part of their code. Causing disrespect to one of them was playing with fire, and in doing so, particularly to Marcello, Bobby had no idea at the time as to just how badly that fire would come back and burn him.

Long after both Kennedys were dead, many suspected and even accused Marcello of direct complicity in Kennedy's assassination. Detractors of Mafia links assert that the only evidence is hearsay. Even though Frank Ragano, Trafficante's lawyer, claimed that Trafficante admitted to him that he and Marcello were deeply involved, Gerald Posner claims that Ragano was actually lying because he'd been mad at Trafficante since 1976.[62] This is certainly possible; Mob men aren't particularly known for their honesty. But Posner bolsters his argument by pointing out that Trafficante and Marcello refused to take out teamsters leader Frank Fitzsimmons because he was too well protected. Posner scoffs: "The same Mafia leaders who shied away from a contract on the teamster's leader supposedly were interested in the most powerful target of all, the President."[63] First of all, very few theorists assert that the U.S. Mafia alone had Kennedy killed. Second, Posner bases this argument on further testimony from Frank Ragano, on the same page where he claims that Ragano is unreliable.

Naturally, Posner believes that Edward Becker is unreliable too, adding that the House Select Committee on Assassinations didn't believe his testimony.[64] Author Michael Benson has a different interpretation, stating, "In 1978, Becker repeated the story to the HSCA, who found him credible."[65] This makes a lot more sense, considering the HSCA's conclusion that "organized crime, as a group, was not involved in the assassination of President Kennedy, but that the available evidence does not preclude the possibility that individual members may have been involved."[66]

Specifically, the HSCA says that "Marcello had the motive, means, and opportunity to have President John F. Kennedy assassinated."[67] That's a far cry from what Posner tells us.[68]

The reason Marcello wasn't pursued more actively was that, at the time, the HSCA could not sufficiently link Oswald and Ruby with Marcello or Marcello's known associates.[69] This was in 1978. Since then, many researchers have established those links.

Ruby worked for Joe Civello, Marcello's lieutenant in Dallas.[70] Ruby had also met with numerous other undisputed Marcello associates such as Frank Caracci, Cleeve Dugas, Nick Graffagnini, and Harold Tannenbaum.[71]

And as for Oswald's connections to Marcello, Oswald's uncle, Dutz Murret, worked for Marcello[72] as a bookmaker; Oswald was a runner for the same operation.[73] Even Oswald's mother had connections to Marcello; she dated some of Marcello's subordinates.[74] Another of Marcello's lieutenants, Nofio Pecora, even bailed Oswald out of jail once.[75]

In other words, by now, there is no shortage of information that links Ruby to Marcello and Oswald to Marcello. We've all heard the interesting allegations that some of Jack Ruby's strippers witnessed Ruby personally meeting with Oswald.

But there's also a 1967 FBI document that reports testimony by ordinary citizens. Mrs. Dwight E. Bailey reported to the FBI that she knew of numerous employees of the Adolphus Hotel—right across the street from one of Ruby's clubs—who had seen Jack Ruby and Lee Harvey Oswald together on many occasions. In fact, Mrs. Bailey's mother had waited on both Ruby and Oswald at the hotel coffee shop.[76] For further consideration, there's a government document that suggests not only that Marcello was connected to Ruby and Oswald but also that he actually met both of them personally.

FBI document CR 137A-5467-69, dated June 9, 1988, is heavily redacted, and it details informant testimony by a man whose name is not revealed for reasons pertaining to his safety. The subject told the FBI:

> Marcello was talking about the Kennedys. He told me and my friend about a meeting with Oswald. He had been introduced to Oswald by a man named Ferris, who was Marcello's pilot [obviously this typo refers to David Ferrie]. He said that the [meeting] had taken place in his brother's restaurant [La Louisiane Restaurant[77]] . . . . He said that Ruby was a homo son of a b—ch but good to have around to report to him what was happening in town . . . . He flew into a rage, cussing the Kennedys. He said yeah I had the little son of a b—ch killed, and I would do it again . . . .[78]

We don't know the identity of this mystery informant, but it's obviously not Edward Becker—Becker's story took place before Kennedy was killed, while this testimony clearly refers to a conversation Marcello had after the assassination. Of course, since the informant is clearly a Mob guy seeking protection, detractors will instantly insist that he's unreliable.

But if he's unreliable, that means his testimony isn't genuine, and if his testimony isn't genuine, then why is the FBI withholding seven pages of the account?[79] And why do three of the pages that were released remained blacked out? In the last unredacted line of the material that was released, the nameless informant agrees to take a polygraph examination. This was in 1988. If the informant failed the polygraph, then there's no reason for the FBI to keep any of the interview transcript classified.

But there's another batch of FBI documents that prove even more interesting. In the aforementioned file, a second source tells us that Marcello admitted to his involvement in the assassination. But in another FBI file, Marcello personally confesses his involvement, and not to Mob guys or informants whom detractors would immediately stamp as unreliable. No, here Marcello confesses to a pair of federal corrections officers. Marcello died in 1993. In 1981, however, the law had finally got him, and Marcello was convicted of violations of the RICO Statute and conspiracy to bribe a federal judge, totaling to a seventeen-year prison sentence for the then seventy-two-year-old man.[80] After his appeals were denied, Marcello finally relinquished his title as Mafia kingfish to become inmate #16225-034-A at the federal correction institution in Texarkana, Texas. Shortly thereafter, nature began to creep up on him, along with all those decades of gluttony, hard drinking, and fried-oyster loaves.

Dizzy spells, senility, and an irregular heartbeat led prison medical officials to fear that Marcello might soon be subject to a stroke or heart attack. In late February of 1989, Marcello was transferred from the prison hospital to the nearby Wadley Regional Medical Center for tests, where he remained under the constant watch of corrections staff.[81]

During the early morning hours of February 28, 1989, James Cates and Vincent Brown, senior federal detention officers, were the men on duty watching Marcello. Marcello himself was asleep, restrained to a hospital bed and hooked up to an IV line and a heart monitor. After a short while he began to thrash around and mumble incoherently. At one point Marcello mistook Cates and Brown as his own Mob bodyguards and mentioned that it was time to get back to New Orleans. But there was something odd about Marcello's verbal rambling, which Cates noted at times "was very incoherent and garbled, but other times clear and concise." (It is not uncommon for patients suffering from certain types of senility to vacillate between confusion and perfect lucidity.)

During their shift, Officers Cates and Brown observed that Marcello continued to mumble and drift in and out of sleep. But then, at about 2:30 A.M., Marcello awoke and said this: "That Kennedy, that smiling motherf—er. We'll fix him in Dallas."

This isn't hearsay; this is documented in an official FBI memorandum.[82] Marcello also told Cates and Brown that he was tired because he and others had just driven back to New Orleans from New York.[83] Marcello also spoke in French for a time.[84] After that, on two more occasions, Marcello said, "We are going to get that motherf—ing Kennedy in Dallas."

Cates immediately reported this information to the warden, who in turn reported it to the FBI. Yet another official FBI document tells us that Marcello was flown out of the Wadley facility in Texarkana the very next day and rushed to the Federal Medical Center in Rochester, Minnesota,[85] whereupon the FBI immediately ordered a troop of agents to Rochester for the express purpose of observing Marcello and determining "the most effective manner in which information can be obtained from him."[86]

To sum up, five people overheard Marcello admit to active involvement in Kennedy's murder. Two of them, Frank Ragano and Edward Becker, had Mob connections. Neither of them had any logical reason to lie, yet a few researchers dismiss them as unreliable simply because of their Mob ties—same for the anonymous witness documented in FBI records. He was probably also Mob-connected and had no reason to lie, but will likewise be deemed unreliable by detractors, even though the FBI found it necessary to withhold three full pages of his testimony and to black out most of what was released.

But there are still two more witnesses—two senior federal detention officers with untainted job performance records and no conceivable reason in the world to lie.

We'll leave the rest to the reader's powers of deduction.

The Headshot Controversy

Thanks to Admiral Burkley's confiscation of President Kennedy's brain, the world will more than likely never know from whence the fatal shot was fired. But most theorists believe it was fired from in front of Kennedy as the motorcade traveled down Elm Street. Robert Groden's book, *The Killing of a President,* asserts this unequivocally; he provides a diagram that shows a bullet track beginning at the stockade fence behind the grassy knoll and ending where Kennedy's head was positioned in the car. Groden states: "The fifth shot, fired from behind the stockade fence on the knoll, struck the president in the right temple . . . . The bullet exited from the rear of the head . . . ."[87]

Groden's book is an oversized trade paperback; it is mostly composed of pictures, is augmented with segments of text, and conveys to the general reader, perhaps more than any other book, all the complications of the Kennedy assassination. With his pictures, Groden provides evidence rather than mere theories, and his effort should be commended. Groden was also a technical advisor on Oliver Stone's film, *JFK*, and in that film we see a portrayal identical to Groden's assertion: a rifleman behind the grassy knoll's stockade fires the fatal headshot.[88]

To believe this, however, one must accept a ballistic anomaly. If a typical high- or medium-velocity rifle bullet hits a human target in the right temple and exists the back of the head, it is doing something very unusual, but not impossible.

Bullets tumble. Bullets follow bonelines. It's possible for a high-velocity bullet to enter a man's ankle and exit through his head. Things like this have happened. Part of the basic design of the M-16, for example, was to make the bullet unstable in combat. It chambered an uncharacteristically thin projectile (only 5.56 millimeters wide) behind a rifle-sized volume of propellant. This increases the likelihood of the bullet tumbling around inside the target's body rather than simply entering and exiting in a straight line, as is far more typical of higher caliber (7.62 millimeter) bullets. A thinner bullet can do all kinds of strange things once it enters the target's body.

The rifle Oswald supposedly used was the infamous Mannlicher-Carcano, which chambered a 6.5 millimeter round, not as thin as the M-16 bullet but definitely thinner than typical rifle bullets. (Of course, Oswald—if he fired at all—did not fire from the grassy knoll.) At any rate, Groden's scenario is unlikely but perfectly plausible. Add to that over a dozen witnesses who claimed to have seen a large exit wound at the back of Kennedy's head.[89]

But all of this must be discussed in the context of a twenty-six-second piece of eight-millimeter film shot on November 22, 1963, by a kind and innocuous dressmaker and home-movie buff named Abraham Zapruder. *Life* magazine, which originally purchased the Zapruder film, aptly defines its importance: "Of all the witnesses to the tragedy, the only unimpeachable one is the 8-mm movie camera of Abraham Zapruder."[90]

Human witnesses are subject to human faults. Some of them become confused, some of them unconsciously allow their testimony to be influenced by the power of suggestion, and some of them simply forget what they saw. Some of them lie, and in the case of the Kennedy assassination, an undue number of them seemed to die prematurely. But the camera doesn't lie and is not subject to these same human defects, and Zapruder's camera captured the very instant of one of American history's most controversial—and appalling—occurrences.

In that film, we see President John F. Kennedy's head explode. But in that explosion, and in the decades since it occurred, the American public has become inundated in confusion. Today, even in spite of such books as Posner's *Case Closed* (which supports the lone gunman theory), the most popular personal assessments seem to support the general theory that Kennedy was killed as a result of a conspiracy, that the Warren Commission Report was a pack of government-generated lies, that crucial evidence and witness testimony would easily refute the Warren Commission Report, and that conclusions of subsequent investigations were forged, tampered with, destroyed, or ignored. The authors of this book agree with these assessments but not with the equally popular assertion that the fatal headshot was fired from the grassy knoll. This theory is based on the evidence in the Zapruder film, in which, on frame 313, we do indeed see Kennedy's head explode. For readers who haven't seen the Zapruder film, we strongly urge you to buy, rent, or borrow a copy of one of the best-quality, best-resolution examples: A&E Home Video's *The Men Who Killed Kennedy* (Volume 1), Oliver Stone's 1991 blockbuster, *JFK* (in the trial-scene toward the end, Stone uses a great print of the Zapruder film), or, most recently, the June 1998 MPI Video, *Image of an Assassination* (a high-tech digital reproduction of the original film).

If you haven't seen this before, be prepared for a shock because it's gruesome, disturbing footage, and you will see blood, chunks of brain-matter, and skull fragments blow out of President Kennedy's right temple.

To us, the emission of cranial matter from Kennedy's right temple looks more like an exit wound, yet proponents of the theory that the headshot was fired from the grassy knoll maintain that it was an entrance wound. Though it's true that the grassy knoll lay to the front-right of Kennedy's car for most of its trek down Elm Street, by the time the midnight-blue open-topped Lincoln arrived at the position when Kennedy was hit, a shot from the grassy knoll would have been nearly perpendicular to Kennedy's head. What we're told, then, in the most popular theory, is that a sniper behind the wooden fence at the grassy knoll fired almost directly into Kennedy's right temple. Yet in all these versions of the Zapruder film, we see cranial matter jettison from the right temple. If a sniper on the knoll had hit Kennedy in the head at that point of the limousine's progress, the jettison of cranial matter would have occurred on the left side of Kennedy's head.

We're not disputing the idea that more than one sniper was in Dealey Plaza that day. We're not even disputing that a sniper was posted behind the fence at the grassy knoll. Dozens of witnesses, including police[91] (in fact, eighty of the witnesses on Dealey Plaza, according to researcher Robert Groden[92]), reported that shots were fired from the grassy knoll area. Gordon Arnold, fresh out of basic training, hit the dirt in front of the knoll's stockade fence when he heard rifle shots behind him.[93] In Robert Groden's *The Killing of a President,* actual pictures show police and citizens rushing up the knoll.[94] Abraham Zapruder himself, when he shot his immortal film footage, was standing on a cement pedestal on the grassy knoll, and even he reported that shots were fired from behind him, i.e. behind the fence at the knoll.[95] Congressional experts, via their analysis of acoustical evidence, determined that there was a 95 percent probability that at least one shot was fired from the grassy knoll, but then another government-sponsored committee (the Committee on Ballistic Acoustics) rendered the previous conclusions as invalid without precisely saying why.[96] That's hogwash as far as the authors of this book are concerned—just more government manipulation. How can the Committee on Ballistic Acoustics not only nullify a technical determination by congressional experts but then ignore the testimony of dozens of witnesses without so much as a word as to why they did so. Were all these people fabricating the same story—citizens and police? Even members of the motorcade said they believed shots were fired from the knoll.[97]

That said, we simply do not believe that the headshot (nor possibly any sucessful shot) was fired from the grassy knoll.

Many have claimed that the right rear of Kennedy's head was blown out,[98] but that's not necessarily what we see in the Zapruder film. The resolution of this old piece of film, even in the digitalized version, is less than great. Details are muted, grainy, shifting; so much occurs in frame 313's split second that it's next to impossible to assess it all with any clarity. Hence it's difficult to say for sure that any portion of the rear of Kennedy's skull was or was not blown out. To us, it looks like the right- temple is blown out. Yes, Kennedy's head does seem to move backward at or just after the moment of impact, but this is more easily explained as an effect of inertia as the car begins to accelerate. From our point of view, at least, a shot from the grassy knoll couldn't have done what we see in the Zapruder film.

And for this to be the case, the headshot must have come from behind Kennedy, not from the knoll in front of Kennedy. In this case the most feasible positions for a sniper would be the Texas Schoolbook Depository, the Dal-Tex Building (both on the left side of Elm Street), the Dallas Records Building, or the Criminal Courts Building (to the left of Elm Street). (Even Robert Groden acknowledges the likelihood of at least one shot being fired from the roof of the Records Building.[99])

In addition, Dr. Marion Jenkins, Dr. Robert McClelland, and Father Oscar Huber, who performed last rites over Kennedy, all observed what they interpreted as an entrance wound over Kennedy's left temple,[100] which would verify an exit wound over Kennedy's right temple. This seems to make sense based on the Zapruder film, but it only further contributes to the overall conundrum by contradicting the witnesses who claim to have seen a substantial exit wound at the rear-right of Kennedy's skull.

Dr. Ronald F. White, in his fascinating contribution to *Assassination Science,* describes Kennedy's murder as "the beginning of a Post-Modern period in the United States," calling it a "'babble of tongues' that comprises the historiography on the assassination."[101] In a sense, this is true: too many flapping mouths, too many witnesses, too many investigations by unqualified investigative bodies have turned aspects of the Kennedy assassination into a phenomenon more akin to an *X-Files* convention. Only recently have reliable, unbiased experts begun to cut a scientific trail into the mystery. One highly recommended example is the previously mentioned *Assassination Science.* This is a must-read for anyone interested in the Kennedy assassination; unfortunately, the reader needs doctorates in physics, criminology, and anatomy to get the most out of it. But such efforts, in spite of the complexity of their lexicon, theory, etc., are exactly what the investigation needs to separate the chaff from the grain, so to speak—a scientific analysis of the evidence and even the speculation.

A more user-friendly example of unbiased expert examination is something that occurred as recently as the late summer of 1998, and it didn't involve scientists in a lab. Here, the lab was Dealey Plaza itself.

Executives for Associated Television (a Los Angeles-based production company) essentially rented Dealey Plaza from the city of Dallas for enough time to get some genuine ballistics experts in there to do something that should have been done a long time ago. With the most modern and sophisticated measuring equipment, these experts set out to examine the headshot controversy more intricately—and scientifically—than has ever been attempted in the past. This landmark endeavor shines the brightest investigative light ever on the topic, and the result may even have proved exactly where the fatal headshot came from. To a majority of theorists, it's a surprising result indeed.

The idea originated when coauthor Brad O'Leary convinced Associated Television to go to Russia to shoot a documentary based on recently procured KGB files involving Oswald and the Kennedy assassination. This show has appeared repeatedly on the Learning Channel. During comprehensive interviews with a variety of some of Russia's premier technical authorities (as well as former KGB chiefs and operatives), Lieutenant Colonel Nikolai Martinnikov, a leading ballistics expert with the Russian Federal Crime Lab, suggested using modern precision test lasers as a means of examining the various headshot theories to determine exactly where in Dealey Plaza the fatal shot was fired from.

The Dealey Plaza Re-Enactment

Only recognized experts were recruited to partake, men with unimpeachable credentials:

- Anthony Larry Paul: a field ballistics expert with over thirty years of experience in crime-scene reconstruction; a ballistics instructor for the FBI and the Los Angeles and Philadelphia Police Departments.
- Heinz Thummel: an applied laser specialist and a pioneer of laser-engineering; Thummel was the first scientist to conceive of laser-sighting for the firearms industry over three decades ago.
- Ronald L. Singer: the chief criminalist for the Tarrant County Criminalist Laboratory.
- Dr. Vincent DiMaio: a nationally renowned forensic pathologist whose numerous textbooks and technical papers have set standards in his field. DiMaio is the chief medical examiner for San Antonio, Texas.
- Robert Groden: perhaps the most famous Kennedy assassination researcher of popular design. Groden has written a number of bestsellers and, via his skills as a photographic technician, has probably best shown to the readership the degree of controversy that revolves around the Kennedy assassination.

Paul defines the basic objectives, designs, and ultimate motive of the re-enactment by explaining, "We're going to re-create the shooting-scenario—as many various scenarios as possible—using laser technology to establish the lines of trajectory." Singer augments the team's particular interest, suggesting that they test "some of the other theories, other locations, and see exactly what we can eliminate." He adds, "I think that really is the way you need to go—with any kind of study like this—you eliminate the fringe theories, and the more theories you eliminate the closer you come to the actual truth. It's like Sherlock Holmes said, once you've eliminated all of the impossible, all that's left is the truth." With the use of laser sights, then, the project would be able to determine which shooting theory best represents what actually happened on November 22, 1963. Ultimately, DiMaio sums up the team's goals to "just present what the objective evidence is in this case, to eliminate some of the mythology about the nature of the wounds and the weapons, then let people make up their own minds. I'm interested essentially in the scientific aspect."

Professional surveyors were brought in to properly spot the test vehicle, a task of crucial importance. Three test positions were determined to mark Kennedy's original progress down Elm Street, one before the president was hit, the second to mark the first shot, and the third to mark the fatal headshot. It was imperative that these test positions be derived independently and not from the Warren Commission figures, so the team went right to the source: the Zapruder film. Using a still blowup of each frame, from a benchmark point of exactly where Abraham Zapruder stood while he took the film, the team was able to calibrate each shooting scenario with exactitude. (Afterwards, the team compared their placement figures to the Warren Commission's—they were the same.)

But even the car itself required the same necessities for precision, so a test vehicle was provided, identical to the open-topped Lincoln that Kennedy rode in on that fatal day, with particular attention to the drive-shaft, suspension, and tires. It was imperative that the vehicle maneuver in the same fashion as the car in which Kennedy was killed.

Next, articulated mannequins were used to serve as Kennedy and Governor Connally, postured into the precise positions that Kennedy and Connally were in when the car was fired upon. Other concerns, too, were taken into critical consideration: tree branches that now blocked trajectories from certain windows, road repaving, even the total body weight of all six passengers in the original limousine.

Laser sights in place and the test vehicle properly positioned, the team then commenced, and the measurements, calculations, and laser-test firings ensued, with surprising results.

The alternate theories were eliminated in short order. Several researchers have long held the suspicion that the headshot may have been fired from the point where the end of the knoll's fence meets a concrete buttress of the triple-overpass, far ahead of Kennedy's car. While this location would have provided a fine firing post for a sniper, the trajectory simply didn't line up. A rifle shot from that location not only would have blown the windshield out of the car but also would not have been able to hit Kennedy's head in a manner that would be consistent with the grievous wound we see in the Zapruder film.

The next was a more obscure theory that the headshot was fired from a storm drain ahead of the car. (This theory lost much of its steam over the years until an episode of *The X-Files*, a television series involving government conspiracies and science fiction plots, re-depicted it.) Again, the team's scientific conclusion was that a headshot from this location would not have been possible.

Thirdly (and probably to the disappointment of many assassination buffs), the majority consensus of the team members quickly eliminated the most famous theory of them all: the grassy knoll theory, most popularly posited in Oliver Stone's film. The grassy knoll is simply not in the correct position to establish any of the necessary lines of trajectory that could explain not only Kennedy's wounds but also John Connally's. There certainly may have been a sniper behind that fence at the knoll, but the team's test results prove beyond a reasonable doubt that no rifle shots from that location hit the president.

So where was the fatal shot fired from? What the team initially determined was that all of the shots that hit Kennedy and Connally were fired from behind the limousine. Perfect laser axes from the rear were established, and the primary shooting post was found to be the far window on the sixth floor of the schoolbook depository—which would have all but verified the original Warren Commission conclusions. But a second perfectly plausible firing post was established as well: the second floor of the Dal-Tex Building. According to Ronald Singer,

The first thing I would say is that I'm very pleased with what we did. I actually got more out of it than I expected. . . . I think the best thing that we did was that based on the laser trajectories that we shot from the grassy knoll area, as well as from the area of the overpass, I think we plainly showed that with good sound scientific evidence, there couldn't have been a shot there that hit President Kennedy in the head.

Though most of the test results indicated that all of the shots that hit Kennedy and Connally probably came from the Texas Schoolbook Depository, the Dal-Tex Building could not be eliminated. Groden best conveys the importance of this scientifically-derived plausibility: "One of the most significant things that we were able to do with this testing was to find that there is additional confirmation of a suspected firing point that has been suspect now for well over thirty years, and that is the second floor of the Dal-Tex Building."

Afterwards, the team's conclusions were then shown to the very man who'd suggested the laser tests in the first place, Russia's ballistic expert Lieutenant Colonel Nikolia Martinnikov of the Russian Federal Police. His opinion doubly confirmed the findings of the U.S. ballistic team. "I would like to attract your attention to the fact that on the basis of this study what can be said for sure is that the shots tracked from the rear," Martinnikov concluded. And he too agreed that the Dal-Tex Building was a post "that could not be eliminated from the study."[102]

Appendices

Appendix A

SECRET

AAZ-22592
1 Apr 64

C ll.51t '05'06

° Jean SOUETRE's expulsion from U.S.

CIA HISTORICAL REVIEW PROGRAM
RELEASE IN FULL 1995

-2-

1964

8. Jean SOUETRE aka Michel ROUX aka Michel MERTZ - On 5 March, Mr.
Papich advised that the French had hit the Legal Attache in Paris
and also the STECS man had queried the Bureau in New York City concerning subject stating that he had been expelled from the U.S. at
Fort Worth or Dallas 48 hours after the assassination.* He was in
Fort Worth on the morning of 22 November and in Dallas in the afternoon. The French believe that he was expelled to either Mexico or
Canada. In January he received mail from a dentist named Alderson
living at 5803 Birmingham, Houston, Texas. Subject is believed to
be identical with a Captain who is a deserter from the French Army
and an activist in the OAS. The French are concerned because of
De Gaulle's planned visit to Mexico. They would like to know the
reason for his expulsion from the U.S. and his destination. Bureau
files are negative and they are checking in Texas and with INS. They
would like a check of our files with indications of what may be passed
to the French. Mr. Papich was given a copy of CSCI-3/776,742 previously
furnished the Bureau and CSDB-3/655,207 together with a photograph of
Captain SOUETRE. WE/3/Dublic; CI/SIG; CI/OPS/Evans

* of President Kennedy

Document Number 632-796

for FOIA Review on   JUN 1976

Probably the most shocking piece of Kennedy assassination evidence ever discovered, CIA
Document #632-796 verifies that a French terrorist/assassin named Jean Rene Souetre was
in Dallas on the day of Kennedy's assassination. It also verifies that "Souetre" was flown
out of the country shortly afterward. As shocking as this document is, it was never turned
over to the Warren Commission.

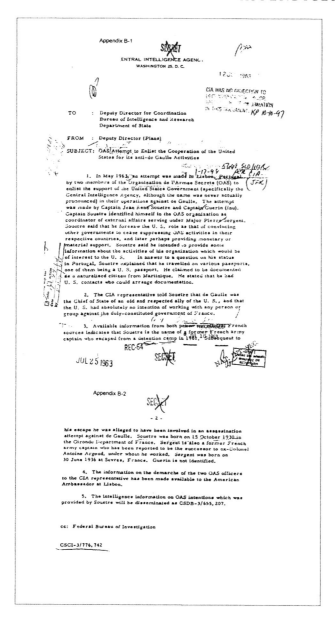

CIA Document #CSCI-3/776,742 reports that French OAS terrorist Jean Rene Souetre approached CIA representatives for help in overthrowing French president Charles de Gaulle. It also reports Souetre's probable participation in an OAS assassination attempt against de Gaulle. Written in July 1963, this document proves that the CIA and FBI were aware of Souetre months before Kennedy was murdered.

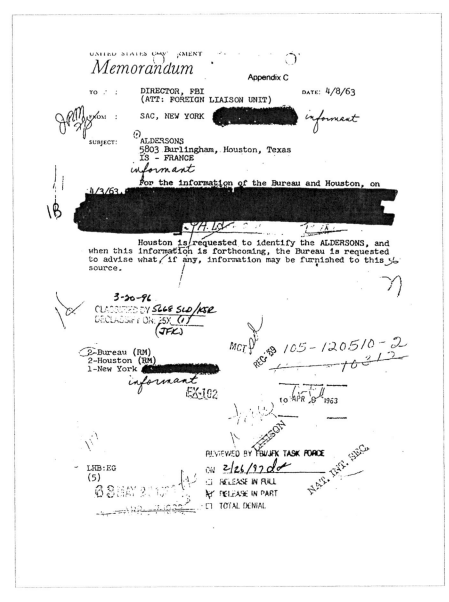

FBI Memorandum (DOC 105-120510-2, 4/8/6). This shocking document verifies FBI orders to investigate Dr. Lawrence Alderson, whom the French Secret Service had identified as knowing Souetre. There's no other plausible reason for the FBI to be investigating Alderson other than Alderson's link to Souetre (which is almost assuredly mentioned in the blacked-out paragraph), the same French terrorist who would later be named as being present in Dallas on the day of Kennedy's murder. Note, however, that this document is dated nearly eight months prior to Kennedy's death.

Appendix D-1
Telephone Interview with Dr. L. M. Alderson
J. Gary Shaw - October 5, 1977, 4:30 pm

Dr: Hello.

GS: Dr. Alderson?

Dr: Yes.

GS: This is Gary Shaw. How are you sir?

DR: Just fine.

GS: Good.

GS: I won't take but a minute, but I'm an Architect, as the girl has probably told you, in Cleburne, Texas. But among the things that I do as a, maybe hobby, is looking into the events surrounding November 22, 1963 and the killing of President Kennedy. One of the things I learned just recently is that a fellow by the name of Jean (and I'm not sure of this pronunciation), Souetre, who's a Frenchman, knew you or received mail from you and he was in Dallas...in Ft. Worth on that morning, and in Dallas that afternoon, and was later on expelled from the United States for reasons as of yet unknown.

Dr: How did you find this out?

GS: From a CIA document that was recently declassified. You're probably been reading somewhat about this. My interest lies in a photograph I have of Souetre and ...

Dr: Swetra (pronouncing)

GS: How is it?

Appendix D-2

GS: Swetra, okay, ...and see if I could identify it as it being he. Could you help me with that?

Dr: Sure. Be happy to.

GS: Okay. Maybe you could even give me a little information about him, I don't know how well you knew him or anything.

Dr: Very well.

GS: Very well?

Dr: Your information is very correct, but there were a few more things involved but all I'm getting is second and third hand because I have not seen him in many many years. As a matter of fact, I have not seen him in quite a bit before that time but...he was flown out of Dallas and I don't know why and don't know by whom.

GS: Do you not even know why he was there?

Dr: I don't have the vaguest idea, according to the CIA when they interviewed me, on their way to see me. I don't know how they knew this or I don't know whether they had even come in contact with him.

GS: What kind of individual was he?

Dr: I don't know, it's hard to explain. He's a career soldier. From what I can gather he was in the French Underground Movement in Algiers. I do know he did leave the French Air Force. When I knew him I was a Security Officer with him in France and lived with him. So, I knew him quite well. He was very well educated. He was very outgoing,

-2-

Appendix D-3

forward, dynamic. He was from a very poor family therefore, in France you don't have a thing if you're from a poor family unless you have a military career behind you.

GS: Right.

Dr: So he was very interested in this and this was why I never did really understand why he left it. But he very definitely left, I presume, his wife. I have not heard from her in well, many years. But she was a very well-to-do, beautiful, Southern French wine-family type situation. And the last time I heard, I heard from her and she was the one that had told me that he had left the French Army and had gone into the underground trying to save Algiers. So evidently he was rather committed or felt committed to leave his career, which was the only career he had. And the next time I heard from him, quite truthfully, was when the CIA, or the FBI rather, had me tailed for about two months following the investigation. And I knew I was being trailed and followed.

GS: And didn't know why?

Dr: And didn't know why. It got interesting after a while, when they finally called and made their show and came in and interviewed me and they were trying to find Jean under any circumstances under any conditions. They just wanted to talk and, you know, and I never heard from him.

GS: Right. What did he look like? Do you...can you give me just a ...

Dr: He was good looking, tall, rather angular, last time I saw him. He had kind-of curly hair, dark brown, good looking guy, Handsome guy.

Appendix D-4

GS: What did he do? Did he have any trade other than professional soldier.

Dr: Not at all, he was a professional soldier. That's why I say, in France, you know, either you're left a trade or left something in life or you have nothing. There's no happy-middle-class-in-between in France. And he was from the lower class, he didn't belong to the happy-middle in-between class which didn't exist, so that is why his whole life was French Air Force. And he was a very prominent upcoming French Security Officer. When I knew him he was a lieutenant.

GS: Well, life's a strange set of circumstances. I'll read you the dispatch if you like.

Dr: I'd be interested in seeing it. If you want me to look at a picture, I'd be happy to identify a picture for you.

GS: Okay.

Dr: I'd be interested in seeing it. I've never heard from the investigation, except I contacted the, I guess, defunct Committee that there isn't anymore or, whether they do exist I really don't know, they've been through so much hassle the last year or so. Because to my knowledge it had never been made public nor had it ever come out that there was someone that had suspected as having been involved or actually assassinating Kennedy. Now this is the way I was approached when I was finally interviewed and approached.

GS: Right.

Dr: They felt that Jean knew who or he himself had assassinated Kennedy. And what they wanted to know in Washington had had him flown out of Dallas ...

Appendix D-5

GS: You don't know?

Dr: I don't have the vaguest idea.

GS: Well, it's a strange affair. When I saw your name and saw that you were still in Houston, I felt the best thing to do was call. Was it in a service connection that you knew him? Was it in Germany?

Dr: No, it was in France. Matter of fact, he was in the, I don't remember, Second French Air Force Headquarters, whatever it was, in   which is uh, just outside of   France.

GS: Well this thing reads like this: Jean Souetre, also known as Michel Roux, I guess that is the way you pronounce that, also known as Michel Mertz on 5 March 64, the FBI advised the French had the legal Attaché in Paris and also the blank had questioned the Bureau in New York City concerning subject stating that he had been expelled from the U.S. at Ft. Worth or Dallas 18 hours after the assassination. He was in Ft. Worth on the morning of 22 November and in Dallas that afternoon. He was expelled to either Mexico or Canada. In January he received mail from a dentist named Alderson living at 5803 Birmingham, Houston, Texas. Subject is believed to be identical with a captain who is a deserter from the French Army and is active in the OAS.

Dr: That's true.

GS: The French are concerned because of DeGaulle's planned visit to Mexico. They would like to know the reason for his expulsion from the U.S. and his destination.

-5-

Appendix D-6

Bureau files are negative and they are checking in Texas and with INS. That's basically it.

Dr: Well, now you will find another report because that's not the one that was filed. You will find one in the FBI files which was my interview.

GS: Okay, I'm running your name down with the Archives. I doubt that I will find it in the National Archives. It is probably a withheld report, because we have not come across it yet.

Dr: The last contact I had with the CIA was in France when I was working with them. So the only contact I had in this country was with the FBI.

GS: I see...well you've been very helpful. I think what I'd like to do if you don't mind is send you these photographs and let you look at them.

Dr: Are they fairly recent?

GS: No, they were taken in 63.

Dr: Okay, the only one I had was taken long before that, but he could be aged.

GS: Do you have a photograph of him?

Dr: Yes.

GS: Well, I would be interested in seeing that too.

Dr: Yes, be happy to. Mail it down if you got it. 10600 Fondren, Suite 102.

The entire transcript of JFK researcher Gary Shaw's October 5, 1977, telephone interview with Dr. Alderson, which verifies that Alderson did indeed know Jean Rene Souetre and that the FBI, shortly after Kennedy's murder, tailed Alderson and eventually interviewed him. The FBI approached Alderson and indicated to him that the FBI suspected Souetre of being involved in Kennedy's assassination.

Dr. Alderson claimed he reported his interview with the FBI, and the FBI's suspicions about Souetre, to the Select Committee, but the matter was never pursued.

196   APPENDICES

Appendix E

I. FINDINGS OF THE SELECT COMMITTEE ON ASSASSINATIONS IN THE
ASSASSINATION OF PRESIDENT JOHN F. KENNEDY IN DALLAS, TEX.,
NOVEMBER 22, 1983

A. Lee Harvey Oswald fired three shots at President John F. Kennedy. The second and third shots fired struck the President. The third
shot he fired killed the President.
    1. President Kennedy was struck by two rifle shots fired from
behind him.
    2. The shots that struck President Kennedy from behind him
were fired from the sixth floor window of the southeast corner of
the Texas School Book Depository building.
    3. Lee Harvey Oswald owned the rifle that was used to fire the
shots from the sixth floor window of the southeast corner of the
Texas School Book Depository building.
    4. Lee Harvey Oswald, shortly before the assassination, had
access to and was present on the sixth floor of the Texas School
Book Depository building.
    5. Lee Harvey Oswald's other actions tend to support the con-
clusion that he assassinated President Kennedy.
B. Scientific acoustical evidence establishes a high probability that
two gunmen fired at President John F. Kennedy. Other scientific evidence does not preclude the possibility of two gunmen firing at the
President. Scientific evidence negates some specific conspiracy allegations.
C. The committee believes, on the basis of the evidence available to
it, that President John F. Kennedy was probably assassinated as a
result of a conspiracy. The committee is unable to identify the other
gunman or the extent of the conspiracy.
    1. The committee believes, on the basis of the evidence available
to it, that the Soviet Government was not involved in the assassination of President Kennedy.
    2. The committee believes, on the basis of the evidence available
to it, that the Cuban Government was not involved in the assassination of President Kennedy.
    3. The committee believes, on the basis of the evidence available
to it, that anti-Castro Cuban groups, as groups, were not involved
in the assassination of President Kennedy, but that the available
evidence does not preclude the possibility that individual members
may have been involved.
    4. The committee believes, on the basis of the evidence available
to it, that the national syndicate of organized crime, as a group,
was not involved in the assassination of President Kennedy, but
that the available evidence does not preclude the possibility that
individual members may have been involved.
    5. The Secret Service, Federal Bureau of Investigation, and
Central Intelligence Agency, were not involved in the assassination of President Kennedy.

(3)

H.R. 1828

Page 3 of The Final Report of the Select Committee on Assassinations. *The Select Committee was the last official government investigation into Kennedy's murder. Note Part I, Paragraph B, which states the Committee's findings of a "high probability that two gunmen" fired at Kennedy. Also note Part I, Paragraph C, stating that Kennedy was "probably assassinated as a result of a conspiracy."*

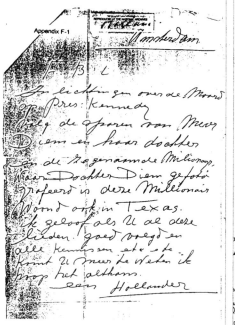

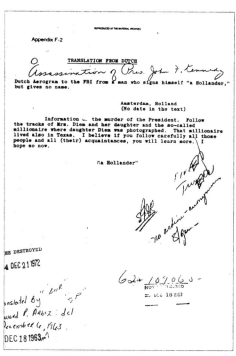

Kennedy was probably assassinated as a result of a conspiracy? This anonymous letter was sent to the FBI from Holland little more than a week after Kennedy's death—yet another document never reported to the Warren Commission. The letter's anonymous author suggests to the FBI that members of South Vietnam's Diem regime were involved in Kennedy's assassination.

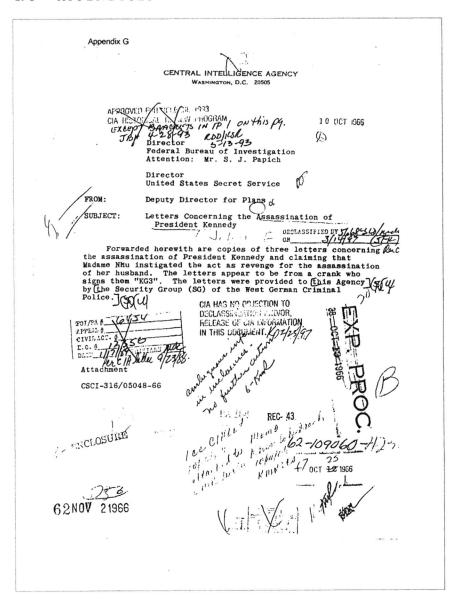

Appendix G

CENTRAL INTELLIGENCE AGENCY
WASHINGTON, D.C. 20505

10 OCT 1966

Director
Federal Bureau of Investigation
Attention: Mr. S. J. Papich

Director
United States Secret Service

FROM: Deputy Director for Plans

SUBJECT: Letters Concerning the Assassination of
President Kennedy

    Forwarded herewith are copies of three letters concerning
the assassination of President Kennedy and claiming that
Madame Nhu instigated the act as revenge for the assassination
of her husband. The letters appear to be from a crank who
signs them "KG3". The letters were provided to this Agency
by the Security Group (SG) of the West German Criminal
Police.

CIA HAS NO OBJECTION TO
DECLASSIFICATION AND/OR,
RELEASE OF CIA INFORMATION
IN THIS DOCUMENT.

Attachment

CSCI-316/05048-66

ENCLOSURE

REC- 43

62 NOV 21 1966

Coincidence? A "crank?" This CIA document reports a series of letters written by an anonymous German who claimed that Madame Nhu instigated Kennedy's assassination as an act
of revenge for her husband Ngo Dinh Nhu and President Diem's assassination at the hands
of a Kennedy-controlled coup.

Appendix H

UNITED STATES DEPARTMENT OF JUSTICE
FEDERAL BUREAU OF INVESTIGATION

Copy to:

Report of:
Date: HENRY A. WELKE   Office: Norfolk, Virginia
                        September 22, 1964
Field Office File #:   Bureau File #:
                        89-17   105-82555
Title:
                        LEE HARVEY OSWALD

Character:
                        INTERNAL SECURITY - R, CUBA

Synopsis:
                        ERICH LINTROP, Z #72988D1, born 11/4/04, Estonia,
        interviewed aboard SS AMERICAN FLYER, Norfolk, Va. He claims
        that about four days after assassination of President JOHN F.
        KENNEDY he was in Constantinople, Turkey, as a crew member
        aboard the SS THUNDERBIRD. He met unidentified Turkish
        Army officer. Officer told him there were rumors in Turkey
        that Madame NHU of South Vietnam may have been responsible
        for assassination; that an unidentified monk from South
        Vietnam had the money for the assassins; but that the monk
        had disappeared with the money. LINTROP felt that this
        information was a poor rumor. LINTROP claims had never met
        LEE HARVEY OSWALD or JACK RUBY and knows nothing about them
        other than what he has read in newspapers and magazines.

                                        - RUC -

One more FBI investigation never reported to the Warren Commission. Merchant mariner Erich Lintrop overheard a Turkish military officer claiming that Kennedy's assassination was ordered by Madame Nhu of South Vietnam.

ſ

Appendix I

AUC-31-98 18-03 FROM-LBJ LIBRARY   10-612 W14 6171   PAGE   2/2

R̶ Pru, K

THE WHITE HOUSE
WASHINGTON

~~TOP SECRET~~   4 December 1963

MEMORANDUM FOR:

        Bromley Smith

Subj: Changes in Defense Readiness Conditions as a Result of
        the Assassination of President Kennedy

1. By the authority granted under the Joint Chiefs of Staff Emergency
Action Procedures (SM-600-63) dated 12 June 1963, the JCS, commanders of unified and specified commands, CINCNORAD or higher
authority are authorized to declare Defense Readiness Conditions
(DEFCONS) 1, 2, 3, 4 and 5. A copy of Chapter Four of this publication
is appended as Tab A.

2. Acting on this authority, the JCS, after news of the Dallas shooting
was received, issued their message 3675, appended as Tab B, at 2:15
p. m., 22 November.

3. Acting on this message, USCINCSO declared an increase in readiness to DEFCON 4 at 2:50 p. m. That command attained DEFCON 4
readiness at 4:28 p. m. and returned to a DEFCON 5 status two days
later, 24 November, at 12:20 p. m. Copies of the three messages
advising of these actions are appended under Tab C.

4. CINCPAC, at 3:13 p. m., 22 November, directed his forces to
take actions consistent with a DEFCON 3 unless those actions would
indicate heightened tensions. A copy of his directive is appended
under Tab D. (*U.S. forces in Viet Nam are in DEFCON 3 on
a continuing basis.)*

5. Each unified or specified commander is required to inform the JCS
whenever he increases or decreases the DEFCON status in his command.
The NMCC received no notifications of such change other than those
specified above and appended. If a commander took precautions within
his command other than changing DEFCON status, he need not necessarily
inform the JCS of them. NMCC received no other message notifications.

L. S. Hallett

O. S. HALLETT

DECLASSIFIED
Authority JFK #173-10091-12000
By fdl . NARA Date 4-17-98

~~TOP SECRET~~

Proof of the little-known fact that Kennedy's assassination may have brought us to the brink of World War III. This recently declassified White House document proves that continental U.S. military forces were brought to alert state DEFCON 3 on the day of Kennedy's murder. President Johnson feared the Soviets might launch a first strike in the event that we suspected them of involvement.

NARA _CC_____   DATE _1/13/95_

Appendix J

SECRET

..ION OF SOVIET AND COMMUNIST
..TY OFFICIALS TO THE ASSASSINATION
OF PRESIDENT JOHN F. KENNEDY

According to our source, Soviet officials claimed that Lee Harvey Oswald had no connection whatsoever with the Soviet Union. They described him as a neurotic maniac who was disloyal to his own country and everything else. They noted that Oswald never belonged to any organization in the Soviet Union and was never given Soviet citizenship. [(CG 5824-S*)](X)(μ)

A second source who has furnished reliable information in the past advised on November 27, 1963, that Nikolai T. Fedorenko, the Permanent Representative to the Soviet Mission to the United Nations, held a brief meeting with all diplomatic personnel employed at the Soviet Mission on November 23, 1963. During this meeting, Fedorenko related for the benefit of all present the news of the assassination of President John F. Kennedy and stated that Kennedy's death was very much regretted by the Soviet Union and had caused considerable shock in Soviet Government circles. Fedorenko stated that the Soviet Union would have preferred to have had President Kennedy at the helm of the American Government. He added that President Kennedy had, to some degree, a mutual understanding with the Soviet Union, and had tried seriously to improve relations between the United States and Russia. Fedorenko also added that little or nothing was known by the Soviet Government concerning President Lyndon Johnson and, as a result, the Soviet Government did not know what policies President Johnson would follow in the future regarding the Soviet Union.(X)(U)

According to our source, Colonel Boris Ivanov, Chief of the Soviet Committee for State Security (KGB) Residency in New York City, held a meeting of KGB personnel on the morning of November 25, 1963. Ivanov informed those present that President Kennedy's death had posed a problem for the KGB and stated that it was necessary for all KGB employees to lend their efforts to solving the problem.(S)(U)

According to our source, Ivanov stated that it was his personal feeling that the assassination of President Kennedy had been planned by an organized group rather than being the act of one individual assassin. Ivanov stated that it was therefore necessary that the KGB ascertain with the greatest possible speed the true story surrounding President Kennedy's assassination. Ivanov stated that the KGB was interested in knowing all the factors and all of the possible groups which might have worked behind the scenes to organize and plan this assassination.(S)(U)

SECRET

- 2 -

Another little-known fact: Page 2 of FBI Document #124-10144-10086 (file #62-109060-4321), written in December 1966, indicates that the Soviets were so afraid that the U.S. might suspect them that the KGB began its own investigation of the Kennedy assassination, and that the KGB believed Kennedy was killed not by a lone gunman but by an organized conspiracy.

```
7._____ DATE 2/.. '. __        REPRODUCED AT THE NATIONAL ARCHIVES

              Appendix K

/ED
CLAS____1 / 6
REG'D____
DATE ___2/19/88                              PRIORITY
VIEW
  _____

FM DIRECTOR FBI                              DEA
                                      REVIEWED BY FBI/JFK TASK FORCE
TO LEGAT PARIS PRIORITY
                                      ON  12.195 da/
     ATTN: BOB FARMER                 ☑ RELEASE IN FULL
BT                                    ☐ RELEASE IN PART
UNCLAS                                ☐ TOTAL DENIAL
                                        (1)
ASSASSINATION OF PRESIDENT JOHN F. KENNEDY; PPSAKA; OO: DALLAS.

     ON JANUARY 22, 1988, MR. MICHAEL TOBIN, HEROIN SECTION,

DEA HQ, ADVISED THAT STEPHEN J. RIVELE HAS APPROACHED HIM WITH

INFORMATION CONCERNING THE ASSASSINATION OF PRESIDENT KENNEDY.

RIVELE BELIEVES THAT THE PRESIDENT WAS KILLED BY LUCIEN JEAN

SARTI (DECEASED), ROGER BOCOGNANI, AND AN INDIVIDUAL NAMED

LEBLANC.  THESE INDIVIDUALS WERE RECRUITED BY ANTOINE GUERINI,

WHO POSSIBLY DID SO AT THE REQUEST OF CARLOS MARCELLO (ORGANIZED

CRIME SUBJECT IN NEW ORLEANS).  RIVELE HAS INDICATED ALL OF

THESE INDIVIDUALS (WITH THE EXCEPTION OF MARCELLO) WERE

ASSOCIATES IN A HEROIN SMUGGLING OPERATION CENTERED IN SOUTH

AMERICA.  RIVELE IS OBTAINING THIS INFORMATION FROM CHRISTIAN


                       DFP:FSD(0)      2/19/88    5042/6    4294

1 - MR. CLARKE             1 - OLIA
1 - MR. NELSON             1 - DALLAS - INFORMATION AIRMAIL
1 - MR. TUBBS
1 - MR. PIERCE
                                          62 - 1010
                                      SEE NOTE PAGE SEVEN

                                          16 MAR 17 1989
```

FBI report of information culled by researcher Stephen Rivele, suggesting that French heroin boss Antoine Guerini hired men to kill Kennedy at the request of New Orleans Mob chieftain Carlos Marcello. Keep in mind that the massive heroin network of both Guerini and Marcello depended on the raw opium that was shipped from Ngo Dinh Nhu in Saigon.

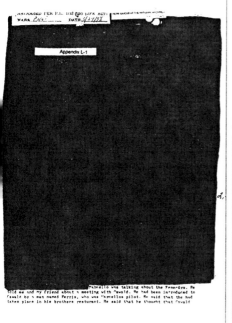

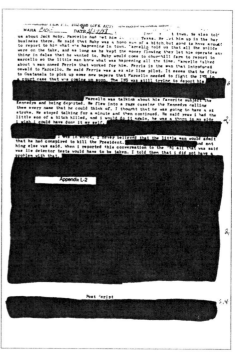

FBI Document 124-10182-10430 (file #CR 137A-5467-69, 70, 72), though hugely redacted, tells of either an FBI undercover agent or informant talking to Marcello. Look closely at the bottom of Page L-1. Marcello admits that he had personally met with Lee Harvey Oswald. Also, look closely at Page L-2. Marcello admits his involvement in the Kennedy assassination. He also admits that he personally knew Jack Ruby.

Appendix M

DL 175-109

Continuation of FD-302 of _____ JAMES ROBERT CATES _____ , on ____ 3/2/89 ____ , Page ___ 2 ___

that MARCELLO was incoherent and that he did not want to get back into bed. CATES stated that Nurse MAJORS then helped them lift MARCELLO back into bed and secure his restraints which consisted of soft fabric belts and handcuffs which secured his left hand to the head of his bed. MARCELLO struggled for a while after these restraints were secured, but they were necessary because he had a heart monitor and IV attached to his body.

CATES stated that MARCELLO did not go into a sound sleep, but began mumbling off and on. Sometimes CATES could understand what MARCELLO was saying and sometimes his comments were garbled and did not make sense. CATES stated that at one point MARCELLO looked at him and said "Tomorrow we are going to have to go back to New Orleans". CATES advised that apparently MARCELLO must have thought that both he and VENCIENT BROWN were MARCELLO's bodyguards or associates. MARCELLO's attitude turned cheerful and he said something to the effect that we are going to party, to have a celebration, and made a reference to the outstanding food they have in New Orleans.

CATES stated that at about this time he and BROWN decided to keep a log or a record of CARLOS MARCELLO's actions and comments. BROWN wrote down on a "separatee folder" that MARCELLO was incoherent, had struggled, and needed to be restrained. He wrote in the Registered Nurse's name as a witness and that MARCELLO was making incoherent statements. However, CATES stated that he does not think that BROWN wrote down any specific statement or comment made by MARCELLO.

CATES advised that at approximately 2:30 a.m. on February 28, 1989, CARLOS MARCELLO was mumbling incoherently and then he got their attention by saying "Mother-fucker". CATES stated he has worked in A unit most of the time and MARCELLO has not previously used any profanity. CATES then paid attention and heard MARCELLO say "That KENNEDY, that smiling mother-fucker, we'll fix him in Dallas". About three or four minutes later MARCELLO said "I want to see PROVENZANO in New York".

Officer CATES advised that the rest of the night CARLOS MARCELLO rambled on about insignificant items like "I need to go over to the other room and get my stuff, I want my New Orleans newspaper, pass me a cigar," and also about his children.

CATES stated that he truly believes that CARLOS MARCELLO thought that both he and BROWN were some type of subordinates

Still another person who overheard Marcello confess to involvement in the Kennedy assassination: federal detention officer James Cates.

Appendix N

4 October 1962

MEMORANDUM FOR RECORD

SUBJECT: Minutes of Meeting of the Special Group (Augmented) on
Operation MONGOOSE, 4 October 1962

PRESENT: The Attorney General; Mr. Johnson; Mr. Gilpatric, General
Taylor, General Lansdale; Mr. McCone and General Carter;
Mr. Wilson

1. The Attorney General opened the meeting by saying that
higher authority is concerned about progress on the MONGOOSE program
and feels that more priority should be given to trying to mount
sabotage operations. The Attorney General said that he wondered if
a new look is not required at this time in view of the meager results,
especially in the sabotage field. He urged that "massive activity"
be mounted within the entire MONGOOSE framework. There was a good
deal of discussion about this, and General Lansdale said that another
attempt will be made against the major target which has been the object
of three unsuccessful missions, and that approximately six new ones
are in the planning stage.

Mr. Johnson said that "massive activity" would have to
appear to come from within. He also said that he hopes soon to be
able to present to the Group a plan for giving Cuban exiles more of a
free hand, with the full realization that this would give more visibility
to their activities. On this latter point, Mr. McCone said that he
reserves judgment as to the feasibility and desirability of such a
program. (Mr. Johnson agreed that he has reservations as well.)

2. Mr. McCone then said that he gets the impression that high
levels of the government want to get on with activity but still wish
to retain a low noise level. He does not believe that this will be
possible. Any sabotage would be blamed on the United States. In this
connection, he cited the enormous number of telephone calls that had
been directed at CIA at the time that the skin divers landed in Eastern
Cuba and at the time Cuban exile students shot up the apartment house.
He urged that responsible officials be prepared to accept a higher noise
level if they want to get on with operations.

In partial rebuttal, the Attorney General said that the
reasons people were so concerned at the times mentioned were: (a) the
fact that the skin divers were Americans, and (b) that the student

DECLASSIFIED
JFK Assass. P̶. ̶ ̶ ̶ ̶tion Act of 1992
NK F 95-1589 - Von Tarel Call 2/27/96
NARA date 2/4/97   By KJH

EYES ONLY

For those who don't believe that Kennedy and his administration would stoop to clandestine
efforts to assassinate a foreign leader, read paragraph 1 of this memorandum, composed
well after the abortive Bay of Pigs Invasion. General Edward Lansdale, the same man whom
Kennedy had asked to kill Diem, outlines for Robert Kennedy that more "attempts" in Cuba
will be made against "the major target." This target could only be Fidel Castro.

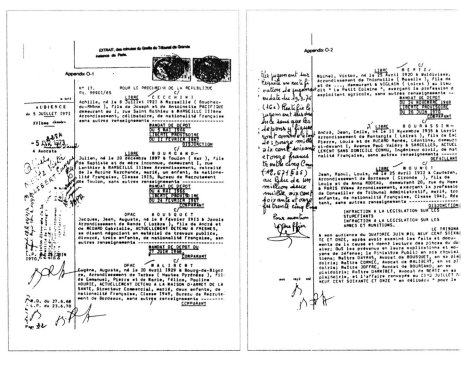

Indisputable official documentation that Mertz served as a primary operator for the Marseille heroin syndicate. These are the cover sheets for the entire French court record of the trial that convicted Mertz and his Marseille partners of international heroin distribution. The heroin that Mertz and these men delivered to U.S. Mafia druglords originated as opium base from Ngo Dinh Nhu and Rock Francisci in Saigon.

IO

concernant : MERTZ Michel, Victor.-

Appendix P

RELEVE DES CONDAMNATIONS

Dates	Tribunaux	Nature du délit	Condamnations
22.2.40	T.C. THIONVILLE	blessures par imprudence.	50 Frs d'amende
.3.41	T.C. NANCY	vol	2 mois de prison et 2? Frs d'amende
5.1.42	T.C. METZ	port d'arme prohibée	100 reich-marks
27.6.42	T.C. METZ	coups et blessures	20 reich-marks
25.9.45	T.M. ORLEANS	blessures involontaires	5000 Frs d'amende
14/4/46	T.C. BEAUNE	d°	1200 Frs d'amende
15/10/46	Ordre d'informer du T.M.	vol,- recel- faux et usage de faux	incompétence du tr? nal dossier tranc: au procureur géné: la Seine le 2?/?/:
22/1/49	6° chambre du T.C.PA-RIS.	violation de domicile	6000 Frs d'amende
30/11/51	T.M. de METZ	exécution d'un nommé JEANN IN	acquitté
2/5/44		vol d'essence	révoqué de son empl: d'inspecteur auxili:. re de police et int? né au camp de MEXC?.
16.12.53	G1 Cdt la Division de FES	abus autorité et menace de mort envers la police	60 jours d'arrêt à forteresse.
Décembre 1965	Tribunal de Simple Police de MONTARGIS	outrages et rebellion à agent de la force publique. -conduite en état d'ivresse	1000 Frs d'amende / 60 Frs d'amende
Juillet 1971	16° Chambre Correctionnelle de la Seine	Trafic de stupéfiants	5 ans de prison - 30.000 F d'amende, ans d'interdiction séjour.

War hero, or just a murderer, thug, and drug peddler? Here is the official French criminal record for Michel Victor Mertz. Mertz spent thirty years vigorously breaking the law, and this file details his long string of infractions: assault and battery, burglary, harboring illegal weapons, homicide, flight to avoid prosecution, inciting riot, forgery, threatening to murder police, plus abundant court fines and jail time. Note the final documented conviction (a five-year prison sentence for trafficking narcotics).

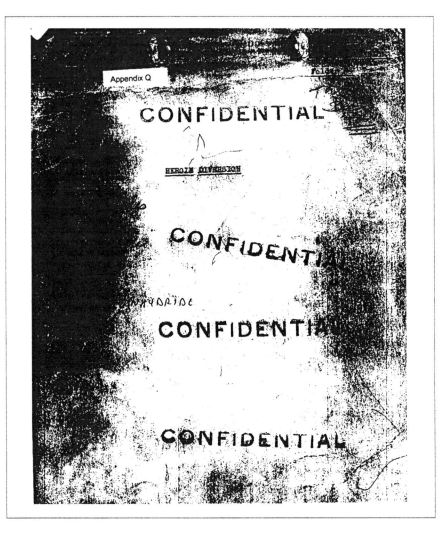

Cover sheet for a 1961 U.S. Bureau of Narcotics report on French heroin operations. This and several other reports on French heroin production and distribution in the late-'50s to early-'60s were strangely difficult to procure from the National Archives (and many more were simply denied release). Why would such records, three to five decades old, be withheld from the public under the auspices of national security? But what's stranger is that Mertz is not mentioned anywhere, even though his complicity is verified by extensive French records during a time when French and U.S. law enforcement organizations worked closely together. Did some element of the U.S. government expunge all mention of Mertz, the same element, perhaps, that saw to his escape from Dallas, Texas, two days after Kennedy's murder?

Endnotes

One — A Young Man in a Hurry

1. *Encylcopaedia Britannica*, s.v. "Kennedy, John F(itzgerald)."
2. Ibid.

Two — Taproot to Chaos

1. *Encylcopaedia Britannica*, s.v. "Vietnam, History."
2. Historical data in Chapter Two from *Encylcopaedia Britannica*, s.v. "Vietnam, History and War"; and *Vietnam: A Television History*. Volume One: "America's Mandarin." A co-production of WGBH Boston, Central Independent Television/UK, and Antenne-2 France and in association with LRE Productions, 1996.

Three — The Puppet Who Pulled His Own Strings

1. Dulles, J.F. *Vietnam: A Television History*. As quoted by high-ranking State Department aide Paul M. Kattenburg.
2. Karnow, Stanley. *Vietnam*. Viking,, 1983: 221.
3. Karnow: 222.
4. McCoy, Alfred W. *The Politics of Heroin: CIA Complicity in the Global Drug Trade*. Lawrence Hills Books, 1991: p. 148; *Vietnam: A Television History*. Volume One: "America's Mandarin."
5. Karnow: 223.
6. Karnow: 223-224.
7. Sheehan, Neil. *A Bright Shining Lie*. Vintage, 1989: 138.

8. *Encylcopaedia Britannica*, s.v. "Ngo Dinh Diem."

9. Sheehan: 192-193.

10. Sheehan: 187-188.

11. Hersh, Seymour M. *The Dark Side of Camelot*. Little Brown, 1997: 415.

12. Karnow: 278.

13. *Vietnam: A Television History*. Volume One: "America's Mandarin."

14. Sheehan: 189.

15. General material in Chapters Three and Four, regarding Diem's attacks on Buddhists, the self-immolations, incarcerations, growing civil unrest, Madame Nhu's ascent into notoriety, etc., are well outlined in most modern history texts. But the authors urge interested readers particularly to consult the video *Vietnam: A Television History*. Volume One: "America's Mandarin"; and the books: Stanley Karnow's *Vietnam: A History* and Neil Sheehan's *A Bright Shining Lie*.

Four — Triumvirate of Hatred

1. Sheehan: 335.

2. Karnow: 279.

3. *Encyclopedia Britannica*, s.v. "Kennedy, John F(itzgerald)."

4. *Vietnam: A Television History*. Volume One: "America's Mandarin."

5. Karnow: 281.

6. Sheehan: 335; Karnow: 285.

7. See Endnote Fifteen in Chapter Three.

Five — The Network

1. McCoy: 203.

2. Ibid.

3. McCoy: 204

4. McCoy: 45.

5. McCoy: 197.

6. McCoy: 296.

Six — Kennedy's Coup

1. U.S. Department of State. *Foreign Relations of the United States, 1961-1963*. Volume IV: 32. (From here on, this source will be referred to as *FRUS*.)

2. Karnow: 285.

3. *FRUS, 1961-1963*. Volume III: 142-143.

4. Herring, George C., ed. *The Pentagon Papers*. McGraw-Hill, 1993;"Intelligence Assessment of 1963 Buddhist Protest," # 53-2-63: 62.

5. Karnow: 285.

6. *Vietnam: A Television History*. Volume One: "America's Mandarin."

7. Karnow: 251.

8 *FRUS, 1961-1963*. Volume IV: 513.

9. This is only a brief synopsis of the technical aspects of the coup that resulted in Diem and Nhu's assassination. For a detailed account, interested readers should consult Karnow's *Vietnam: A History*: 302-311.

10. Sheehan: 362.

11. Karnow: 283.

12. Corey, C.L. "Whoever Shot Ngo Dinh Diem, It Couldn't Have Been the CIA." *Insight on the News* (March 15, 1999), Correspondece Section: 3.

13. Karnow: 305.

14. Bird, Kai. "Cries and Whispers." *Washingtonian* (October 1998): 48.

15. From a Conein interview seen in *Vietnam: A Television History*. Volume One: "America's Mandarin."

16. Hersh: 416.

17. Herring, *The Pentagon Papers*: 78.

18. "The Dislodging of Diem." *Boston Globe* (December 1, 1998): A18.

19. Brinkley, Douglas. "Of Ladders and Letters." *Time* (April 24, 2000): 40-41.

20. Karnow: 309.

21. Fussel, James A. "Conein...Lucien Conein. Who Was He?" *Kansas City Star* (September 20, 1998): G1; Karnow: 283.

22. Sheehan: 363.

23. Corey, C.L. "Whoever Shot Ngo Dinh Diem, It Couldn't Have Been the CIA." *Insight on the News* (March 15, 1999), Correspondence Section: 3.

24. Rust, William J. *Kennedy in Vietnam*. New York: Da Capo Press, 1985: 171-172.

25. *FRUS, 1961-1963*. Volume IV: 521.

26. Herring, *The Pentagon Papers*. "Washington Moves Toward Coup": 63.

27. Karnow: 287.

28. *FRUS, 1961-1963*. Volume IV: 21.

29. Karnow: 301.

30. Hersh: 419.

31. Sheehan: 371.

32. Karnow: 295.

33. *FRUS, 1961-1963*. Volume IV: 577.

34. Bouscaren, Anthony T. *The Last of the Mandarins: Diem of Vietnam*. Pittsburgh: Duquesne University Press, 1965: 94.

35. *FRUS, 1961-1963*. Volume IV: 580.

Seven — Building the Case

1. "Tapes Reveal Nixon Blaming JFK in Killing." *Times-Picayune* (February 26, 1999), National Section: A14.

2. Lane, Mark. *Plausible Denial*. ThunderMouth Press, 1991: 269-271.

3. Sheehan: 371.

4. Karnow: 310.

5. Karnow: 309.

6. Hersh: 429.

7. Hersh: 416.

8. Hersh: 430.

9a. *FRUS, 1961-1963.* Volume IV: 337-338.

9b. *FRUS, 1961-1963.* Volume IV: 370

10. *FRUS, 1961-1963.* Volume IV: 371.

11. *FRUS, 1961-1963.* Volume IV: 372.

12. *FRUS, 1961-1963.* Volume IV: 608-624.

13. *FRUS, 1961-1963.* Volume IV: 637-640.

14. Roberts, Craig. *Kill Zone.* Consolidated Press International, 1994: 208.

15. Groden, Robert J. *The Killing of a President.* Viking Penguin, 1993: 214.

16. Bird, Kai. *The Color of Truth.* Simon & Schuster, 1998: 264.

17. Prouty, L. Fletcher. *JFK: The CIA, Vietnam and the Plot to Assassinate John F. Kennedy.* Citadel Press, 1996: 267.

18. Prouty: 269.

19. Prouty: 267.

20. Prouty: (third set of photo plates) 4.

21. Prouty: 280.

22. Lind, Michael. *Vietnam: The Necessary War.* Simon & Schuster, 1999: 196.

23. Shultz, Dick. "How Kennedy Launched His Secret War in Vietnam." *Boston Globe* (January 31, 2000): A16.

24. Duffy: 478-479.

25. Bishop, Jim. *The Day Kennedy Was Shot.* HarperPerennial, 1992: 81.

26. Sheehan: 8.

27. Sheehan: 186.

28. Hersh: 429.

Eight — The Usual Suspects

1. *Summary of Findings and Recommendations.* "Findings of the Select Committee on Assassination in the Assassination of President John F. Kennedy in Dallas, Tex., November 22, 1963." January 1979: 1.

2. Duffy, James P. and Vincent L. Ricci. *The Assassination of John F. Kennedy.* Thunder's Mouth Press, 1992: 489.

3. Duffy: 233-234.

4. Groden, *The Killing of a President*: 159-161.

Nine — The French Assassin

1. Hurt, Henry. *Reasonable Doubt.* New York: Holt, Rinehart, and Winston, 1986: 414-419.

2. Benson, Michael. *Who's Who in the JFK Assassination.* Citadel Press, 1993: 132.

3. Hurt: 414.

4. Summers, Anthony: *Conspiracy.* McGraw-Hill, 1980: 605.

5. Summers: 605.

Ten — The Secret Army

1. Porch, Douglas. *The French Secret Services.* Farrar, Straus and Giroux, 1995: 398.

2. *Encylcopaedia Britannica*, s.v. "Salan, Raoul (-Albin-Louis)"; Porch: 358-398.

Eleven — SDECE and the French Mafia

1. Becket, Henry S.A. *The Dictionary of Espionage.* Stein and Day, 1986: 158.

2. Porch: 396.

3. Becket: 158.

4. *Newsday*, staff and editors. *The Heroin Trail.* Holt, Rinehart and Winston, 1973, 1974: 111.

5. Porch: 400.

6. McCoy: 31-38.

7. McCoy: 25. (An interesting note: on pages 60-61 of McCoy's book, he cites that a few years later, in 1947, SDECE was not the only group involved with Marseille's organized crime element. America's own CIA "dealt directly with Corsican syndicate leaders through the Guerini brothers. The CIA's operatives supplied arms and money to Corsican gangs for assaults on Communist picket lines. . . ." McCoy is probably the foremost expert in this field; interested readers should consider his book a must.)

8. *The Heroin Trail*: 81.

9. Porch: 400.

10. *The Heroin Trail*: 113.

Twelve — The Mysterious Souetre

1. *The Heroin Trail*: 112.

2. CIA Document CSCI-3/776,742. (See Appendix B.)

3. CIA Document CSCI-3/776,742.

4. Benson: 416.

5. "Telephone Interview with Dr. L.M. Alderson and J. Gary Shaw - October 5, 1977; 4:30 P.M." (See Appendix D.)

6. "Memorandum of Interview by J. Gary Shaw with Dr. Lawrence M. (Larry) Alderson, D.D.S." October 6, 1977, 4:00 P.M.

7. Ibid.

8. "Telephone Interview with Dr. L.M. Alderson and J. Gary Shaw - October 5, 1977; 4:30 P.M."

9. Ibid

10. FBI Document 105-128-529, 3/6/64.

11. Hurt: 416.

12. In Oliver Stone's film *JFK,* it is posited that a telex notice was transmitted to the FBI's New Orleans Field Office on November 17, 1963, stating that the FBI had become aware of a threat to assassinate Kennedy in Dallas. HSCA dismissed this information on the grounds that the initial claimant, FBI security clerk William S.

Walter, was lying (Summers: 311) in spite of researcher Mark Lane's procurement of a copy of the telex in 1976 via the Freedom of Information Act (Benson: 469-470). Some detractors claim that the telex is a forgery even though there is no credible evidence to suggest that.

13. Hurt: 418.

14. FBI Document 105-120510-2, 4/8/63. This document establishes that the FBI was actively seeking information on Alderson. It states: "Houston is requested to identify the Aldersons, and when this information is forthcoming, the Bureau is requested to advise what, if any, information may be furnished to this source." (See Appendix C.)

Thirteen — The Quagmire of Paper

1. Telephone interview between coauthor Seymour and Justice Department classification officer who asked that his name not be revealed in print for fear of repercussions.

2. Associated Press. "Government Faulted for JFK Secrecy." September 28, 1998.

3. Duffy: 234.

4. "Memorandum of Interview by J. Gary Shaw with Dr. Lawrence M. (Larry) Alderson, D.D.S." October 6, 1977, 4:00 P.M.

5. FBI Document 105-120510-1, 5/3/63; and follow-up attachment dated 5/21/63.

6. Hurt: 415.

7. FBI Document 105-120510-2, 4/8/63.

Fourteen — Alias Michel Roux

1. Porch: 401.

2. Porch: 400.

3. FBI Document 105-128529-3, 3/11/64.

4. FBI Document 105-128529-15, 3/12/64.

5. FBI Document 105-128529-12, 3/13/64.

Fifteen — A Man Named Mertz

1. *The Heroin Trail*: 112.
2. *The Heroin Trail*: 109-121.

Sixteen — Crisis in France

1. Porch: 410.
2. *The Heroin Trail*: 81.
3. *The Heroin Trail*: 78.
4. McCoy: 25.
5. *The Heroin Trail*: 101, 110; McCoy: 64.
6. Porch: 401.

Seventeen — Codename: QJ/WIN

1. Roberts: 44.
2. McCoy: 15. (McCoy also cites CIA alliances with Laotian heroin dealers and Chinese opium dealers operating in Burma.)
3. Hurt: p. 419; Chambaz, Jacques. "French Terrorist Accused of Murdering Kennedy." *Le Quotidien de Paris* (January 1, 1984). (This was the only accessible interview with Souetre for many years. Our own interview with Souetre, however, made by Monique Lajournade, took place on June 9, 1999, and remains the latest and most comprehensive to date.)
4. *Final Report of the Assassination Records Review Board.* Chapter Five, subsection entitled "CIA crypts." September, 1998.
5. Becket: 46.
6. Duffy: 524.
7. Roberts: 45.
8. *Final Report of the Assassination Records Review Board.* Chapter Five, subsection entitled "CIA sluglines." September, 1998.
9. Duffy: 427.
10. Benson: 104.

11. Roberts, Craig and John Armstrong. *JFK: The Dead Witnesses.* Consolidated Press International, 1995: 98.

12. Summers: 493-494.

13. Scott, Peter Dale. *Deep Politics and the Death of JFK.* University of California Press, 1993: 352.

14. Material detailing SDECE's direct accommodations to Mertz after his OAS duties were finished; material detailing Mertz's Swiss bank accounts and material and property holdings all on a captain's salary and implications that SDECE refused to jail Mertz for heroin distribution even after repeated complaints by the U.S. Federal Bureau of Narcotics; and further implications that Mertz served minimal prison time for major crimes; *The Heroin Trail*: 113-119. (The suggestion that SDECE accepted money from the same heroin syndicate it protected, however, is not cited in *The Heroin Trail* but is instead a logical conclusion of the authors of this book.)

15. *The Heroin Trail*: 119.

16. *The Heroin Trail*: 111.

17. *The Heroin Trail*: 119.

18. *The Heroin Trail*: 117.

Eighteen — Kernels of Truth

1. FBI Document, Record Number 124-10001-10395, Records Series: HQ, Agency File Number 62-109060-8260, 02/19/88: 2.

2. Stone, Oliver. *JFK*; Turner, Nigel. *The Men Who Killed Kennedy.* The segment entitled "The Forces Of Darkness." (Note: The best account of Rivele's hypothesis based on his interviews with Christian David is the interview with Rivele himself also found in "The Forces Of Darkness" segment of *The Men Who Killed Kennedy.*) Additionally, a good synopsis can be found in Michael Benson's *Who's Who in the JFK Assassination*: 100-101, 313, 381; an official synopsis is found in FBI Document, Record Number 124-10001-10395, Records Series: HQ, Agency File Number 62-109060-8260, 02/19/88. And there's still another FBI document in which can be found a complete chronological outline of Rivele's investigation of David and Nicoli: FBI Document, Record Number 124-10001-10391, Agency File Number 62-109060-8264, 12/14/87.

3. UPI. PM cycle, October 26, 1988: International Section.

4. FBI Document, Record Number 124-10001-10395, Agency File Number 62-109060-8260, 02/19/88: 1-3.

5. Ibid: 1.

6. Ibid: 3-4.

7. "Empty Revelations over Kennedy's Assassination." *Manchester Guardian Weekly* (November 6, 1988): Le Monde Section, 13.

8. FBI Document, Record Number 124-10001-10391, Agency File Number 62-109060-8264, 12/14/87: 3.

9. *Encyclopaedia Britannica*, s.v. "Lumumba, Petrice (Hemery)."

Nineteen — The Real Conspiracy

1. Benson: 222-223.

2. Groden, *The Killing of a President*: 114.

3. Senator J. W. Fulbright, Chairman, Committee on Foreign Relations, writing in the preface to "U.S. Involvement in the Overthrow of Diem, 1963" prepared by the Senate Committee on Foreign Relations, July 20, 1972.

4. *The Pentagon Papers.* The Department of Defense History of the United States Decision Making on Vietnam, Senator Gravel Edition, Volume II. Boston: Beacon Press, 1972: 207.

5. Dodds, Paisley. "37 JFK Tapes Made Public." Associated Press (November 25, 1998).

6. Synopsis of Madame Nhu's upbringing, life, marriage, and activities are best detailed in Karnow's *Vietnam: A History*: 265-267, 281.

7. *FRUS*. Volume III: 142-143.

8. National Security Council Document (via the Rockefeller Commission), Record Number 1781000210406, Agency File Number "Assassination Materials–Misc. Rock/CIA (2)," Minutes of Special Group on Operation Mongoose, 4 October 1962. (See also Appendix N: a shorter version of incontrovertible proof that Kennedy and his administration had many more plots on the board to assassinate Castro long after the Bay of Pigs failure.)

9. Howard, Alison. "Suspect in 2 Deaths Resists Drugs." *Washington Post* (December 6, 1991).

10. "Pope To Have First Meeting With Vietnamese Catholics." Associated Press (August 14, 1993).

11. *FRUS*. Volume IV: 273.

Twenty — Shadow Men

1. Telephone interview with Dr. L. M. Alderson by J. Gary Shaw, October 5, 1977, 4:30 P.M.: 4.

2. CIA Document 632-796.

3. CIA Document CSCI-3/776,742.

4. Hurt: 419; Interview with Souetre by Monique Lajournade, June 9, 1999.

5. Hurt: 418-419.

Twenty-One — Souetre Speaks

1. McCoy: 157.

2. McCoy: 250.

Twenty-Two — Brother Bobby's Cover-Up

1. Nechiporenko: 136.

2. National Security Council Document (via the Rockefeller Commission), Record Number 1781000210406, Agency File Number "Assassination Materials–Misc. Rock/CIA (2)," Minutes of Special Group on Operation Mongoose, 4 October 1962; Posner, "Cracks in the Wall of Silence."

3. Hurt: 416.

4. FBI Document, Record Number 180-10022-10291, Agency File Number 62-109060-5819, Title: "De Gaulle Viewed Death of JFK as a Conspiracy;" 10/20/67.

5. See Appendix N.

Twenty-Three — Saigon

1. FBI Document, Record Number 124-10054-10045, Agency File Number 62-109060-4257, Subject: "JFK, Suspect, Madame Nhu," 06/22/66; FBI Document, Record Number 124-10052-10263, Agency File Number 62-109060-4257, Subject: "JFK, Suspect, Madame Nhu," 11/14/66 (This is one of several documents recounting testimony of professional seaman Erich Lintrop, who repeatedly informed the FBI that he had overheard Turkish military officers discussing Madame Nhu's involvement in the Kennedy Assassination.); FBI Translation on December 6, 1963, of anonymous letter sent to the FBI from the Netherlands in which the letter's author asserts that Madame Nhu was involved in Kennedy's assassination. (See Appendices F, G, and H.)

2. Kornbluh, Peter, ed. *Bay of Pigs Declassified*. New York: The New Press, 1998): 285.

3. National Security Council Document (via the Rockefeller Commission), Record Number 1781000210406, Agency File Number "Assassination Materials–Misc. Rock/CIA (2)," Minutes of Special Group on Operation Mongoose, 4 October 1962; Posner, "Cracks in the Wall of Silence."

4. Document entitled "Commission on CIA Activities within the United States." Interview with CIA Colonel Sheffield Edwards (via the Rockefeller Commission), Record Number 1778-10002-10352, Agency File Number "A-II (A) CHRON–Assassinations," 04/09/75. This is a fascinating document which not only proves that the CIA recruited Mafia assets to attempt to assassinate Castro with botulin poison but also proves that Bobby Kennedy was fully aware of the operation, that he did not object to the operation in any way, and that he ordered Colonel Sheffield to brief him on any other Castro-assassination plans.

5. FBI Translation on December 6, 1963, of anonymous letter sent to the FBI from the Netherlands in which the letter's author asserts that Madame Nhu was involved in Kennedy's assassination. (See Appendix F.)

6. FBI Document, Record Number 124-10052-10263, Agency File Number 62-109060-4257, 11/14/66.

7. FBI Document, Record Number 124-10054-10045, Agency File Number 62-109060-4257, 06/22/66. The body of this document relates letters sent to the FBI by a German man known only as "KG3"; the letters maintain that Madame Nhu was part of the conspiracy to kill Kennedy.

8. Tran Le Xuan, aka Madame Ngo Dinh Nhu. "Statement by Madame Nhu on the Death of South Vietnam's President." *New York Times* (November 2, 1963).

9. Karnow: 296.

10. Hughes, Ken. "The Tale of the Tapes: JFK and the Fall of Diem; Three Weeks before His Own Assassination, President Kennedy Launched a Cover-up in the Assassination of the President of South Vietnam." *Boston Globe* (October 24, 1999): Magazine Section, 14.

11. Karnow: 304.

Twenty-Four — Suspicions of LBJ and the KGB

1. Humphrey, Hubert H. *The Education of a Public Man.* University of Minnesota Press, 1991: 196.

2. Nechiporenko: 111.

3. Powers, Thomas. *The Man Who Kept Secrets: Richard Helms and the CIA.* Alfred A. Knopf, 1979: 121.

4. Shesal, Jeff. *Mutual Contempt.* Norton, 1997: 131.

5. Summers, Anthony. *Conspiracy.* Paragon House, 1989: 410.

6. Mahoney, Richard D. *Son's & Brothers.* Arcade, 1999: 302-303.

7. Duffy: 254.

8. FBI Document, Record Number 124-10144-10086, Agency File Number 62-109060-4321, 12/01/66 (declassified on 8/15/95): 2.

9. Ibid: 4.

10. Interview with KGB General Nikolai Leonov, on video *The Secret KGB/JFK Assassination Files.* Associated Television, 1998.

11. Interview with former President of the Soviet Union Mikhail Gorbachev, on video *The Secret KGB/JFK Assassination Files.* Associated Television, 1998.

12. Interview with KGB Colonel Ilya Semyonovitch Pavlotsy, on video *The Secret KGB/JFK Assassination Files.* Associated Television, 1998.

Twenty-Five — Epilogue

1. Dodds, Paisley. "37 JFK Tapes Made Public." Associated Press (November 25, 1998).
2. Benson: 313.

Afterword

1. Horne, Douglas. ARRB Memorandum for File: "Questions Regarding Supplementary Brain Examination(s) Following the Autopsy of President John F. Kennedy." August 28, 1996 (Final Revision: June 2, 1998): 5. (Transcript excerpt from interview with Dr. J. Thornton Boswell.)
2. Benson: 316-317.
3. Nechiporenko, Colonel Oleg Maximovich. *Passport to Assassination.* Birch Lane Press, 1993: 111.
4. Interview with Kalugin, from video *The Secret KGB/JFK Assassination Files.* Associated Television, 1998.
5. FBI Document Record Number 124-10144-10086, Agency File Number 62-109060-4321, 12/01/66: 4. (Declassified on 8/15/95.)
6. Ibid: 1; White House Document, 4 December 1963. Memorandum for Bromely Smith, Subject: "Changes in Defense Readiness Conditions as a Result of the Assassination of President Kennedy." Signed by O.S. Hallett. (Declassified on 4/7/98 as JFK #177-10001-10000.)
7. FBI Document Record Number 124-10144-10086, Agency File Number 62-109060-4321, 12/01/66: 2.
8. *The KGB/Oswald Files.* Associated Television, November 1998.
9. FBI Document Record Number 124-10144-10086, Agency File Number 62-109060-4321, 12/01/66: 2.
10. Ibid.
11. Ibid.

12. Ibid: 3.

13. Benson: 332.

14. Posner, Gerald. *Case Closed*. Arbor Books, 1993: 20.

15. Fetzer: 145-146

16. *The Warren Commission Report*. New York: St. Martin's: 191.

17. Posner: 20.

18. Posner: 508. (The note reads: Testimony of John E. Donovan, WC Volume VIII: 296.) We're not denying the legitimacy of this testimony; we're just saying that we seriously question the opinion of Mr. Donovan in this regard because our own sources contradict it.

19. Interview with "Randy Martin." December 1, 1998. The interviewee asked to be quoted with a pseudonym due to his admission of combat kills as a sniper in Vietnam.

20. Summers, 1989: 45-46.

21. Hogg, Ian and Rob Adam. *Jane's Guns Recognition Guide*. HarperCollins, 1996: 325.

22. Summers, 1989: 46.

23. Though the subject of Kennedy's missing brain has been reported by researchers in many excellent books, we feel that the mystery is best portrayed in Nigel Turner's video series *The Men Who Killed Kennedy*.

24. Posner, Gerald. "Cracks in the Wall of Silence." *Newsweek* (October 4, 1998).

25. Russo, Guy. *Live By The Sword*. Bancroft Press, 1998: 387-390.

26. Lardner, George Jr. "Archive Photos Not of JFK's Brain, Concludes Aide to Review Board." *Washington Post* (November 10, 1998): National New section.

27. Horne, Douglas. ARRB Memorandum for File: "Questions Regarding Supplementary Brain Examination(s) Following the Autopsy of President John F. Kennedy." August 28, 1996 (Final Revision: June 2, 1998): 1-30.

28. Horne, Douglas. ARRB Memorandum: "Chain-of-Custody Discrepancy Re: Original Copy of President John F. Kennedy's Autopsy Protocol." August 2, 1996: 1.

29. Ibid: 2.

30. ARRB summary titled "Draft: Assassination Records Review Board, Staff Report to Accompany Release of Medical and Autopsy Records." July 31, 1998: 1.

31. Ibid.

32. Associated Press. "Photos Renew Dispute About JFK Autopsy." 1998.

33. Posner, *Case Closed*: 407.

34. Associated Press. "Photos Renew Dispute About JFK Autopsy." 1998.

35. Posner, "Cracks in the Wall of Silence."

36. Posner, *Case Closed*: 402-420.

37. Posner, *Case Closed*: 465.

38. Hurt: 346.

39. Posner, *Case Closed*: 412-413.

40. Fetzer, James H. *Assassination Science*. Chicago: Catfeet Press, 1998: 146.

41. Weisberg, Harold. *Case Open*. Carrol & Graf, 1994.

42. *The Warren Commission Report*: 801.

43. Readers interested in Ruby's incontestable involvement with organized crime should investigate the following sources: Hurt's *Reasonable Doubt*: Chapter Eight; Summers's *Conspiracy*: Chapter Twenty-three; Davis's *Mafia Kingfish*: Chapter Twenty-four; to name just a few.

44. Bonanno, Bill. *Bound by Honor*. St. Martin's Press, 1999: 110-111.

45. Benson: 103-104.

46. Duffy: 196.

47. Benson: 151-152.

48. Roberts: 141.

49. Duffy: 198.

50. Benson: 151.

51. Benson: 455.

52. Benson: 455-456.

53. Benson: 456.

54. Benson: 456.

55. Davis: 19-21, 30-131.

56. Davis: 58-61.

57. Davis: 65-67.

58. Davis: 575.

59. Davis: 118-122.

60. Davis: 103-105.

61. Benson: 277.

62. Posner, *Case Closed*: 461.

63. Ibid.

64. Posner, *Case Closed*: 458-460.

65. Benson: 34.

66. *Report on the House Select Committee On Assassinations*: 1.

67. Benson: 279.

68. In notes on pages 459-460 of *Case Closed,* Posner tells us that the only thing that made HSCA Chairman Blakey suspicious of Marcello was an FBI surveillance tape on which Marcello seemed concerned that electronic eavesdropping devices may have been installed in the room. On the very next page, Posner excerpts an interview with an FBI agent who claims that "Giancana and the people around him were complete virgins when it came to electronic surveillance."

69. Benson: 279.

70. Davis: photo, 2.

71. Davis: 158, 451.

72. Benson: 279.

73. Davis: 484-485.

74. Benson: 279.

75. Davis: 451.

76. FBI File Number 62-109060-4391, Record Number 124-10057-10273, 1/9/67.

77. Davis: photo, 23.

78. FBI File Number CR 137A-5467-69,70,72, Record Number 124-10182-10430, 06/09/88 (released in part on 3/27/98).

79. FBI Postponement Information Sheet (JFK Materials). The second coversheet for CR 137A-5467-69,70,72.

80. Davis: 548-558.

81. FBI Airtel from Dallas SAC to Director, FBI. Agency File Number 175A-DL-109-7, Record Number 124-10267-10456, 4/11/89: 1.

82. Attachment to FBI Airtel. Agency File Number 175A-DL-109-7. United States Government Memorandum to J.D. Swinson Jr. 2/28/89.

83. Attachment to FBI Airtel. Agency File Number 175A-DL-109-7. Transcription on 3/13/89 of FBI investigations interview with Senior Correctional Officer Vincent Earl Brown, 3/2/89. File #DALLAS 175-109: 1.

84. Ibid: 2.

85. Attachment to FBI Airtel; Agency File Number 175A-DL-109-7. Transcription on 3/13/89 of FBI investigations interview with Dr. Jerry B. Stringfellow, 3/2/89. FILE #DALLAS 175-109: 1-2.

86. FBI Teletype. Agency File Number 175A-DL-109-3, Record Number 124-10267-10460, 3/10/89: 2.

87. Groden, *The Killing of a President*: 32.

88. Stone, Oliver. *JFK*.

89. Groden, *The Killing of a President*: 86-88.

90. *Image of an Assassination*. A cover endorsement for this documentary video by MPI Teleproductions, 1998.

91. Duffy: 202.

92. Groden, *The Killing of a President*: 32.

93. Benson: 17-18.

94. Groden, *The Killing of a President*: 47, 50-51.

95. Duffy: 523.

96. FBI Document, Record Number 124-10006-10144, Agency File Number 62-109060-2ND NR 8235.

97. Duffy: 202.

98. Groden, *The Killing of a President*: 86-87.

99. Groden, *The Killing of a President*: 41.

100. Duffy: 216.

101. Fetzer: 407.

102. All information and interview material regarding the Dealey Plaza re-enactment is from the documentary video *The Secret KGB/JFK Assassination Files*. Associated Television, 1998. Used by permission of Associated Television.

Bibliography

Assassination Records Review Board summary, entitled "Draft: Assassination Records Review Board, Staff Report to Accompany Release of Medical and Autopsy Records." July 31, 1998.

Assassination Records Review Board. *The Final Report of the Assassination Records Review Board.* September, 1998.

Becket, Henry S.A. *The Dictionary of Espionage.* Stein and Day, 1986.

Benson, Michael. *Who's Who in the JFK Assassination.* Citadel Press, 1993.

Beschloss, Michael R. "An Assassination Diary." *Newsweek* (November 23, 1998): 42.

Bird, Kai. *The Color of Truth.* Simon & Schuster, 1998.

Bird, Kai. "Cries and Whispers." *Washingtonian* (October, 1998): 48.

Bishop, Jim. *The Day Kennedy Was Shot.* HarperPerennial, 1992.

Bly, Nellie. *The Kennedy Men.* Kensington, 1996.

Bonanno, Bill. *Bound by Honor.* St. Martin's Press, 1999.

Bouscaren, Anthony T. *Diem of Vietnam.* Duquesne University Press, 1965.

Brinkley, Douglas. "Of Ladders and Letters." *Time* (April 24, 2000).

Cawthorne, Nigel. *Sex Lives of the Presidents.* St. Martin's, 1998.

Corey, C.L. "Whoever Shot Ngo Dinh Diem, It Couldn't Have Been the CIA." *Insight on the News* (March 15, 1999): Correspondence Section, 3.

Davis, John H. *Mafia Kingfish: Carlos Marcello and the Assassination of John F. Kennedy.* Signet, 1989.

"The Dislodging of Diem." *Boston Globe* (December 1, 1998): A18.

Dodds, Paisley. "37 JFK Tapes Made Public." Associated Press (November 25, 1998).

Duffy, James P., and Vincent L. Ricci. *The Assassination of John F. Kennedy.* Thunder's Mouth Press, 1992.

"Empty Revelations over Kennedy's Assassination." *Manchester Guardian Weekly* (November 6, 1988): Le Monde Section, 13.

Fetzer, James H., ed. *Assassination Science.* Catfeet Press, 1998.

Fussel, James A. "Conein...Lucien Conein. Who Was He?" *Kansas City Star* (September 20, 1998).

"Government Faulted for JFK Secrecy." Associated Press (September 28, 1998).

Groden, Robert J. *The Killing of a President.* Viking Penguin, 1993.

Groden, Robert J. *The Search for Lee Harvey Oswald.* Viking Penguin, 1995.

Herring, George C., ed. *The Pentagon Papers.* McGraw-Hill, 1993.

Hersh, Seymour M. *The Dark Side of Camelot.* Little Brown, 1997.

Hogg, Ian, and Rob Adam. *Jane's Guns Recognition Guide.* Harper Collins, 1996.

Horne, Douglas, ARRB Memorandum: "Chain-of-Custody Discrepancy Re: Original Copy of President John F. Kennedy's Autopsy Protocol." August 2, 1996.

Horne, Douglas. ARRB Memorandum for File: "Questions Regarding Supplementary Brain Examination(s) Following the Autopsy of President John F. Kennedy." August 28, 1996 (Final Revision: June 2, 1998).

Howard, Alison. "Suspect in 2 Deaths Resists Drugs." *Washington Post* (December 6, 1991).

Hughes, Ken. "The Tale of the Tapes: JFK and the Fall of Diem; Three Weeks before His Own Assassination, President Kennedy Launched a Cover-up in the Assassination of the President of South Vietnam." *Boston Globe* (October 24, 1999): Magazine Section.

Humphrey, Hubert H. *The Education of a Public Man.* University of Minnesota Press, 1991.

Hurt, Henry. *Reasonable Doubt.* Holt, Rinehart and Winston, 1986.

Karnow, Stanley. *Vietnam.* Viking, 1983.

Kornbluh, Peter, ed. *Bay of Pigs Declassified.* New York: The New Press, 1998.

Lane, Mark. *Plausible Denial.* ThunderMouth Press, 1991.

Lardner, George Jr. "Archive Photos Not of JFK's Brain, Concludes Aide to Review Board." *Washington Post* (November 10, 1998): National New Section.

Lind, Michael. *Vietnam: The Necessary War.* Free Press, 1999.

Mahoney, Richard D. *Sons & Brothers.* Arcade, 1999.

McCoy, Alfred W. *The Politics of Heroin: CIA Complicity in the Global Drug Trade.* Lawrence Hills Books, 1991.

Nechiporenko, Colonel Oleg Maximovich. *Passport to Assassination.* Birch Lane Press, 1993.

Newsday Staff and Editors. *The Heroin Trail.* Holt, Rinehart and Winston, 1973, 1974.

"Photos Renew Dispute About JFK Autopsy." Associated Press (September, 1998).

"Pope To Have First Meeting With Vietnamese Catholics." Associated Press (August 14, 1993).

Porch, Douglas. *The French Secret Services.* Farrar, Straus and Giroux, 1995.

Posner, Gerald. *Case Closed.* Arbor Books, 1993.

Posner, Gerald. "Cracks in the Wall of Silence." *Newsweek* (October 4, 1998).

Powers, Thomas. *The Man Who Kept Secrets: Richard Helms and the CIA.* Alfred A. Knopf, 1979.

Prouty, L. Fletcher. *JFK: The CIA, Vietnam and the Plot to Assassinate John F. Kennedy.* Citadel Press, 1996.

Reymond, William. *JFK: Autopsie d'un Crime D'Etat.* Flammarion, 1998.

Roberts, Craig. *Kill Zone.* Consolidated Press International, 1994.

Roberts, Craig and John Armstrong. *JFK: The Dead Witnesses.* Consolidated Press International, 1995.

Robinson, Linda. "What Didn't We Do To Get Rid of Castro?" *U.S. News & World Report* (October 28, 1998).

Ruedy, John. *Modern Algeria*. Indiana University Press, 1992.

Russell, Dick. *The Man Who Knew Too Much*. Carroll & Graf, 1992.

Russo, Guy. *Live by the Sword*. Bancroft Press, 1998.

Rust, William J. *Kennedy in Vietnam*. Da Capo Press, 1985.

Scott, Peter Dale. *Deep Politics and the Death of JFK*. University of California Press, 1993.

Sheehan, Neil. *A Bright Shining Lie*. Vintage, 1989.

Shesal, Jeff. *Mutual Contempt*. Norton, 1997.

Shultz, Dick. "How Kennedy Launched His Secret War in Vietnam." *Boston Globe* (January 31, 2000).

Stone, Oliver. "Was Vietnam JFK's War?" *Newsweek* (October 21, 1996).

Summers, Anthony. *Conspiracy*. McGraw-Hill, 1980.

Summers, Anthony. *Conspiracy*. Paragon House, 1989.

"Tapes Reveal Nixon Blaming JFK in Killing." *Times-Picayune*. February 26, 1999: A14.

Tolchin, Martin. "John G. Tower, 65, Longtime Senator from Texas." *Washington Times* (April 6, 1991).

Tran Le Xuan, aka Madame Ngo Dinh Nhu. "Statement by Madame Nhu on the Death of South Vietnam's President." *New York Times* (November 2, 1963).

UPI, PM cycle. October 26, 1988: International Section.

U.S. Department of State. *Foreign Relations of the United States, 1961-1963*. Volume III & IV/Vietnam: August-December 1963.

The Warren Commission, *The Warren Commission Report*. St. Martin's, 1964.

Weisberg, Harold. *Case Open*. Carrol & Graf, 1994.

White, Peter T. "South Viet Nam Fights the Red Tide." *National Geographic* (October, 1961).

VIDEOS

Best Evidence. Rhino Home Video, 1990.

Image of an Assassination. MPI Home Video, 1998.

JFK. A film by Oliver Stone. Warner Bros, 1991.

Lords of the Mafia: Marcello. Associated Television, 1999. (For more information, check ATINews.com.)

The Men Who Killed Kennedy. Arts & Entertainment Network, 1993.

The Secret KGB/JFK Assassination Files. Associated Television, 1998. (For more information, check ATINews.com.)

Vietnam: A Television History. Volume One: "America's Mandarin." A co-production of WGBH Boston, Central Independent Television/UK, and Antenne-2 France and in association with LRE Productions, 1996.

DOCUMENTS

CIA Document, CSCI-3/776,742, 7/12/63.

CIA Document, Number 62-10960, 10/10/66 (declassified 3/14/97).

CIA Document, Number 632-796, 4/1/64. Handwriting at top reads: AAZ-22592.

Department of State Agency File # POL 15-1 US/Kennedy. Excerpt of condolence from General Duong Van Minh to President Johnson, regarding Kennedy's death.

Department of State Memorandum, 11/5/61. From Alexis Johnson to the deputy undersecretary, Subject: "General Taylor's Recommendations," (Stamped Category A, 10/7/68), classified "Top Secret." First subject line reads: "Attached is a copy of General Taylor's recommendations." (Declassified by Authority # NND 949535, 1/27/03.)

Department of State Memorandum, 12/29/61. From Executive Secretary L.D. Battle for Roger Hilsman to Secretary McGeorge Bundy, Subject:" Coup Plotting in South Vietnam," classified "Secret." Reference Number 751K.00/11-2961 (declassified by National Archives, Authority # NND 949535, 1/21/03).

Department of State Memorandum, 8/26/63. A pre-coup summary of plans classified "Top Secret": 3-4. (Declassified by Authority # NND 939543, 12/4/02.)

Department of State Telegram, 12/22/61. To Gov. Harriman from W.W. Rostow via the Chief of MAAG, Saigon 210957Z, Subject: "Diem's Fears of a Coup and Command Arrangements," classified "Secret." Post Reference Number 21282, other Reference Number 751K.00/12-2261 (declassified by Authority # NND 949535, 1/2/03).

FBI Document 62-109060. Translated by Edward P. Arbez. December 6, 1963.

FBI Document 62-109060-4257, 11/14/66.

FBI Document 105-120510, 5/3/63.

FBI Document 105-82555-492, 9/22/1964.

FBI Document, Agency File Number: Lee H. Oswald 1; 62-109060-2518.

FBI Document, Record Number 124-10001-10391, Agency File Number 62-109060-8264, 12/14/87.

FBI Document, Record Number 124-10001-10395, Agency File Number 62-109060-8260, 02/19/88 (declassified 1/21/95).

FBI Document, Record Number 124-10144-10086, Agency File Number 62-109060-4321, 12/01/66 (declassified on 8/15/95).

FBI Document, Record Number 124-10267-10456, Agency File Number 175A-DL-109-7, 4/11/89 (declassified 3/30/98).

FBI Investigative File on Assassination of John Kennedy, Agency File Number 62-109060-5819.

FBI Reference Number DL 137A-5467-70, 5/26/1988: 1-7. Cover sheet reads "FBI Postponement Information Sheet (JFK Materials)" (declassified 2/21/94).

FBI Teletype 3/12/64, Document Number 105-128529-11 (declassified 2/26/97).

Foreign Service Dispatch #255, 12/22/61. From the Saigon Embassy to the State Department, signed by Joseph A. Mendenhall, counselor of embassy for political affairs, classified "Confidential." (Declassified by Authority # NND 949535, 1/27/03.) (Details Madame Nhu's support of social purification law, Bill No. 60.)

Letter from Nguyen Thai Binh to Thomas F. Johnson, 1st District, Maryland, 11/20/61, forwarded from Johnson to Secretary of State Dean Rusk on 11/28/61. (Declassified by Authority # NND 94935,

1/21/03.) (Informs Congressman Johnson of Diem's misappropriation of U.S. aid by Diem and his close associates and also refers to opium traffic approved of by Diem.)

Letter from Roger Hilsman to Department of State assistant secretary, 8/30/63. Subject: "Possible Diem-Nhu Moves and U.S. Responses." (Declassified by Authority # NND 939543, date of declassification not legible but probably January 2003.) (This letter is a list of contingencies regarding a Diem coup with possible U.S. responses to various scenarios prepared by Roger Hilsman.)

Memorandum for Mr. Alexis Johnson, assistant secretary of defense, international security affairs, 10/12/61. Cover letter signed by William P. Bundy, classified "Confidential." Reference Number 751K.00/10-1261 (declassified by Authority # NND 949535, 1/27/03).

Memorandum from Joseph A. Mendenhall, political counselor, American embassy Saigon, to Edward E. Rice, deputy assistant secretary, 8/16/62. Subject: "Viet-Nam—Assessment and Recommendations." (Declassified by Authority # NND 939543, 1/21/03.) (This memorandum from chief U.S. political advisor in Saigon, Joseph Mendenhall, is a list of recommendations to Kennedy advisor Edward Rice, which bluntly recommends that the U.S. "Get rid of Diem, Mr. And Mrs. Nhu, and the rest of the Ngo family.)

"Memorandum of Interview by J. Gary Shaw with Dr. Lawrence M. (Larry) Alderson, D.D.S." October 6, 1977, 4:00 P.M.

Possible Contingencies in Viet Nam, Alternate Situations, 11/28/61. Signed by Robert H. Johnson, classified "Top Secret—Limited Distribution." (Declassified by Authority # NND 949535, 1/21/03.)

"Telephone Interview with Dr. L.M. Alderson and J. Gary Shaw - October 5, 1977; 4:30 P.M."

United States Government Memorandum, 3/9/64, Document Number 105-128529-9. Released in part by FBI/JFK Task Force, 2/26/97

United States Government Memorandum, 5/3/63, Document Number 105-12051(or 4—illegible)0. Released in part by FBI/JFK Task Force, 2/26/97.

United States Government Memorandum to FBI Director from New York SAC, 4/8/63, Document Number 105-120510-2. Released in part by FBI/JFK Task Force, 2/26/97.

White House Document, 12/4/63. Memorandum For Bromely Smith, Subject: "Changes in Defense Readiness Conditions as a Result of the Assassination of President Kennedy." Signed by O.S. Hallett (declassified 4/7/98 as JFK #177-10001-10000).

Index

237

LaVergne, TN USA
12 November 2009
163913LV00001B/29/P